PSYCHOTROPIC
DRUGS
FAST
FACTS

THE REFERENCE SOURCE FOR THE 1990s

PSYCHOTROPIC
DRUGS
FAST
FACTS

Jerrold S. Maxmen, M.D.

W · W · Norton & Company · New York · London

First Edition

Library of Congress Cataloging-in-Publication Data

Maxmen, Jerrold S.
  Psychotropic drugs : fast facts / Jerrold S. Maxmen.
    p.   cm.
  "A Norton professional book"—P. pacing t.p.
  Includes bibliographical references.
  ISBN 0-393-70118-2
  1. Psychotropic drugs.   I. Title.
  [DNLM: 1. Psychotropic Drugs—handbooks.   QV 39 M464p]
  RM315.M355   1991
  615'.788—dc20
  DNLM/DLC
  for Library of Congress   91–3018

W. W. Norton & Company, Inc., 500 Fifth Avenue, New York, N.Y. 10110
W. W. Norton & Company, Ltd., 10 Coptic Street, London WC1A 1PU

                    4   5   6   7   8   9   0

Introduction

Wisdom arrived one afternoon. Drs. Donald F. Klein and John M. Davis' brand-new 1969 *Diagnosis and Drug Treatment of Psychiatric Disorders* came by mail. The book was splendid. Yet what electrified were pages 96 and 97, which listed the percentages of side effects of ten antipsychotics. Granted, four neuroleptics were now obsolete, and a fifth was for vomiting. Nevertheless, I was the only psychiatric resident to possess these cherished numbers.

Cherished? Well, although they were not exactly psychoanalytic theory or pharmacologic conjecture, they did reveal that chlorpromazine disturbed menstruation 16.3% of the time, thioridazine induced akathisias 8.9% of the time, and perphenazine blurred vision 17.8% of the time. When I met a patient who feared a dry mouth on neuroleptics, page 96 told me whether trifluoperazine, fluphenazine, or perphenazine caused it the least.[1]

Were these two pages number-crunching? Definitely. Were the data skewed, outmoded, or dead wrong? Occasionally. Did these figures cover vast territory? Absolutely. (Klein's second edition of this book jokes that chlorpromazine sedates 9–92% of the time.) Nonetheless, patients *do* want to know which medications cause more weight gain and which ones reduce libido; and clinicians *should* know the answers. With Klein and Davis, I finally had some informed answers.

For 16 years, Klein and Davis stuck to me. When I wrote a textbook in 1985, I wanted it stuffed with pages 96 and 97. Yet I quickly discovered that this was exasperating: data diverged, disagreed, and didn't exist. Instead, I wrote a "normal" textbook.

Even still, this idea of a "dictionary of details" continued. For routine clinical work, I wanted *one* place to get the *facts*. I was tired of hunting through a dozen books to unearth a mere fact: the half-life of protriptyline versus nortriptyline, or the dose of amoxapine versus bupropion, or the cost of triazolam versus quazepam. What's more, new drugs kept arising; *Newsweek* announced them; so would patients. I heard too often, "I want Prozac." But aside from what pharmaceutical houses told me, or the *PDR* (written by the drug companies) told me,

---

[1] It's trifluoperazine at 2.3%.

By the way, there was also page 229, but it was less cherished. Although affording side-effect percentages for antidepressants, it displayed *broad* numbers—imipramine gave dry mouth 10–30% of the time, tranylcypromine triggered dizziness 5–20% of the time. Broad figures were common sense, but that fluphenazine on page 96 induced hypotension precisely 0.79% of the time—that was enlightenment.

or even what Ted Koppel told me, I did not know whether Prozac sedated more or less than doxepin, amitriptyline, or clomipramine. I needed one source with all this information. What I wanted was not a textbook that explains everything, but a single *reference.* I wanted *Fast Facts.* Norton obliged.

Fast Facts simply presents the facts of clinical psychopharmacology. It describes nine categories of medications: antipsychotics, anticholinergics, antidepressants, MAOIs, lithium, anticonvulsants, anti-anxiety agents, hypnotics, and stimulants. Every chapter details the drugs' names, forms, pharmacologies, dosages, indications, predictors, clinical applications, therapeutic levels, outcomes, alternatives, side effects (and their percentages), pregnancy and lactation data, drug/food interactions, adverse responses in children, the elderly, and the sick, medication alterations of laboratory studies, withdrawal hazards, overdoses (and remedies), toxicities, suicide potentials, precautions, contraindications, nurses' information, patients' concerns, and costs. And yet, with all this information, this drug almanac still posed problems.

Fast Facts is a Book Without Verbs (BWV). (I do not consider "increase" and "decrease" to be verbs, but attitudes. Excoriate, guffaw, swoon, and sashay—these are verbs.) Good writing, "good-writing" manuals tell me, highlights good verbs. If so, a BWV could be very dull. I hope it will inform and stimulate.

Although a BWV, it is a BWP—a book with pronouns. This meant I had to decide whether to refer to a patient as a "he" or a "she." I chose "he."

A bigger dilemma was the same number problem faced by Klein and Davis. The literature bursts with scientific "facts"; numbers conflict, contradict, and confuse; they measure similar, but different, parameters; they lie. Correct numbers can be "incorrect," as when the "correct" dose can be incorrect for a particular patient. Definitions baffle. If I write that a drug generates weight gain, how much weight has to be gained? The criteria depend on the pounds increased, the period's duration, the person's size, etc. Aside from how carefully a scientist defined dizziness, how could I reconcile dissimilar "truths," as when researcher A found dizziness in 47 of 100 patients while researcher B uncovered it in 5 out of 1000 patients? These problems are endless. Ultimately, I did what most authors do: I reviewed the printed material, averaged the findings, factored in personal experience, and compromised on the best clinical information. For the errors, I alone bear responsibility. Nevertheless, some people really helped. Drs. Greg Dalack, Brian Fallon, Laurence Greenhill, David Kahn, Neil Kavey, Ron Rieder, Holly Schneier, Michael Sheehy, and David Strauss made suggestions that greatly improved the book.

The enclosed data are generalizations: they do not, or could not, suit every patient under all circumstances. Patients are allergic to drugs, react atypically to the same agents, and respond paradoxically to others. Moreover, the doses, neurotransmitter actions, and other specifications must be altered to the newest scientific developments and tapered to specific patient's requirements.

Although *Fast Facts* focuses on drugs, this does not mean that only drugs are effective. Medications function best to alleviate specific *symptoms* (e.g., delusions, panic attacks). Psychotherapy, in contrast, functions best to resolve specific *issues* (e.g., marital fights); issues may accompany, cause, or result from symptoms. Psychotherapy addresses the content of symptoms (e.g., "the homeless spy on me"). Psychotherapy clarifies how medications reduce symptoms (e.g., "I understand why I'm taking this drug"). Psychotherapy puts life into perspective (e.g., "My elevator phobia is fearsome, but my wife is fantastic!"). Psychotherapy explores how to behave with a mental disorder (e.g., to tell one's husband, not one's boss, about hallucinating). If one has diabetes, a medication, insulin, would reduce blood sugar; a self-help group, a psychotherapy, would discuss the stresses of living with diabetes. Insulin and a self-help group do not conflict, but serve different, albeit complementary, purposes. The same applies for psychotropic drugs and psychotherapy. To compare the two is akin to asking whether the length *or* the width of a football field determines its size.

In short, *Psychotropic Drugs: Fast Facts* is an up-to-date reference with tables and charts for psychiatrists, psychologists, nurses, social workers, activities therapists, internists, psychotherapists, and anyone I forgot. It is *not* a beginner's manual or a "how to prescribe" book, but a comprehensive guide for experienced clinicians. Enjoy this BWV.

Jerrold S. Maxmen, M. D.
New York, January 1991

P. S. Please send me your well-needed improvements. Thanks.

Organization

Each chapter contains 16 sections—give or take a few depending on the circumstances. Here are some details:

INTRODUCTION

This section presents the general category of medications, their broad indications, the disorders they treat in this and other chapters. It's a traffic guide.

NAMES, CLASSES, MANUFACTURERS, DOSE FORMS, AND COLORS

Only drugs currently sold in the United States are listed.

PHARMACOLOGY

This part sketches a medicine's basic clinical pharmacology: its absorption, distribution, metabolism, and elimination. Several terms are often employed:

Bioavailability is the percentage of an oral dose that can act pharmacologically.

Plasma Binding is the percentage of drug bound clinically to plasma proteins.

Volume of Distribution (liters/kg) is the total body volume of distribution at the steady state level in the plasma.

Half-life, usually expressed in hours, is when 50% of the drug has been eliminated. The book's figures usually represent the drug's major active fractions, including metabolites; the broader numbers in parentheses are ranges.

Excretion is typically the percent of drug unchanged in the urine.

DOSES

Prescribed here are the standard doses, ranges, initial dosages, therapeutic serum levels, drug amounts for different age groups, and so on.

CLINICAL INDICATIONS AND USE

This section conveys when a drug is specifically indicated. It addresses what can predict a drug's clinical potential, how to employ practically these medications, when (and how) to use different forms of the drug, what to do when problems arise, how to maintain and terminate these agents, and how to apply these drugs for other conditions.

SIDE EFFECTS

This section affords a reasonably comprehensive, but not complete, description of side effects and what to do about them. Although these agents are presented under organ categories, this does not suggest that each side effect belongs exclusively to a single system. Weight gain—prompted by brain, gut, and hormones—was placed under "Gastrointestinal." Categories are for convenience.

PERCENTAGES OF SIDE EFFECTS

This section offers the incidence of specific drug side effects. The first number is the best average I could determine from the literature, whereas the parenthesized number is the range of these side effects. I have only included ranges that I thought might clarify a side effect's frequency. For instance, if the average is 18%, but the range is 10–90%, this suggests that most of the side effects are usually closer to 10%.

For uniformity's sake, and also because most studies don't display placebo comparisons, these percentages include placebo findings. The sign "—" exists throughout these tables. It refers to the nonexistence of information and *not* to the nonexistence of the side effect. If, under vomiting, three drugs are —, —, and 5.5, this does not mean that only the third drug causes the vomiting. The other two might, or might not, but there are no data to decide. If a study has demonstrated that a drug does not create a problem, the chart reads "0.0." The enclosed numbers reflect both exact percentages (e.g., 13.7%) and broad ranges (e.g., 10–30%).

The chief aim here is to compare the frequency of adverse reactions. People will have no trouble finding exceptions to these figures. If you find some, please send them along.

PREGNANCY AND LACTATION

This section summarizes these agents' adverse effects on newborns and from breast milk.

The *Milk/Plasma Ratio* underscores that milk and plasma drug concentrations are not parallel throughout breast feeding.

The *Time of Peak Concentration in Milk* is the hours between the medication's ingestion until it peaks in the milk. It is generally safest to feed the infant at the trough of maternal plasma concentration—that is, just prior to the next dose—to minimize the baby's ingestion of the drug.

Infant Dose (μg/kilogram/day) is calculated from peak milk concentrations, unless stated otherwise. It represents the maximum likely exposure the child has to the drug.

Maternal dose percentage is the infant dose compared to the maternal dose controlled for weight.

Safety Rating conveys how relatively safe it is for a mother to consume a drug while breast-feeding during the first year.

DRUG-DRUG INTERACTIONS

This section indicates the major drug interactions with psychotropic agents. This list is thorough, but not complete; it stresses clinical effects and interventions, not mechanisms.

EFFECTS ON LABORATORY TESTS

This section outlines how these medications influence laboratory tests.

WITHDRAWAL

If problems emerge on withdrawal of the drug, this section depicts what happens and what to do about them.

OVERDOSE: TOXICITY, SUICIDE, AND TREATMENT

This section dispenses the opposite. It portrays clinical overdose symptoms, gives toxic and suicide blood levels, signifies how many days' supply can be lethal, outlines drug-abuse signs and how to remedy intoxications and overdoses.

PRECAUTIONS

When should a drug *not* be taken? That's addressed here—the contraindications and dangers clinicians should exercise when prescribing these medications.

NURSES' DATA

Much of what has already been written will be of great assistance to all staff, including nurses, but this section informs staff about observing patients on medication, showing them how to handle side effects, and using the various dose forms of the drug.

ORGANIZATION

PATIENT AND FAMILY NOTES

This book is written for professionals, not laymen. This section affords the key information staff should insure patients receive: whether to consume medications in relation to meals, how to deal with forgetting a dose, how to cope with immediate side effects, when to call a doctor regarding a crisis, etc.

If one member of a family is affected by a mental disorder, all members are affected. Some of these concerns, therefore, are for the entire family.

COST INDEX

These cost ratings are determined based on relative wholesale prices of roughly equivalent quantities of similar or identical medications. The higher the cost rating, the higher the price. The cost index is *not* a rating of safety or efficacy; it is simply a comparison of cost, derived largely from the 1990 and 1991 editions of *Facts and Comparisons.*

APPENDICES

A *drug information guide,* describing the major action of all drugs mentioned in the book.

A *symptom check list,* to be given to patients before and during their drug taking to see which symptoms arose before or after the drug was begun.

The references of this book—and there are many—provide these data.

ABBREVIATIONS

ACA	Anticholinergic agents
ADR	Adverse drug reaction
bid	Twice a day
CBC	Complete blood count
d	Days
DST	Dexamethasone suppression test
D/S	Dextrose and saline
D/W	Dextrose and water
ECG	Electrocardiogram
ECT	Electroconvulsive therapy
EEG	Electroencephalogram
EPS	Extrapyramidal side effects
EUCD	Emotionally Unstable Character Disorder
g	Gram

GABA	Gamma-aminobutyric acid
GAD	Generalized Anxiety Disorder
HCAs	Heterocyclic antidepressants
h/o	History of
h	Hours
hs	At sleep
IM	Intramuscular injection
IV	Intravenous injection
kg	Kilogram
LFT	Liver function tests (SGOT, SGPT, LDH, bilirubin, alkaline phosphotase)
μg	Microgram (10^{-6} grams)
mg	Milligrams (10^{-3} grams)
MAOI	Monoamine-oxidase inhibitor
NDI	Nephrogenic diabetes insipidus
ng	Nanograms (10^{-9} grams)
NIMH	National Institute of Mental Health
NMS	Neuroleptic malignant syndrome
NSAIA	Nonsteroidal anti-inflammatory agents
OCD	Obsessive-Compulsive Disorder
po	Oral dose
qd	Once a day; daily
qid	Four times a day
qod	Every other day
r/o	Rule out
SC	Subcutaneous
TCAs	Tricyclic antidepressants
TD	Tardive dyskinesia
tid	Three times a day
TSH	Thyroid-stimulating hormone
T_3	Triiodothyronine
T_4	Thyroxine

ORGANIZATION

Contents

Chapter	Page	Drugs Stressed	Disorders Stressed
Introduction	v		
Organization	ix		
1. Antipsychotics	1		
INTRODUCTION	1	Chlorpromazine	Schizophrenia
NAMES, CLASSES,		Chlorprothixene	Delirium
MANUFACTURERS,		Clozapine	Dementia
DOSE FORMS,		Fluphenazine	Neuroleptic
COLORS	2	Haloperidol	malignant
PHARMACOLOGY	3	Loxapine	syndrome
DOSES	5	Mesoridazine	Tardive
CLINICAL		Perphenazine	dyskinesia
INDICATIONS		Pimozide	
AND USE	6	Thioridazine	
SIDE EFFECTS	12	Trifluoperazine	
PERCENTAGES OF		Enanthates and	
SIDE EFFECTS	26	Decanoates	
PREGNANCY AND		Bromocriptine	
LACTATION	32	Dantrolene	
DRUG-DRUG		Physostigmine	
INTERACTIONS	33		
EFFECTS ON			
LABORATORY			
TESTS	35		
WITHDRAWAL	35		
OVERDOSE: TOXICITY,			
SUICIDE, AND			
TREATMENT	36		
PRECAUTIONS	38		
NURSES' DATA	39		
PATIENT AND FAMILY			
NOTES	40		
COST INDEX	41		

Chapter	Page	Drugs Stressed	Disorders Stressed
2. Anticholinergics	43	Amantadine	Extrapyramidal
INTRODUCTION	43	Benztropine	reactions:
NAMES,		Biperiden	Dystonia
MANUFACTURERS,		Diphenhydramine	Akathisia
DOSE FORMS,		Procyclidine	Parkinsonism
COLORS	44	Trihexyphenidyl	Rabbit
PHARMACOLOGY	44	Bromocriptine	syndrome
DOSES	45	Dantrolene	
CLINICAL		Diazepam	
INDICATIONS		Lorazepam	
AND USE	45	Propranolol	
SIDE EFFECTS	47		
PERCENTAGES OF			
SIDE EFFECTS	49		
PREGNANCY AND			
LACTATION	50		
DRUG-DRUG			
INTERACTIONS	50		
EFFECTS ON			
LABORATORY			
TESTS	51		
WITHDRAWAL	52		
OVERDOSE: TOXICITY,			
SUICIDE, AND			
TREATMENT	52		
PRECAUTIONS	52		
NURSES' DATA	53		
PATIENT AND FAMILY			
NOTES	54		
COST INDEX	55		
3. Antidepressants	57	Amitriptyline	Major
INTRODUCTION	57	Amoxapine	depression
NAMES, CLASSES,		Bupropion	Chronic
MANUFACTURERS,		Clomipramine	physical
DOSE FORMS,		Desipramine	disorders
COLORS	58	Doxepin	(e.g.,
PHARMACOLOGY	60	Fluoxetine	Cataplexy,
DOSES	63		

Chapter	Page	Drugs Stressed	Disorders Stressed
CLINICAL		Imipramine	Ulcers,
INDICATIONS		Imipramine	Diarrhea,
AND USE	64	pamoate	Congestive
SIDE EFFECTS	73	Maprotiline	heart failure,
PERCENTAGES OF		Nortriptyline	Migraine,
SIDE EFFECTS	82	Protriptyline	Parkinson's
PREGNANCY AND		Trazodone	disease,
LACTATION	88	Trimipramine	Sleep apnea)
DRUG-DRUG			"Pseudodemen-
INTERACTIONS	89		tia"
EFFECTS ON			Eating disorders
LABORATORY			Childhood
TESTS	92		stage-4
WITHDRAWAL	92		Sleep disorders
OVERDOSE: TOXICITY,			(e.g.,
SUICIDE, AND			Enuresis,
TREATMENT	93		Night terrors,
PRECAUTIONS	95		Sleepwalking)
NURSES' DATA	95		
PATIENT AND FAMILY			
NOTES	97		
COST INDEX	97		
4. Monoamine-Oxidase Inhibitors	99		
INTRODUCTION	99	Isocarboxazid	Major
NAMES, CLASSES,		Phenelzine	depression
MANUFACTURERS,		Tranylcypromine	Atypical
DOSE FORMS,			depression
COLORS	100		
PHARMACOLOGY	100		
DOSES	101		
CLINICAL			
INDICATIONS			
AND USE	101		
SIDE EFFECTS	106		
PERCENTAGES OF			
SIDE EFFECTS	118		
PREGNANCY AND			
LACTATION	119		

CONTENTS

Chapter	Page	Drugs Stressed	Disorders Stressed
DRUG-DRUG INTERACTIONS	119		
EFFECTS ON LABORATORY TESTS	121		
WITHDRAWAL	122		
OVERDOSE: TOXICITY, SUICIDE, AND TREATMENT	122		
PRECAUTIONS	124		
NURSES' DATA	125		
PATIENT AND FAMILY NOTES	125		
COST INDEX	126		
5. Lithium	127		
INTRODUCTION	127	Lithium carbonate	Bipolar disorder
NAMES, MANUFACTURERS, FORMS, COLORS	128	Lithium citrate	Major depression
PHARMACOLOGY	128		Schizoaffective disorder
DOSES	129		Emotionally unstable character disorder
CLINICAL INDICATIONS AND USE	130		Borderline personality disorder
SIDE EFFECTS	136		
PERCENTAGES OF SIDE EFFECTS	143		
PREGNANCY AND LACTATION	145		Premenstrual dysphoria
DRUG-DRUG INTERACTIONS	146		Alcoholism
EFFECTS ON LABORATORY TESTS	148		
WITHDRAWAL	148		
OVERDOSE: TOXICITY, SUICIDE, AND TREATMENT	148		

Chapter	Page	Drugs Stressed	Disorders Stressed
PRECAUTIONS	150		
NURSES' DATA	151		
PATIENT AND FAMILY			
NOTES	151		
COST INDEX	152		
6. Anticonvulsants	153		
INTRODUCTION	153	Carbamazepine	Bipolar disorder
NAMES,		Valproic acid	Unipolar
MANUFACTURERS,		Clonazepam	depression
DOSE FORMS,			Aggression
COLORS	154		
PHARMACOLOGY	154		
DOSES	155		
CLINICAL			
INDICATIONS			
AND USE	155		
SIDE EFFECTS	160		
PERCENTAGES OF			
SIDE EFFECTS	166		
PREGNANCY AND			
LACTATION	167		
DRUG-DRUG			
INTERACTIONS	169		
EFFECTS ON			
LABORATORY			
TESTS	171		
WITHDRAWAL	171		
OVERDOSE: TOXICITY,			
SUICIDE, AND			
TREATMENT	172		
PRECAUTIONS	173		
NURSES' DATA	174		
PATIENT AND FAMILY			
NOTES	175		
COST INDEX	176		

CONTENTS

Chapter	Page	Drugs Stressed	Disorders Stressed
7. Antianxiety Agents	177		
INTRODUCTION	177	Alprazolam	Anticipatory
NAMES, CLASSES,		Buspirone	anxiety
MANUFACTURERS,		Chlordiazepoxide	Generalized
DOSE FORMS,		Clomipramine	anxiety
COLORS	178	Clonazepam	disorder
PHARMACOLOGY	179	Clonidine	Panic disorder
DOSES	183	Clorazepate	Phobic disorder
CLINICAL		Diazepam	Obsessive-
INDICATIONS		Hydroxyzine	compulsive
AND USE	184	Lorazepam	disorder
SIDE EFFECTS	193	Meprobamate	Post-traumatic
PERCENTAGES OF		Oxazepam	stress
SIDE EFFECTS	197	Prazepam	disorder
PREGNANCY AND		Propranolol	Tobacco
LACTATION	199		withdrawal
DRUG-DRUG			
INTERACTIONS	202		
EFFECTS ON			
LABORATORY			
TESTS	208		
WITHDRAWAL	208		
OVERDOSE: TOXICITY,			
SUICIDE, AND			
TREATMENT	209		
PRECAUTIONS	213		
NURSES' DATA	214		
PATIENT AND FAMILY			
NOTES	215		
COST INDEX	215		
8. Hypnotics	217		
INTRODUCTION	217	Barbiturates	Insomnia
NAMES, CLASSES,		Chloral hydrate	Hypnosedative
MANUFACTURERS,		Disulfiram	withdrawal
		Estazolom	

Chapter	Page	Drugs Stressed	Disorders Stressed
DOSE FORMS,		Ethchlorvynol	Alcohol
COLORS	218	Flurazepam	withdrawal
PHARMACOLOGY	218	Methyprylon	Alcohol
DOSES	220	Quazepam	prevention
CLINICAL		Temazepam	
INDICATIONS		Triazolam	
AND USE	220	Tryptophan	
SIDE EFFECTS	225		
PERCENTAGES OF			
SIDE EFFECTS	226		
PREGNANCY AND			
LACTATION	229		
DRUG-DRUG			
INTERACTIONS	230		
EFFECTS ON			
LABORATORY			
TESTS	232		
WITHDRAWAL	232		
OVERDOSE: TOXICITY,			
SUICIDE, AND			
TREATMENT	239		
PRECAUTIONS	241		
NURSES' DATA	242		
PATIENT AND FAMILY			
NOTES	242		
COST INDEX	243		
9. Stimulants	245		
INTRODUCTION	245	Dextroampheta-	Attention-deficit
NAMES,		mine	hyperactivity
MANUFACTURERS,		Methylphenidate	disorder
DOSE FORMS,		Pemoline	Treatment-
COLORS	245		resistant
PHARMACOLOGY	246		depression
DOSES	247		Narcolepsy
CLINICAL			AIDS
INDICATIONS			
AND USE	247		
SIDE EFFECTS	250		

CONTENTS

Chapter	Page	Drugs Stressed	Disorders Stressed
PERCENTAGES OF SIDE EFFECTS	253		
PREGNANCY AND LACTATION	254		
DRUG-DRUG INTERACTIONS	255		
EFFECTS ON LABORATORY TESTS	256		
WITHDRAWAL	257		
OVERDOSE: TOXICITY, SUICIDE, AND TREATMENT	258		
PRECAUTIONS	259		
NURSES' DATA	259		
PATIENT AND FAMILY NOTES	260		
COST INDEX	261		
Appendices	262		
DRUG IDENTIFICATION	262		
SYMPTOM CHECK LIST	267		
References	269		
Index of Drugs by Brand Names	278		

PSYCHOTROPIC DRUGS FAST FACTS

1. Antipsychotic Agents

INTRODUCTION

Antipsychotics block psychosis, whereas hypnosedatives do not.

Both antipsychotics and hypnosedatives sedate, which accounts for their being named "major" and "minor" "tranquilizers," respectively. To avoid confusion, this book avoids the term "tranquilizer."

Antipsychotics, also called "neuroleptics," primarily treat schizophrenia.

This chapter focuses on

- Schizophrenia (see pages 6–11)
- Delirium (see page 11)
- Dementia (see pages 11–12)
- Neuroleptic Malignant Syndrome (NMS) (see pages 20–22)
- Tardive dyskinesia (TD) (see pages 22–24)

Other chapters discuss using neuroleptics for

- Aggression (Anticonvulsants, pages 158–60)
- Anorexia nervosa (Antidepressants, page 70)
- Anxiety (Anti-anxiety, page 186)
- Borderline personality disorder (Lithium, page 136)
- Depression (Antidepressants, pages 64, 68–69)
- Mania (Lithium, pages 131–32)

NAMES, CLASSES, MANUFACTURERS, DOSE FORMS, AND COLORS

Generic Names	Brand Names	Manufacturers	Dose Forms (mg)*	Colors
PHENOTHIAZINES				
Aliphatics				
Chlorpromazine	Thorazine	SmithKline Beecham	t: 10/25/50 100/200; SR: 30/75/150/ 200/300; o: 30/100; p: 25 mg/ml; s: 10 mg/5 ml; sp: 25/100	t: all orange
Piperidines				
Mesoridazine	Serentil	Boehringer Ingelheim	t: 10/25/50 100; o: 25 mg/ml; p: 25 mg/ml	t: all red
Thioridazine	Mellaril	Sandoz	t: 10/15/25/ 50/100/150/200; o: 30/100:	t: chartreuse/ pink/tan/white green/yellow/pink
	Mellaril-S	Sandoz	su: 25/100 mg/5 ml	
Piperazines				
Fluphenazine	Permitil	Schering	t: 2.5/5/10; o: 5 mg/ml	t: light orange/ purple-pink/ light red
	Prolixin	Princeton	t: 1/2.5/5/10; e: 0.5 mg/ml; o: 5 mg/ml; p: 2.5 mg/ml	t: pink/yellow/ green/red
Fluphenazine decanoate	Prolixin Decanoate	Princeton	p: 25 mg/ml	—
Fluphenazine enanthante	Prolixin Enanthate	Princeton	p: 25 mg/ml	—
Perphenazine	Trilafon	Schering	t: 2/4/8/16; o: 16 mg/5 ml; p: 5 mg/ml	t: all gray
Trifluoperazine	Stelazine	SmithKline Beecham	t: 1/2/5/10; o: 10 mg/ml; p: 2 mg/ml	t: all blue
BUTYROPHENONES				
Haloperidol	Haldol	McNeil	t: 0.5/1/2/5/ 10/20; o: 2 mg/ml; p: 5 mg/ml	t: white/yellow/ pink/green/aqua/ salmon
Haloperidol decanoate	Haldol Decanoate	McNeil	p: 50/100 mg/ml	—

Generic Names	Brand Names	Manufacturers	Dose Forms (mg)*	Colors
THIOXANTHENES				
Chlorprothixene	Taractan	Roche	t: 10/25/50/100; o: 100 mg/5 ml; p: 25 mg/2 ml	t: orange/pink/ orange/red; o: fruit
Thiothixene	Navane	Roerig	c: 1/2/5/10/20; o: 5 mg/ml; p: 2/5 mg/ml	c: orange-yellow/ blue-yellow/ orange-white/ blue-white/ dark blue-light blue
DIPHENYLBUTYLPIPERDINES				
Pimozide	Orap	Lemmon	t: 2 mg	t: white
DIBENZAZEPINE				
Loxapine	Loxitane	Lederle	c: 5/10/25/50;	t: dark green/ yellow-green/ light green- dark green/ blue-dark green
	Loxitane-C	Lederle	o: 25 mg/ml;	—
	Loxitane-IM	Lederle	p: 50 mg/ml	—
DIHYDROINDOLONE				
Molindone	Moban	Du Pont	t: 5/10/25/50/ 100; o: 20 mg/ml	t: orange/ lavender/light green/blue/tan; o: cherry
DIBENZODIAZEPINE				
Clozapine	Clozaril	Sandoz[1]	t: 25/100	t: all yellow

*c = capsules, e = elixir, o = oral concentrate; p = parenteral concentrate; s = syrup; sp = suppository; SR = sustained release spansules; su = suspension; t = tablets
[1] Must prescribe clozapine through Sandoz.

PHARMACOLOGY

Antipsychotics are dopamine antagonists; they also elevate prolactin.

Most neuroleptic metabolites are inactive, but a few retain antipsychotic actions (e.g., mesoridazine's 7-hydroxychlorpromazine).

Oral form

- Antipsychotics' peak concentrations usually occur around 2–4 hours.
  √ Pimozide peaks at 6–8 hours, and ranges from 4–12 hours.
- Neuroleptics are highly lipophilic.

- They accumulate in the brain, which permits a once-a-day dose for psychosis.
  √ Aside from ·antipsychotic actions, oral neuroleptics have side effects, which can arise early (e.g., dry mouth in 30 minutes) or later (e.g., 2 years in tardive dyskinesia).
- Do not prescribe 2 neuroleptics concurrently.

IM form

- Peak concentrations at 15–30 minutes after injection.
- Expect 3–4 fold greater potency in IM over po doses.

Clozapine differs from other neuroleptics because it apparently does not

- Elevate prolactin and
- Cause extrapyramidal symptoms (EPS), including tardive dyskinesia (TD).

Pharmacology of Antipsychotics

Generic Names	Bio-availability (%)	Plasma Binding (%)	Onset of Action (hours)	Half-life (hours)	Excretion (%)*
Chlorpromazine	32 ± 19	95–98	4–6	30 ± 7	25 ± 15 R 70–80 F
Chlorprothixene	?	?	?	?	R/F
Clozapine	50–60	95	—	8 ± 4 12(4–66)	50 R 30 F
Fluphenazine	?	80–90	1	14.7–15.3 (16—24)	R/F
Haloperidol	70 ± 18	91 ± 1.4	—	17.9 ± 6.4	40 R
Loxapine	?	90	0.25–0.5	3.4 (1–19)	61.6 R 22.6 F
Mesordiazine	?	70	—	24–84	R/F
Molindone	?	98	—	1.5 (4–12)	R/F
Perphenazine	low	high	—	9.5 (8–21)	R/F
Pimozide	>50	99	—	55	38–45 R
Thioridazine	30	70–99	—	16 (7–42)	?
Thiothixene	?	?	—	34	?
Trifluoperazine	?	>80	2–3 weeks	9.3	R/F

* B = bile; F = fecal; R = renal; ? = unavailable or inconsistent.

DOSES

General Neuroleptic Doses

Generic Names	Chlorpromazine Equivalent Doses	Acute Doses (mg/day)	Ranges (mg/day)	P.R.N. (mg/po)	P.R.N. (mg/IM)
Chlorpromazine	100	200–1600	25–2000	25–100	25–50
Chlorprothixene	75	50–400	30–600	25–100	25–50
Clozapine	80	150–500	75–700	—	N/A
Fluphenazine	2	2.5–20	1–60	0.5–10	1–5
Haloperidol	3	2–40	1–100	0.5–5	2–5
Loxapine	12	60–100	30–250	10–60	12.5–50
Mesoridazine	30	75–300	30–400	10–100	25
Molindone	10	50–100	15–200	5–75	N/A
Perphenazine	8	16–32	4–64	4–8	5–10
Pimozide	1	2–10	2–10	N/A	N/A
Thioridazine	95	200–600	40–800	20–200	N/A
Thiothixene	5	6–30	6–60	2–20	2–4
Trifluoperazine	5	6–50	2–80	5–10	1–2

Specific Neuroleptic Doses

Generic Names	First Oral Dose (mg)	First Day Total Dose (mg/day)	Therapeutic Plasma Levels (ng/ml)
Chlorpromazine	50–100	300–400	100–400
Chlorprothixene	25–50	100–200	—
Clozapine	25	50	141–204*
Fluphenazine	1–2	2.5–10	0.1–3
Fluphenazine decanoate	12.5	12.5	0.05–2.7
Haloperidol	1–5	3–20	2–20
Loxapine	10–25	20–50	—
Mesoridazine	50	150	—
Molindone	?	50–75	—
Perphenazine	4–8	16–32	0.8–2.4
Pimozide	1–2	2	—
Thioridazine	50–100	150–300	1–1.5
Thiothixene	5	4–13	2–15*
Trifluoperazine	2–5	4–20	1–2.3

* Women statistically higher than men.

Age-Related Doses

| Generic Names | Childhood | | Geriatric Dose Range (mg/day) |
	Weight (mg/Kg/day)	Dose Range (mg/day)*	
Chlorpromazine	3–6	45–430 (196)	25–200
Chlorprothixene	2–5	30–215 (203)	—
Clozapine	—	—	—
Fluphenazine	0.05–0.1	4.9–50 (10)	2–10
Haloperidol	0.05	1–4.5	1–6
Loxapine	0.5–1	25–60	—
Mesoridazine	?	(153–174)	75–200
Molindone	0.5–1	25–50	50–150
Perphenazine	0.05–0.1	4–24	4–48
Pimozide†	—	—	10–50
Thioridazine	2–5	160–500 (282)	25–200
Thiothixene	0.5–1	2–24 (16)	2–15
Trifluoperazine	0.5	6–10 (0.5–15)	2–15

* Mean in parenthesis.
† Not recommended for psychiatric disorder; is used for Tourette's.

CLINICAL INDICATIONS AND USE

Neuroleptics generally relieve schizophrenia's "positive" (e.g., hallucinations) and "negative" (e.g., blunted affect) symptoms.

Target Symptoms for Antipsychotic Agents

Anorexia	Agitation	Assaultive behavior
Blunted affect	Bizarre thinking	Catatonic behavior
Confusion	Delusional thinking	Disorientation
Hallucinations	Insomnia	Manic symptoms
Paranoid thinking	Psychomotor agitation	Social withdrawal
	Thought withdrawal	

Initiating Therapy

Start with large enough dose to squelch symptoms, but low enough to minimize side effects.

Good and Bad Predictors of Antipsychotic Treatment for Schizophrenia

Good Outcome	Poor Outcome
Later age of onset	Earlier age of onset
Short duration of illness	Long duration of illness
Acute onset	Chronic onset
Good premorbid functioning and social competence	Poor premorbid functioning and social competence
Anxiety, tension, or other affective symptoms	Emotional blunting
Highly systematized and focused delusions whose symbolism is clear	Unsystematized and unfocused delusions
Confusion and disorientation	Clear sensorium
Precipitating factors	No precipitating factors
Married	Single
Family h/o affective disorder	No family h/o affective disorder
Family without h/o schizophrenia	Family with h/o schizophrenia

ANTIPSYCHOTIC AGENTS

Since the efficacy among antipsychotics is roughly equivalent, choosing the "right" antipsychotic can be elusive. Best to

- Select an agent that has previously helped the patient, but if none exists:
  √ If the first dose seems to help the patient, continue it;
  √ If not—patient is dangerously woozy—try another neuroleptic.
- If patient is already sleepy or drowsy, give a less sedative antipsychotic (e.g., fluphenazine, trifluoperazine) in a single dose 30 minutes before bedtime.
- Bedtime doses lessen the experience of side effects, since they arise during sleep.
- If the patient requires sedation or is actively disturbed
  √ Prescribe a more sedative oral neuroleptic (e.g., 100–200 mg of chlorpromazine or thioridazine), tid or qid; or escalate to
  √ IM neuroleptic (e.g., chlorpromazine 25–50 mg, haloperidol 5 mg) or
  √ Add benzodiazepines (e.g., lorazepam, 1–2 mg po, diazepam 5 mg IM) to neuroleptics.

What happens if patient does not improve sufficiently?

- Psychotic symptoms may vanish in days, but many require 2–12 weeks (or more) to disappear.
- If symptoms remain after initial 2 weeks, consider
  √ Is patient taking the oral medication?
    □ If patient does not have a common side effect (e.g., dry mouth), he probably is *not* ingesting the medication.
    □ To be certain, obtain a plasma level by drawing blood 12 hours after an oral dose.

√ Liquid medication is more readily swallowed than pills, which are "cheeked."
- If patient is taking the pills, but without a good response, then
  √ Re-examine diagnosis and make sure there are clear target symptoms.
  □ Raise (or lower) the dose of the same neuroleptic.
  □ Try a liquid form.
  □ Switch to depot medication (see below).
  □ Consider adding lithium or ECT.

Maintenance Program

After the initial schizophrenic break

- Do not change medications without a clear, consistent reason for 3–6 months after discharge.
  √ With the same drug and dose, changing the pill's form—size, shape, or color—may distress patient.
- From 6–9 months after discharge (or point of maximum improvement), start to taper gradually the dose to 20% of the highest dose.
  √ If symptoms recur, increase dose.
- If patient will be under high stress (e.g., new job), do not alter medication until stress is past.

Depot neuroleptics, which are IM antipsychotics lasting 2–4 weeks, are employed for maintenance therapy.

- Their advantages are
  √ Patient does not have to take pills every day;
  √ Certainty that drug is taken;
  √ Less staff work.
- Their disadvantages are
  √ Once injected, they are injected, and patient must deal with any adverse consequences, such as an EPS.
- Avoid the following
  √ Starting any treatment with depot neuroleptics;
  √ IV administration of all depot forms.
  √ Suddenly switching from oral to depot forms; this can radically alter serum level.
    □ For instance, 4 weeks of fluphenazine 10 mg/day po was stopped, replaced by fluphenazine decanoate 12½ mg IM; 2 weeks later the serum level dropped from 0.51 ng/ml to 0.08 ng/ml and symptoms appeared.
- Safety favors
  √ *Gradual* shift from oral to depot forms and
  √ Test dose.

Sample of Gradual Change from Oral to Depot Form of Fluphenazine Decanoate*

Original Oral Dose (mg/ml)	Week 0		Week 2		Week 4		Week 6		Week 8		Week 10	
	po	FD	po	FD	po	FD	po	FD	po	FD	po	FD
5	4.0	6¼	2½	6¼	1.0	6¼	—	6¼	6¼	—	—	6¼
10	7½	6¼	5.0	6¼	2½	12½	—	12½	12½	—	—	12½
20	15.0	6¼	10.0	6¼	7½	12½	5.0	12½	2½	12½	—	12½
30	25.0	6¼	20.0	12½	15.0	25.0	10.0	25.0	5.0	25.0	—	25.0
40	30.0	6¼	25.0	12½	20.0	25.0	15.0	25.0	10.0	25.0	—	25.0

* po = daily; FD = every other week

* Method
  ✓ No depot form is clearly better than another.
  ✓ First, stabilize the patient on a dose of oral fluphenazine or haloperidol.
  ✓ To detect rare sensitivity to vehicle (sesame oil) or side effects, inject 6.25 mg (by insulin syringe for accurate measurement) of fluphenazine decanoate (or any depot form).
  ✓ Dose schedules include
    □ Fluphenazine decanoate (FD) (see page 9).
    □ Fluphenazine enanthate (FE) can follow a similar table.
    □ Haloperidol decanoate (HD) dose should equal 10–15 times the daily dose of haloperidol orally.
  ✓ When depot forms reach peak levels at 2–6 days after injection, may add antiparkinsonian—that is, anticholinergic—agents (ACA).
  ✓ Avoid delivering more than 50 mg IM or SC.
* Depot neuroleptics have not been approved for children under 12.

*The Use of Depot Neuroleptics**

	Fluphenazine Decanoate	Fluphenazine Enanthate	Haloperidol Decanoate
Usual dose (mg)	25 (6¼–100)	25–75 (12½–100)	50–100 (50–300)
Usual frequency of injections (weeks)	3 (3–6)	2 (1–3)	4 (2–5)
Antipsychotic action begins (days)	1–3	1–3	6–7
Peak plasma level (days)	1–2	2–4	3–9
Protein binding	80	80	92
Half-life (days)	6.8–9.6 (one injection) 14.3 (many doses)	3½–4 (one injection)	21 (one injection)
Maximum dose recorded	400 mg/week	1250 mg/week	1200 mg/injection

* Ranges in parentheses.

Indications for long-term antipsychotic therapy

* After 3–4 schizophrenic episodes, may need neuroleptics for years (if not for life), always weighing the risks of psychosis against those of tardive dyskinesia and other side effects. Consider clozapine.
* Maintenance antipsychotic therapy is superior to placebo; after 2 years it prevents relapses in 40–70% of patients.

Anticonvulsants may relieve schizophrenia

- Clonazepam may diminish schizophrenia, although findings are unclear.
  - √ For instance, 31% improvement in 4 studies;
  - √ Decreased paranoid thinking and hallucinations when combined with neuroleptic.
  - √ Helped 4 patients with atypical psychosis who were unresponsive to neuroleptics.
  - √ Dose
    - □ Start at 0.5 mg bid-tid,
    - □ Increase 0.5–1.0 mg every 3 days until stabilization occurs,
    - □ Dose may reach 3 mg/day.
- Carbamazepine offers mixed results.
- Valproic acid, when added to other agents, assisted 12–30% schizophrenics.

Delirium

A delirium is a clouding of consciousness, disorientation, and loss of recent memory.

- It usually lasts no more than several days.
  - √ Patients improve or die.
- Insure that medications are not causing the delirium.

To manage combative, disorganized, or confused behavior, haloperidol is useful.

- Haloperidol affords limited anticholinergic and hypotensive effects.
- Avoid toxicity by avoiding standing regular orders.
- Haloperidol 1–5 mg po or IM,
  - √ Wait one hour, and
  - √ Titrate repeat doses q 2–8 hours.
- Delirious patients rarely need > 10 mg of haloperidol.
  - √ 2–4 mg/day typically suffices.
- Avoid adding ACAs, since
  - √ Increased anticholinergic actions can worsen delirium, and
  - √ Only 20% of delirious patients develop dystonia.

Benzodiazepines are an alternative to antipsychotic agents.

- Example: lorazepam 1-2 mg po or 2–4 mg IM.

Dementia

A dementia is the loss of intellectual abilities, especially judgment, memory, abstract thinking, control over impulses, and language.

- Unlike in delirium, in dementia there is no clouding of consciousness.
- Dementias are often long-term and permanent.

Dementias (so far) benefit little from medication.

Antipsychotic agents may reduce agitation and confusion.

- Haloperidol ½–2 mg po or IM q 4–6h
  √ Bedtime dosing might help regulate sleep cycle.
  √ Low potency neuroleptics (e.g., chlorpromazine) risk further cognitive impairment, hypotension, and seizures.
  √ Avoid adding ACAs, since they may augment toxicity.

Short-acting hypnosedatives (lorazepam ½ mg po) induce less confusion than do longer-acting hypnosedatives (chlordiazepoxide).

SIDE EFFECTS

The greater the drug's antipsychotic potency, the fewer its side effects. The big exception is that increased potency causes more intense and frequent extrapyramidal symptoms (EPS).

Neuroleptics generate anticholinergic side effects.

Degree of Anticholinergic Effects

Most Anticholinergic	Medium Anticholinergic	Least Anticholinergic
Chlorpromazine	Loxapine	Fluphenazine
Chlorprothixene	Molindone	Haloperidol
Clozapine	Perphenazine	Pimozide
Mesoridazine		Thiothixene
Thioridazine		Trifluoperazine

Most anticholinergic symptoms taper off in 1–2 weeks.

Anticholinergic actions occur in many systems, and include

- Hypotension
- Dry mouth
- Constipation
- Paralytic ileus
- Urinary hesitancy or retention
- Blurred vision
- Dry eyes
- Narrow-angle glaucoma
- Photophobia
- Nasal congestion

These anticholinergic effects are discussed with their respective organ systems.

Cardiovascular Effects

Hypotension

Degree of Hypotensive Side Effects Among Antipsychotics

Most	Medium	Least
Chlorpromazine	Clozapine	Fluphenazine
Chlorprothixene	Loxapine	Haloperidol
Mesoridazine	Perphenazine	Molindone
Thioridazine	Thiothixene	Pimozide
	Trifluoperazine	

- *Dizziness, lightheadness, weakness, fainting, and syncope* on standing up.
- Hypotension is more frequent with low salt intake and parenteral use.
- Management
  - √ Suggest patient sit and then stand after 15–60 seconds,
  - √ If more severe hypotension, lower head and elevate legs
  - √ If medically serious, employ volume expanders, and if necessary
    - □ Pressor agents, such as metaraminol, phenylephrine, or norepinephrine.
    - □ *Do not use epinephrine.*

Tachycardia
Non-specific ECG changes
Arrythymia (especially with thioridazine and pimozide)

Gastrointestinal Effects

Dry mouth

- Management
  - √ Sugar-free gum and candy,
  - √ Cool drinks (minimal sugar, e.g., Crystal Light, Gatorade),
  - √ Biotène—sugar-free cool mints,
  - √ Xero-lube, a saliva substitute,
  - √ Ice chips,
  - √ Brush teeth frequently,
  - √ Wash mouth with
    - □ Pilocarpine 1% solution, or
    - □ Gradually dissolve (cholinergic) bethanechol 5–10 mg tablets.

Anorexia, nausea, vomiting, dyspepsia
Diarrhea (occasionally)
Constipation

- Management
  √ Increase bulk (e.g., bran, salads) and fluids (water, milk),
  √ Improved diet (e.g., prunes),
  √ Stool softener (e.g., docusate), laxative (e.g., psyllium), or
  √ Bethanechol 10–25 mg tid-qid.

Paralytic ileus
Allergic obstructive hepatitis

- This cholestatic jaundice is much less common now than when chlorpromazine (and its impurities) were introduced,
- Occurred in <0.1% of patients in 1st month of treatment,
- This disorder rarely led to hepatic necrosis or permanent damage,
- Reversible if drug stopped, and
- Routine LFT do not predict.

Weight gain

- Due to increased appetite or decreased activity,
- More common with chlorpromazine, chlorprothixene, thioridazine, and mesoridazine.

Weight loss

- Molindone and loxapine may lower weight.

Renal Effects

Urinary hesitancy or *retention*

- Urinary retention increases urinary tract infections, which requires periodic urinalyses and cultures.
- Management
  √ Bethanechol 10–25 mg tid-qid or 5–10 mg every hour until symptom abates.
  √ May prescribe IM/SC bethanechol 5–10 mg for more serious cases.

Endocrine and Sexual Effects

Increased blood prolactin may produce

- *Breast enlargement* and *tenderness*
- *Galactorrhea* (rare)

- *Diminished libido*
  - √ Changed quality of orgasm for men and women
  - √ Diminished ability to reach orgasm
- *Gynecomastia* in both sexes
- *Amenorrhea, menstrual irregularities,* and *delayed ovulation*

Management

- Bromocriptine, which inhibits prolactin secretion, exists as $2\frac{1}{2}$ mg tablets or as 5 mg capsules.
  - √ Start at $1\frac{1}{4}$–$2\frac{1}{2}$ mg/day,
  - √ Add $2\frac{1}{2}$ every 3–7 days as tolerated,
  - √ Until optimal dose of 5–$7\frac{1}{2}$ mg/day is reached, or
  - √ The therapeutic range of $2\frac{1}{2}$–15 mg/day is satisfied.

Diminished sexuality

- Reported in 25% of patients taking neuroleptics.
- Affects 60% of patients on thioridazine.

Retrograde ejaculation

- May be physically painful.
- Occurs with patients on all neuroleptics, but especially common with thioridazine (other neuroleptics in parentheses):
  - √ 44% had difficulties achieving an erection (19%).
  - √ 35% had troubles maintaining an erection (11%).
  - √ 49% had "changes" in erections (0%).

Priapism

- Occurs with alpha-adrenergic antipsychotics.

Hypoglycemia, hyperglycemia, glycosuria, high or *prolonged glucose tolerance tests*

Hematologic Effects

Agranulocytosis (Schultz syndrome)

- Agranulocytosis is WBCs < 1000–2000/mm^3, with neutrophils < 500/mm^3.
- Occurs suddenly, often within hours, usually in the first month of treatment, but can erupt any time during the initial 12 weeks of therapy.
- Arises in < 0.02% of patients on neuroleptics.
- Results most frequently with clozapine (1.3%) and chlorpromazine (0.7%).
- Statistically, more frequent in white females over 40 years old.

ANTIPSYCHOTIC AGENTS

- Major signs are
  - ✓ Acute sore throat
  - ✓ High fever
  - ✓ Mouth sores and ulcers
- Also possible are
  - ✓ Upset stomach
  - ✓ Weakness, lethargy, malaise
  - ✓ Lymphadenopathy
  - ✓ Asthma
  - ✓ Skin ulcerations
  - ✓ Laryngeal, angioneurotic or peripheral edema
  - ✓ Anaphylactic reactions
- Management
  - ✓ Do not start any patient on neuroleptic if WBC is < 3000–3500/mm^3.
  - ✓ With onset of sore throat and fever, *stop* all non-life sustaining drugs (e.g., neuroleptics).
  - ✓ Routine or frequent CBCs do not help, except with clozapine.
- Mortality high if drug not ceased and treatment initiated.

Leukopenia

- WBC from 2000–3500/mm^3
- Symptoms similar to agranulocytosis

Management

- Reduce or stop antipsychotic, depending on the severity.

Eyes, Ears, Nose, and Throat Effects

Blurred vision

- Difficulty for vision close up, not far away
- Management
  - ✓ Pilocarpine 1% eye drops or
  - ✓ Bethanechol 5–10 mg po.
  - ✓ Eye glasses can be used temporarily, but they need frequent changing.

Photophobia

- From dilated pupils

Pigmentation

- Long-term neuroleptic use, especially chlorpromazine, places granular deposits chiefly in the back of the cornea and the front of the lens.

- Vision usually unimpaired.
  √ Eye pigmentation often co-exists with neuroleptic-induced skin pigmentation or photosensitivity reactions.
- Eye pigmentation does not require slit-lamp examination,
  √ But if shining a light into the eye displays an opaque pupil, patient should consult ophthalmologist.

Pigmentary retinopathy

- Caused almost always by chronic use of > 800 mg/day of thioridazine.
- Reduced visual acuity and blindness.
- Management
  √ Stop thioridazine.
  √ Symptoms may disappear, if caught early.
  √ *Never* prescribe > 800 mg/day of thioridazine for more than a few days.

Dry eyes

- This anticholinergic disturbance particularly bothers the elderly or those wearing contact lenses.
- Management
  √ Artificial tears
    ▫ Employ cautiously with soft contact lenses or
    ▫ Apply patient's usual wetting solution or comfort drops.

Narrow-angle glaucoma

- Highly anticholinergic neuroleptics can trigger narrow-angle glaucoma.
- A h/o eye or facial pain, blurred vision, or halos circling outside lights suggests acute narrow-angle glaucoma.
  √ When shining a penlight across the eye's anterior chamber, if the entire eye does not illuminate, suspect narrow-angle glaucoma.

Nasal congestion, dry throat

Dry bronchial secretions and *strained breathing* aggravate patients with respiratory ailments.

Skin, Allergies, and Temperature Effects

Photosensitivity

- Chlorpromazine, as well as other neuroleptics, foster severe sunburn after 30–60 minutes of direct sunlight.

- Management
  - √ Cautious exposure and increase to the sun and
  - √ Apply sun screens with para-aminobenzoic acid.

Skin rashes

- Stop neuroleptic.

Hypothermia more common than *hyperthermia.*

Management

- Warn patients about this in advance so they can protect themselves,
- Proper heated (or cooled) environment.
- Avoid overexercising or working in hot places.
- Fluids, etc.

Decreased sweating

- May cause a secondary, and sometimes fatal, *hyperthermia.*
- Be careful with patients who
  - √ Work in hot weather,
  - √ Take neuroleptics with high-anticholinergic effects,
  - √ Drink excessive alcohol, or
  - √ Suffer from CNS disease.

Central Nervous System Effects

Extrapyramidal Symptoms

Most EPS	Medium EPS	Least EPS
Fluphenazine	Chlorpromazine	Clozapine
Haloperidol	Chlorprothixene	Mesoridazine
Pimozide	Loxapine	Molindone
Thiothixene	Perphenazine	Thioridazine
Trifluoperazine		

Dystonia

- Acute contractions of tongue, face, neck, and back.
  - √ Patient may describe stiff tongue as a "thick" tongue.
- Spasms of tongue, jaw, and neck are the first to erupt, typically in a few hours or days.
- Other dystonic symptoms include
  - √ *Opisthotonos,* a tetanic tightening of the entire body with head back and belly up

Types of Extrapyramidal Symptoms

Type	Onset	Risk Groups	Clinical Course
Dystonia	1–5 days	Young males	Acute, spasmodic, painful
Parkinsonism	5–30 days	12–45% of patients; elderly women	Occurs throughout treatment
Akathisia	5–60 days	20–50% of patients; elderly women	Persists during treatment
Neuroleptic Malignant Syndrome (NMS)	Weeks	0.5–1% of patients develop NMS; 80% are under 40; affects 2X men > women; high potency neuroleptics	Mortality rate is 20–30%; symptoms typically persist 5–10 days on oral forms and 20–30 days after depot injections
"Rabbit" Syndrome	Months– years	4% of patients untreated with ACAs	Usually reversible with ACAs
Tardive Dyskinesia (TD)	6–24 months	20–25% of patients with range of 0.5–60%; women, the elderly, and patients with affective disorders	Treat best with prevention; often irreversible

ANTIPSYCHOTIC AGENTS

   √ *Oculogyric crisis* with eyes locked upward
   √ *Laryngospasm* with respiratory difficulties
   √ *Torticollis*—a twisting of cervical muscles with an unnatural head position
   √ More common among piperazines (e.g., fluphenazine enanthate, trifluoperazine) than among aliphatics (e.g., chlorpromazine, thioridazine).
  • More common with manics (26%) than with schizophrenics (6%).

Parkinsonism (a.k.a. Pseudoparkinsonism)

  • Symptoms include
   √ Stiffness, stooped posture
   √ Masklike facies
   √ Bradykinesia
   √ Shuffling, festinating gait (with small steps)
   √ Cogwheel rigidity
   √ Drooling, seborrhea
   √ Tremor
   √ Coarse pill-rolling of thumb and fingers at rest
   √ Micrographia
  • Parkinsonism frequently shows *akinesia*—a paucity of spontaneous gestures or voluntary useful movements with
   √ Apathy
   √ Rigid posture

√ Diminished or no conversation
√ A decreased arm swing
√ Walk with a shorter stride
* Parkinsonism contributes to passive inactivity, which can be misdiagnosed as catatonia, withdrawn schizophrenia, or depression.

Akathisia

* The least obvious, but the most prevalent EPS, is akathisia.
* Symptoms include
√ Motor, inner-driven restlessness
√ The "jitters," fidgety, or "inner itch"
√ Tapping feet incessantly, "restless legs"
√ Rocking forward and backward in chair
√ Shifting weight from side to side when standing
√ Standing and sitting
* May present as a muscular discomfort in an agitated, frightened, dysphoric, pacing, hand-wringing, and weeping individual.
* Patients might not notice, or be bothered by, their regular, rhythmic leg-jiggling.
* Akathisia can be misdiagnosed as anxiety.
√ If the diagnosis is unclear, ask patient if restlessness is a "muscle" feeling or a "head" feeling; the "muscle" feeling suggests akathisia, the "head" feeling, anxiety.

Neuroleptic Malignant Syndrome (NMS)

* Uncommon, yet hardly rare, disorder; potentially fatal, unless recognized and treated early.
* NMS affects ½–2.4% of patients treated with antipsychotics.
* Deaths, which usually result in 3–30 days, occur in 11–18% of NMS patients.
√ Estimated that 1000–4000 NMS fatalities happen in America every year.
* Typically erupts in 24–72 hours.
* Displays
√ Severe parkinsonism with
□ Muscle (akinesic) rigidity, catatonic appearance,
□ Tremors, dyskinesias,
□ Akinesias, "lead-pipe" muscle tone,
□ Flexor-extensor posturing, or
□ Festinating gait.
√ Hyperpyrexia (101°F → 107°F)
√ Altered consciousness, which may present first, can be
□ "Alert look,"
□ "Dazed mutism,"

□ Agitated, confused,
□ Obtunded, incontinent, or
□ Comatose.

√ Autonomic dysfunction with
□ Tachycardia (> 30 beats/per/minute),
□ Increased BP (> 20 points diastolic),
□ Profuse sweating, more salivation,
□ Tachypnea (> 25 respirations/minute),
□ Pallor, or
□ Dysphagia.

√ Severe abnormalities on laboratory tests
□ High creatine phosphokinase (347 → 4286 U/ml),
□ Myoglobinuria, renal decline or failure,
□ Raised WBCs (15,000–30,000/mm³), and/or
□ Often elevated LFTs.

More common with

- People under 20 and over 60 years of age have higher mortality rates from NMS.
- Patients with organic brain syndromes, mental retardation, and drug addiction have greater fatality rates from NMS.
- High neuroleptic doses.
- Rapid neuroleptization.
- Depot antipsychotic agents generate more NMS, but the same number of deaths from NMS.
- Higher—rather than lower—potentcy antipsychotics, although greater use of high-potency drugs may inflate the frequency; one-third of NMS patients develop it again if placed on any antipsychotic.
- Fatalities from NMS in percentage of patients on a specific antipsychotic are
  √ Trifluoperazine (43%)
  √ Chlorpromazine (40%)
  √ Thiothixene (40%)
  √ Fluphenazine (depot) (33.3%)
  √ Fluphenazine (8.3%)
  √ Haloperidol (5.5%)
  √ Thioridazine (0.0%)
- Taking 2 or more neuroleptics.
- Supportive measures must be instituted immediately
  √ Stop neuroleptics and anticholinergic agents.
  √ Maintain hydration by oral or IV routes.
  √ Correct electrolyte abnormalities.
  √ Cool body to reduce fever.
  √ Diagnose and treat pneumonia or pulmonary emboli.

   √ If patient has survived and requires antipsychotic agents, they
     may be re-introduced cautiously.
- Drug treatment favors bromocriptine over dantrolene.
   √ Bromocriptine
     □ Rigidity quickly disappears.
     □ Temperature, BP instability, and creatine phosphokinase levels
       normalize after a few days.
     □ Most effective and safest treatment for NMS.
   √ Dantrolene
     □ Lowers hyperthermia and creatine phosphokinase, while in-
       creasing muscle relaxation, often in hours.
     □ Initial dose may be 2–3 mg/kg/day.
     □ Hepatic toxicity occurs with doses > 10 mg/kg/day.
- ACAs do not help.

Drugs Used to Treat NMS

Generic Name	Dose	Number Treated	Number Successful
Anticholinergic agents	—	20	8
Bromocriptine	7.5–60 mg/day po	3	3
Dantrolene	0.8–10 mg/kg/IV; 50 mg qd-qid po	5	4
Levodopa	100 mg bid po	1	1
Carbidopa-levodopa	25 mg tid-200 qid po	3	2
Amantadine	100 mg bid po	2	2
Lorazepam	1.5–2 mg IV, then po	2	2

"Rabbit Syndrome" (a.k.a., Perioral tremor)

- Arises late during neuroleptic treatment.
- Consists of rapid lip movements that mimic a rabbit.
- Responds well to ACAs.

Tardive Dyskinesia (TD)

- TD consists of involuntary face, trunk, and limb movements.
- TD typically arises when antipsychotics are lowered or stopped.
   √ Symptoms emerge in weeks, months, or sometimes years after
     reducing the dose.
- TD arises after 6–24 months of treatment.
   √ Rarely occurs before 3 months.
- Frequently varies enormously between studies, but usually ranges
  between ½–56%.
   √ Probably closest to 20–25% of patients treated with antipsy-
     chotics for over 2 years.

√ (Dyskinesia—of some type—affects 1–5% of people *never* exposed to neuroleptics.)
* TD presents with 3 major types of symptoms
  √ *Facial-lingual-oral involuntary hyperkinesis* with
    □ Frowning, blinking, smiling, grimacing, puckering, pouting, blowing, smacking, licking, chewing, clenching, mouth opening, rolling and protruding ("fly catcher's") tongue, and spastic facial distortions.
  √ *Limb choreoathetoid movements* with
    □ Choreic movements that are rapid, purposeless, irregular, and spontaneous;
    □ Athetoid movements that are slow, irregular, complex, and serpentine;
    □ Tremors that are repetitive, regular, and rhythmic;
    □ Lateral knee movements; or
    □ Foot tapping, squirming, inversion, and eversion.
  √ *Trunk movements* with
    □ Movements of neck, shoulders, dramatic hip jerks;
    □ Rocking, twisting, squirming, pelvic gyrations, and thrusts.
* Alternatively, patients may experience
  √ Tardive akathisia (with persistent restless feelings),
  √ Tardive dystonia (with recurrent muscle contractions of neck and shoulders), or
  √ Tardive tics.
* TD patients may
  □ Grunt,
  □ Normally have TD disappear while asleep,
  √ Suppress symptoms temporarily by intense voluntary effort and concentration, and/or
  √ Exacerbate TD under stress.
* Milder TD arises in people consuming larger neuroleptic doses, whereas more severe forms afflict patients ingesting smaller doses.
* Unclear if drug-free holidays cause or prevent TD.
* Severity of TD reaches a plateau and does not worsen, despite conservative neuroleptic management.
* All neuroleptics can cause TD, except perhaps clozapine.
  √ Thioridazine and molindone theoretically yield less TD.
  √ Other drugs may generate TD, such as
    □ Amoxapine, an antidepressant
    □ Prochlorperazine, an anti-emetic phenothiazine
    □ Metoclopramide, another anti-emetic.
* Make sure "TD" does not stem from ill-fitting dentures.
* Prevention best treats TD.
  √ Neuroleptics should *never* be used longer than 6 continuous months in *non*schizophrenic patients.

√ At least every 6 months, assess long-treated patients to see if neuroleptics can be reduced or stopped.

√ If antipsychotic discontinued and TD emerges, allow at least 3–7 months for TD to disappear or to lessen on its own.

  □ After 18 months, abnormal movements diminish by 50%.

√ ACAs do not alleviate TD and often aggravate it.

√ Neuroleptics can temporarily halt TD, but TD eventually re-emerges, frequently worse than before.

√ Lacking convincing evidence, drugs that might inhibit TD include

  □ Amantadine (100 mg bid-tid)
  □ Baclofen (5–20 mg tid)
  □ Benzodiazepines (e.g., diazepam, clonazepam)
  □ Carbamazepine (100–800 mg/day)
  □ Choline (2–8 grams/day)
  □ Clonidine (0.3–0.7 mg/day)
  □ Lecithin (10–40 grams/day)
  □ Levodopa (100–2000 mg/day)
  □ Lithium (300 mg tid-qid)
  □ Reserpine (1–6 mg/day)
  □ Valproic acid (1000–1500 mg/day)
  □ Vitamin E

Seizures

• Uncommon,
• Flare up by abruptly raising or lowering antipsychotics, and
• Less common with molindone and fluphenazine.
• Seizures common in epileptics, although epileptics can usually tolerate neuroleptics without seizures.

Sedation, Drowsiness

Most Sedative	Medium Sedative	Least Sedative
Chlorpromazine	Loxapine	Fluphenazine
Chlorprothixene	Molindone	Haloperidol
Clozapine	Perphenazine	Pimozide
Mesoridazine		Thiothixene
Thioridazine		Trifluoperazine

• Sedation especially fatigues during first 2 weeks of therapy.
• Management
  √ Prescribe full dose at bedtime.
  √ Diminish daytime doses.
  √ Switch to less sedating neuroleptic.

Confusion, delirium, disturbed concentration, disorientation

- This toxicity occurs more often in high doses and in the elderly.
- To insure that it is an *anticholinergic toxicity*, should see
  - √ Dilated pupils
  - √ Hot dry skin
  - √ Dry mucous membranes
  - √ Tachycardia
  - √ Absent bowel sounds
- Can be a medical emergency.
- Management
  - √ Stop all neuroleptic and antiparkinsonian agents.
  - √ IM/IV physostigmine can diagnose and treat this toxicity.
  - √ Physostigmine's (cholinergic) risks include
    - □ Increased salivation, sweating, bradycardia, abdominal cramps, desire to urinate or defecate, seizures
    - □ Transient sinus arrest in cardiac patients
    - □ Bronchospasm in asthmatics
  - √ Before and after injecting physostigmine, obtain BP and pulse rate.
  - √ Give 1–2 mg IM/IV physostigmine no faster than 1 mg/minute.
  - √ Anticholinergic delirium clears in 15–20 minutes after injection.
    - □ Physostigmine's effects last 30–60 minutes.
    - □ If patient does not improve with 1 mg of physostigmine, may repeat 1 mg dose in 30–40 minutes.
    - □ May inject up to 4 mg IV of physostigmine in one day.
  - √ Switch to amantadine and/or to less anticholinergic neuroleptic
  - √ If patient is agitated during anticholinergic delirium, may use lorazepam to calm, since it is a shorter-acting benzodiazepine without significant anticholinergic activity.

Side Effects from Depot Neuroleptics

Side Effects	Fluphenazine Decanoate (FD)	Fluphenazine Enanthate (FE)	Haloperidol Decanoate (HD)
Anticholinergic	Occasional	More anticholinergic than FD	Occasional
Cardiovascular	Hypotension occasionally	Hypotension and some hypertension reported at start of therapy	Occasional hypotension; no severe hypertension reported
Weight gain	11% of patients had a 10% weight increase; 4-times more patients gain weight than on oral fluphenazine	Similar to FD	Weight loss and weight gain noted

Side Effects	Fluphenazine Decanoate (FD)	Fluphenazine Enanthate (FE)	Haloperidol Decanoate (HD)
Endocrine effects	Menstrual disturbances, galactorrhea, and amenorrhea	Same as FD	Same as FD
Eye changes	17% (11/63) of patients after 5 years displayed lens and/or corneal opacities	None reported	None reported
Skin and local reactions	One case of induration at high doses; skin reactions arise	No indurations reported; skin reactions occur	Inflammation at injection site; one case of photosensitivity; "tracking" observed
EPS	EPS frequent, FD > HD; 25% have dystonias; NMS more common than with po forms	EPS more frequent (30–50%) than with FD, but 11.7% have dystonias; more NMS than po forms	EPS common, but equal to po form; 65% have dystonias; TD in HD > FD; more NMS than with po form
CNS	Drowsiness and insomnia	Same as FD	Same as FD
Mood	May increase depression in vulnerable patients	Same as FD	No data
Laboratory changes	One case of jaundice; ECG changes noted	No account of jaundice; some ECG changes	Within normal variation

PERCENTAGE OF SIDE EFFECTS

Part I

Side Effects	Chlorpromazine	Chlorprothixene	Clozapine	Fluphenazine	Haloperidol
CARDIOVASCULAR EFFECTS					
Hypotension	2.6	>30	6.4 (0.55–13)	0.79	1
Hypertension	0.0	—	3.5	—	1
Dizziness, lightheadedness	10 (6–14)	15	12.6 (1.7–22)	7	14 (10–30)
Fainting, syncope	2	—	4 (0.62–7)	—	4
Tachycardia	11 (10–30)	6	14.3 (5.3–25)	2	1
ECG abnormalities	20	6	0.5 (0.17–1)	2	<2

Side Effects	Chlorpromazine	Chlorprothixene	Clozapine	Fluphenazine	Haloperidol
Cardiac arrhythmias	6	<2	—	—	<2
Sweating	9	—	7.3 (0.9–13)	—	15
GASTROINTESTINAL EFFECTS					
Dry mouth and throat	23 (10–30)	20	6.6	8	16 (10–30)
Anorexia, lower appetite	2 (0.5–.29)	—	0.6	—	0.0
Nausea, vomiting	6	—	6.4 (1.1–11)	4.3	12
Diarrhea	1.1	—	1.1	1.1	—
Constipation	13	—	10.6 (1.9–16)	9.6	6
Jaundice	0.64	<2	1	0.0	<2
Salivation	11	—	32	—	16
Weight gain	13.3 (0–30)	20	1.9 0.73–3	20.0	1
Edema	2.8	—	—	0.0	—
RENAL EFFECTS					
Urinary hesitancy or retention	3	20	2	1.3	15
Enuresis	—	—	0.23	—	—
ENDOCRINE AND SEXUAL EFFECTS					
Menstrual changes	16.3	—	—	4.4	—
Breast swelling	1.1	—	—	2.2	—
Lactation	0.72	—	—	3.3	—
Inhibited ejaculation	6	<2	1	2	<2
Disturbed sexual function	—	—	0.19	—	—
HEMATOLOGIC EFFECTS					
Agranulocytosis	0.67 (0.32–1.1)	—	1.3 (0.004–3.0)	—	—
Leukopenia	3 (1–10)	<2	1.7 (0.63–3.0)	1	—
EYES, EARS, NOSE, AND THROAT EFFECTS					
Blurred vision	14.4	9.8	5	4.3	6.8
Lenticular pigmentation	6	6	—	<2	<2
Pigmentary retinopathy	6	0.0	0.0	<2	0.0
Nasal stuffiness	2.5	15	—	9.2	15

ANTIPSYCHOTIC AGENTS

Side Effects	Chlorpro-mazine	Chlorpro-thixene	Clozapine	Fluphen-azine	Haloperidol
SKIN, ALLERGIES, AND TEMPERATURE					
Allergies	6.6	—	0.1	2.6	0.0
Photosensitivity	6	<2	—	<2	<2
Rashes	4	15	1.5	<2	1.2
Abnormal skin pigment	15	<2	—	<2	<2
Fever, hyper-thermia	1	—	5.3 (1–13)	—	1
CENTRAL NERVOUS SYSTEM EFFECTS					
Dystonia	3	12	0.0	5 (2.5–8)	30 (16–65)
Parkinsonism	12.5	10	—	15.4	>30
Akinesia	10	10	2 (0.36–5.0)	–	16
Akathisia	8.4 (6–12.1)	10	3.5	21.6	29
NMS	0.6	0.5	—	0.5	0.9
Weakness	1	—	1	—	1
Rigidity	6	—	3	—	30
Seizures	1 (0.5–1.5)	6	2.3 (0.36–5)	0.0	1
Headache	8	—	4.9 (0.86–7)	—	6
Slurred speech	1	—	1	—	0.0
Tremor	12	—	7	—	25
Drowsiness, fatigue	39.8 (23.4–50)	22	23.8 (9–44)	16.2 (13–19.5)	21.8 (2–39)
Confusion, disorientation	6.8 (5–6.8)	—	2.4 (0.74–4)	—	4
Insomnia	22	—	3 (0.19–6)	—	36
Restlessness, agitation (i.e., motoric)	8	—	5	—	24
Anxiety, nervousness (i.e., mental)	10	—	4	—	24
Excitement	0.5	—	2	—	12
Depression	13.9	—	1	—	—

Part II

Side Effects	Loxapine	Mesoridazine	Molindone	Perphenazine	Pimozide
CARDIOVASCULAR EFFECTS					
Hypotension	20	8.4 (1–11.7)	6	1	20
Dizziness	20	8 (1–10.2)	20	12	12 (0–30)
Tachycardia	20	1.8	<2	—	6
ECG abnormalities	<2	20	<2	—	6
Cardiac arrhythmias	—	—	—	—	<2
GASTROINTESTINAL EFFECTS					
Dry mouth and throat	20	13.7 (7.4–30)	20	18.8	22.5 (10–30)
Anorexia, lower appetite	—	—	—	4.2	—
Increased appetite	—	—	—	—	5
Nausea, vomiting	—	2.3	—	0.9	0.0
Taste changes	—	—	—	—	5
Diarrhea	—	—	—	—	5
Constipation	—	10 (1–20)	—	4.2	20
Jaundice	<2	<1	<2	0.0	—
Thirst	—	—	—	—	5
Weight gain	2	20	<2	5.9	4
Edema	—	—	—	0.8	—
RENAL EFFECTS					
Urinary hesitancy or retention	15	5	15	—	15
ENDOCRINE AND SEXUAL EFFECTS					
Menstrual changes	—	5	—	—	0.0
Breast swelling	—	5	—	—	0.0
Lactation	—	—	—	0.9	15
Inhibited ejaculation	6	—	—	—	—
Disturbed sexual function	—	5.5	—	—	15
HEMATOLOGIC EFFECTS					
Agranulocytosis	—	—	—	0.0	—
Leukopenia	<2	—	—	—	—

Side Effects	Loxapine	Mesori-dazine	Molindone	Perphen-azine	Pimozide
EYES, EARS, NOSE, AND THROAT EFFECTS					
Lenticular pigmentation	<2	—	—	—	<2
Increased light sensitivity	—	—	—	—	5
Blurred vision	15	8.9 (2.8–20)	15	17.8	20
Nasal stuffiness	20	20	20	18	20
SKIN, ALLERGIES, AND TEMPERATURE					
Allergies	—	—	—	0.8	—
Photosensitivity	<2	—	—	—	<2
Rashes	6	5.5	6	—	6
Itch	—	0.9	—	—	—
CENTRAL NERVOUS SYSTEM EFFECTS					
Dystonia	14 (8–30)	3.4 (1.7–5)	>30	4.2 (2.8–5.6)	16.3 (10–30)
Parkinsonism	23 (2–37)	5.5	>30	21.1	16.3 (10–30)
Akinesia	—	—	—	—	26.3 (10–40)
Akathisia	24 (17–>30)	0.8	>30	27.3	19.9 (7.3–40)
NMS	—	—	—	0.5	—
Weakness	—	9.5	—	—	—
Muscle cramps	—	—	—	—	15
Rigidity	—	1.4	—	—	10
Seizures	1.8	—	<2	0.7	6
Headache	—	—	—	—	5
Slurred speech	—	1.4	—	—	10
Tremors	—	4	—	—	—
Drowsiness, fatigue	24 (16–>30)	15.7 (6–25)	>30	16.3	36.3 (10–70)
Insomnia	—	—	—	—	10
Agitation restlessness (i.e., motoric)	—	1.5	—	—	5
Depression	—	—	—	6.2	10

Part III

Side Effects	Thioridazine	Thiothixene	Trifluoperazine
CARDIOVASCULAR EFFECTS			
Hypotension	11.2	>30	2.4 (0.8–4)
Dizziness	23.3	20	28.1 (21.2–35)
Tachycardia	6	6	—
ECG abnormalities	15	<2	6
Cardiac arrhythmias	15	<2	—
GASTROINTESTINAL EFFECTS			
Dry mouth and throat	28.1	20	2.3
Anorexia, lower appetite	0.0	—	27.7 (12.3–43)
Nausea, vomiting	29.3	—	2.4
Diarrhea	3.3	—	1.1
Constipation	16.8	—	1.1
Jaundice	<2	<2	0
Weight gain	15	20	5.6
Edema	2.3	—	1.4
RENAL EFFECTS			
Urinary hesitancy or retention	12.8 (5.5–30)	15	0.6
ENDOCRINE AND SEXUAL EFFECTS			
Menstrual changes	3.3	—	4.4
Breast swelling	0.6	—	—
Lactation	3.1	—	—
Inhibited ejaculation	37 (10–44)	<2	—
Disturbed sexual function	—	—	3.4
HEMATOLOGIC EFFECTS			
Agranulocytosis	0.0	—	—
Leukopenia	—	<2	—
EYES, EARS, NOSE, AND THROAT EFFECTS			
Lenticular pigmentation	—	6	—
Blurred vision	18.1	20	4
Nasal stuffiness	20	20	3
SKIN, ALLERGIES, AND TEMPERATURE			
Allergies	3.2	—	4.2
Photosensitivity	6	<2	6
Rashes	15	20	14
Abnormal skin pigment	6	<2	<2

Side Effects	Thioridazine	Thiothixene	Trifluoperazine
CENTRAL NERVOUS SYSTEM EFFECTS			
Dystonia	0.7	14.2 (8.3–30)	5.1 (3–8.2)
Parkinsonism	11.8	30	35.9 (23.7–48)
Akathisia	8.9	>30	15.9 (4.8–27)
NMS	<0.1	0.6	0.7
Weakness	—	—	40
Seizures	1.2	6	1.3
Drowsiness, fatigue	28.6 (21–36.2)	19.5 (10–30)	24.5 (3–61)
Confusion, disorientation	5.2	—	—
Depression	0.0	—	4.3

PREGNANCY AND LACTATION

Teratogenicity
(1st trimester)

- Some risk of anomalies if used during weeks 6–10.

- 3½–5.4% of infants with congenital malformations.

Direct Effect
on Newborn
(3rd trimester)

- EPS, excessive crying, hyperreflexia, hypertonicity vasomotor instability can occur.

- Up to 18% of patients on chlorpromazine have had a marked fall in BP during last 10 days of pregnancy; this can harm mother and newborn.

- Although chlorpromazine is usually safe during pregnancy, other neuroleptics are preferred.

Lactation

- Present in milk or no available reports.

Drug Dosage in Mother's Milk

Generic Names	Milk/ Plasma Ratio	Time of Peak Concentration in Milk (hours)	Infant Dose (μg/kg/day)	Maternal Dose (%)	Safety Rating*
Chlorpromazine	?	2	44	0.2	A
Chlorprothixene	?	4–4.5	4.7	0.14	A
Haloperidol	?	?	0.75–3.2	0.15–2	B

* A: Safe throughout infancy, but unsafe for infants suspected of a glucose-6-dehydrogenase deficiency; B: Reasonably unsafe before 34 weeks, but safe after 34 weeks.

DRUG-DRUG INTERACTIONS

Drugs (X) Interact with:	Antipsychotics (A)	Comments
Acetaminophen	X ↓	May abuse acetaminophen.
*Alcohol	X ↑ A ↑	CNS depression.
Aluminum hydroxide	A ↓	Give aluminum hydroxide at least one hour before, or 2 hours after, antipsychotic agents. See calcium carbonate.
Anesthetics (general)	X ↑	CNS depression, hypotension.
Anticholinergics	X ↑ A ↓ ?	Consider amantadine.
Anticonvulsants	X ↓	Seizures.
Antihistamines	X ↑ A ↑	CNS depression.
Calcium carbonate	O	No effect, unlike aluminum and magnesium hydroxides.
Clonidine	X?	Hypotension.
*Dextroamphetamine	X ↓ A ↓	Chlorpromazine treats dextroamphetamine overdose, but amphetamines should never treat chlorpromazine overdose.
Dichloralphenazone	A ↓	Hastens neuroleptic metabolism.
Diuretics (thiazides)	X ↑	Hypotension, shock.
†Epinephrine	X ↓	Hypotensive phenothiazine-treated patients might do better on levarterenol or phenylephrine.
Estrogen	A ↑	May increase phenothiazine level.
Griseofulvin	A ↓	Speeds neuroleptic metabolism.
*Guanethidine	X ↑	Hypotension, especially with thioridazine and mesoridazine.
Hypnosedatives	X ↑ A ↑	CNS depression.
*Isoproterenol	X ↓	Marked hypotension.
*Levodopa	X ↓	Especially with chlorpromazine.
*Lithium	X ↑ A?	Acute neurotoxicity especially with haloperidol or thioridazine. Chronic combination a smaller problem. Toxic at normal serum levels.
Magnesium hydroxide	A ↓	Give magnesium hydroxide at least one hour before, or 2 hours after, antipsychotic agents. See calcium carbonate.
MAOIs	X ↓ A?	Hypotension may result. MAOIs may trigger EPS.
Norepinephrine	X ↓	Hypotension.
*Opiates	X ↑ A ↑	CNS depression.
*Orphenadrine	X ↓ A ↓	Lowers neuroleptic and anticholinergic levels.
Phenylbutazone	X ↑ A ↑	More drowsiness.
Phenytoin	X?	Toxicity may occur. Obtain phenytoin level and adjust.
*Propranolol	X ↑ A ↑	Hypotension, toxicity, and seizures. Monitor serum levels; decrease dose.
Rifampin	A ↓	Speeds neuroleptic metabolism.
*TCAs	X ↑ A?	Possible toxicity or hypotension; TCAs may diminish EPS.
Warfarin	X ↓	Increased bleeding time.

Drugs (X) Interact with:	Chlorpromazine (C)	Comments
*Barbiturates	X↑ C↓	CNS depression acutely; antipsychotic effects lowered chronically.
Captopril	X↑	Hypotension.
Cimetidine	C↓	Avoid cimetidine, try ranitidine.
Enalapril	X↑	Hypotension.
Insulin	X↑	Change neuroleptics.
Meperidine	X↑ C↑	Hypotension, lethargy, depression; switch one drug.
*Phenmetrazine	X↓	Use another weight reducing method.
Sulfonylureas	X↑	Change neuroleptics.
Tobacco	C↓	May lower antipsychotic effect and induce more drowsiness.

Drugs (X) Interact with:	Haloperidol (H)	Comments
*Carbamazepine	H↓	Psychosis.
Indomethacin	H↑	Drowsiness, tiredness, and confusion. Change one agent.
Methyldopa	H↑	Dementia; switch one medication.

Drugs (X) Interact with:	Loxapine (L)	Comments
Lorazepam	X↑	Rare respiratory depression, stupor, and hypotension. Switch one drug. No other benzodiazepines apparently interact with loxapine.

Drugs (X) Interact with:	Thioridazine (T)	Comments
*Phenylpropanolamine	X↑	One sudden death. Name common over-the-counter drugs with PPA (e.g., Dexatrim, Allerest, Dimetapp) for patients to avoid.
Quinidine	X↓	Arrhythmias, myocardial depression; switch one drug.

Codes: *Moderately important; † Extremely important; ↑ Increases; ↓ Decreases; O = No effect; ? Unsure or increases and decreases.

EFFECTS ON LABORATORY TESTS

ANTIPSYCHOTIC AGENTS

Generic Names	Blood/Serum Tests*	Results	Urine Tests	Results
Chlorpromazine	LFT	↑	VMA	↓
	Glucose	↑↓	Urobilinogen	↑
	Prolactin	↑		
			5-HIAA	↓
			Catecholamines	Interferes
			17-KS, 17-OHCS	Interferes
Clozapine	WBC	↓	?	
	LFT	↑		
Fluphenazine	LFT	↑	VMA	↓
	Cephalin flocculation,	↑	Urobilinogen	↑
	Prolactin	↑	5-HIAA	↓
			Catecholamines	Interferes
			17-KS, 17-OHCS	Interferes
Haloperidol	None		None	
Loxapine	LFT	↑	None	
Molindone	LFT	↑	?	
	Eosinophils,	↑		
	Leukocytes,	↓		
	Fatty acids	↑		
Perphenazine	Glucose, PBI	↑ ↑	Pregnancy tests	False ↑↓
Pimozide	?		?	
Thioridazine	None		Pregnancy tests	False ↑↓
Thiothixene	LFT	↑	None	
	Uric acid	↓		
Trifluoperazine	LFT	↑	VMA	↓
	Glucose	↑↓	Urobilinogen	↑
	Prolactin	↑	5-HIAA	↓
			Catecholamines	Interferes
			17-KS, 17-OHCS	Interferes

↑ Increases; ↓ Decreases; ↑↓ Increases and Decreases; ? Undetermined or unclear.
* LFT = Liver function tests refer to SGOT, SGPT, alkaline phosphatase, bilirubin, and LDH.

WITHDRAWAL

Neuroleptics do not cause

- Dependence
- Tolerance
- Addiction
- Withdrawal

Suddenly stopping high antipsychotic doses may produce

- Gastritis, nausea, vomiting, diarrhea
- Headaches
- Insomnia, and nightmares

Less often it generates

- Sweating
- Rhinorrhea
- Increased appetite
- Giddiness
- Dizziness
- Warm or cold sensations
- Tremors
- Tachycardia

These symptoms

- Begin 2–4 (up to 7) days after discontinuing antipsychotics.
  √ Symptoms worse when patients on both antipsychotics *and* ACAs.
- Can persist 2 weeks.
- Are not life-threatening.
- Can cease by more gradually withdrawing neuroleptics over 1–2 weeks.

Maintain ACAs a week after terminating antipsychotics to prevent EPS. When long-term neuroleptics are rapidly stopped or quickly lowered a long-term TD can develop, as discussed above. But also, a *short-term withdrawal dyskinesia* can arise occasionally if antipsychotics are quickly halted.

- It resembles a long-term tardive dyskinesia with abnormal movements of the neck, face, and mouth.
- Antiparkinsonian drugs do not relieve withdrawal dyskinesia.
- Withdrawal dyskinesia stops with
  √ Re-establishing maintenance neuroleptic dose and
  √ Reducing neuroleptics more gradually (1–3 months).

OVERDOSE: TOXICITY, SUICIDE, AND TREATMENT

If consumed all at once, antipsychotics are relatively nonlethal drugs.

- A 30–60 day supply of antipsychotics can be fatal.
  √ This amount is 10 times less dangerous than TCAs or MAOIs.
- Neuroleptics can still create serious problems.

Suicide more common with less potent antipsychotics (e.g., chlorprom-azine).

* The therapeutic index—the ratio of the lethal to the effective—ranges from
  √ 25–200 for low-potency phenothiazines to
  √ > 1000 for high-potency piperazines and haloperidol.

More serious symptoms emerge when antipsychotics are consumed with another drug, such as a CNS depressant. In one series

* A chlorpromazine overdose induced coma in 4% whereas
* A chlorpromazine and TCA overdose taken together produced coma in 13%.

The general management of neuroleptic overdoses includes

* Stop all neuroleptics and ACAs.
  √ Be alert to dystonias.
* Hospitalize, if needed.
* Obtain ECG, temperature, vital signs, and, if needed, an airway.
* Arousal may not occur for 48 hours,
* Observe patient for 8–12 hours after ingestion.
* Discover other drugs ingested during past 2–10 days.
* Speak soon with family or friends who might afford life-saving information.
* If patient is alert, give an emetic, such as ipecac 15 ml or 10 ml to infant < 1 year.
  √ Followed by 8–16 ounces of water.
  √ If vomiting has not occurred, repeat ipecac in 20 minutes.
  √ Provide no more than 2 doses.
  √ Do not give milk; it interferes with ipecac.
* If patient is unconscious, is likely to become unconscious, or has a sluggish or absent gag reflex, start gastric lavage.
  √ Before initiating gastric lavage, employ cuffed endotracheal in-tubation to prevent aspiration and pulmonary complications.
    □ Stop convulsions before passing stomach tube.
* Emesis and lavage best if overdose transpired within 4 hours; yet they can remove drugs consumed 24–36 hours earlier.
* *After* emesis or lavage, supply activated charcoal (40–50 g in adults, 20–25 g in children) by mouth or through lavage tube to prevent further absorption.
  √ Charcoal inactivates ipecac; it must follow ipecac.

Most overdoses accentuate side effects, and so their treatment is akin to treating side effects. Other treatment includes

- For hypotension, dizziness
  √ May appear in 2–3 days.
  √ May evolve into shock, coma, cardiovascular insufficiency, myocardial infarction, and arrhythmias.
  √ First treatment is fluids.
  √ Second treatment is sympathomimetics, such as levarterenol (norepinephrine), metaraminol, phenylephrine.
  √ *Do not use epinephrine.*
- For severe urinary retention
  √ Catheterize patient if no recent voiding.
  √ Hemodialysis is relatively useless because of low drug concentrations.
  √ Hematuria, which arises later, often derives from chlorprothixene and loxapine.
- For seizures
  √ Common in children.
  √ Manage with standard interventions
    □ IV diazepam is first choice.
    □ Avoid barbiturates; they risk respiratory depression.
    □ Avoid pentylenetrazol, picrotoxin, and bemegride.

Toxicity and Suicide Data

Generic Names	Toxicity Doses Average (Highest) (g)	Mortality Doses Average (Lowest) (g)
Chlorpromazine	25.0 (30.0)	(1.250)
Chlorprothixene	(8.0)	—
Clozapine	(4.0)	2.50
Fluphenazine	—	—
Haloperidol	—	—
Loxapine	—	1.5–3
Mesoridazine	—	—
Molindone	—	—
Perphenazine	—	—
Pimozide	—	—
Thioridazine	20.0	5–10 (2.0)
Thiothixene	20.0	(0.736)
Trifluoperazine	—	—

PRECAUTIONS

Hypotension occurs most with parenteral use and high doses, especially > 50 mg of IM chlorpromazine.

Use antipsychotics cautiously with

- Narrow-angle glaucoma
- Prostatic hypertrophy
- CNS depressive agents
- Bone marrow depression, blood dyscrasias
- Parkinson's disease
- Neuroleptic hypertensitivity
- Extreme hypotension or hypertension
- Acutely ill children (e.g., chickenpox, measles, Reye's syndrome, gastroenteritis, dehydration)
  - √ Increased EPS, particularly dystonias and akathisias
- The elderly with
  - √ Hepatic disease
  - √ Cardiovascular illness
  - √ Chronic respiratory disease
  - √ Hypoglycemic conditions
  - √ Seizures

Avoid pimozide in patients with

- Tics other than Tourette's Disorder
- Medications stimulating tics (e.g., methylphenidate, dextroamphetamine), and
- Prolonged QT interval

Sudden death has occurred with patients on neuroleptics.

- Sudden death has also occurred in seemingly healthy adults for no obvious reason.
- Ventricular fibrillation, aspiration from food or vomit, and grand mal seizures may have been culpable.

NURSES' DATA

Discuss with the patient the reasons and myths for taking medications.

Oral medication
- Dilute with milk, orange juice or semi-solid food to reduce bitter taste.
  - √ Haloperidol is a tasteless and colorless elixir, unlike chlorpromazine and thioridazine.
- Protect oral liquids from the light.
- Discard markedly discolored solutions (slight yellowing does not alter potency).

ANTIPSYCHOTIC AGENTS

Injections
- Do not hold drug in syringe for > 15 minutes as plastic may adsorb drug.
- Very slowly administer IM injections.
- To thwart contact dermatitis, keep antipsychotic solution off of patient's skin and clothing.
- Give IM injections into upper outer quadrant of buttocks or deltoid.
  - √ Deltoid speeds absorption because of faster blood perfusion.
  - √ Tell patient injection may sting.
  - √ Massage slowly after injections to prevent formation of sterile abscesses.
  - √ Alternate sites.
- Watch for orthostatic hypotension, especially with parenteral administration.
  - √ Show patients how to stand when dizzy (see page 75).

Depot injection
- Use dry needle (at least 21 gauge).
- Give deep IM injection into a large muscle using Z-track method.
- Rotate sites and specify in charting.
- Can inject SC.
- Do not let drug remain in syringe for more than 15 minutes.
- Do *not* massage injection sites.

PATIENT AND FAMILY NOTES

Patients and family should notify doctor if

- Patient has a sore throat during first several months of treatment.
- NMS appears.
- Patient is having general or dental surgery.

Tell patient and families
- About TD, especially *before* 6 months of neuroleptic treatment.
- When starting neuroleptics, carefully drive cars, work around machines, and cross streets. Patients initially should check "reflexes" to ensure their "timing" is okay.
- May drink alcohol with antipsychotics, but "one drink often feels like 2 drinks."
- Avoid overexposure to sun; use sunscreens.
- Do not keep medication at bedside to avoid accidental ingestion.
  - √ Keep safely away from adventurous, hungry children.
- If forget a dose, patient can take up to 2 hours late, but
  - √ If more than 2 hours late, wait for next scheduled dose.
  - √ Do not double the dose.

COST INDEX

General Neuroleptic Doses

Generic Names	Brand Names	Equivalent (mg) Dosage	Dose Assessed (mg)	Cost Rating*
Chlorpromazine	Thorazine	50	50	84
	generics	50	50	>8
Chlorprothixene	Taractan	50	50	189
Clozapine	Clozaril†			
Fluphenazine	Permitil	1	1	103
	Prolixin	1	1	178
Fluphenazine decanoate	Fluphenazine Decanoate	1	25 mg/ml	194
	generics	1	25 mg/ml	112
Fluphenazine enanthate	Fluphenazine Enanthate	1	25 mg/ml	207
Haloperidol	Haldol	1	1	141
	generics	1	1	>69
Haloperidol decanoate	Haldol Decanoate	1	50 mg/ml	198
Loxapine	Loxitane	10	10	226
Mesoridazine	Serentil	25	25	126
Molindone	Moban	10	10	145
Perphenazine	Trilafon	4	4	274
	generics	4	4	183
Pimozide	Orap	2	2	179
Thioridazine	Mellaril	50	50	120
	generics	50	50	>97
Thiothixene	Navane	2	2	124
	generics	2	2	>79
Trifluoperazine	Stelazine	2	2	200
	generics	2	2	>45

* The higher the number, the higher the cost.

† Sandoz is the only American firm to market clozapine. In December 1990, it promised to slash each patient's annual clozapine price from $8,944 to $4,500. Meanwhile, the drug's yearly cost in Germany was $2,500, and in England, $1,100.

2. Anticholinergic Drugs

INTRODUCTION

Neuroleptic-induced extrapyramidal side effects (EPS) are diminished by anticholinergic agents (ACAs).

Some ACAs (e.g., benztropine) are prescribed almost exclusively for EPS, while others (e.g., propranolol) are given for nonEPS and EPS.

EPS fall into 4 major categories described on pages 18–20, 22

- Dystonia
- Pseudoparkinsonism (including akinesia)
- Akathisia
- Rabbit syndrome

Other EPS not treated with ACAs are discussed in the antipsychotic chapter, and are

- Neuroleptic Malignant Syndrome (NMS) (see pages 20–22)
- Tardive Dyskinesia (TD) (see pages 22–24)

NAMES, MANUFACTURERS, DOSE FORMS, AND COLORS

Generic Names	Brand Names	Manufacturers	Dose Forms (mg)*	Colors
Amantadine	Symmetrel	Du Pont	c: 100; s: 50 mg/5 ml	c: red
Benztropine	Cogentin	Merck Sharp & Dohme	t: 0.5/1/2; p: 1 mg/ml	t: all white
Biperiden	Akineton	Knoll	t: 2; p: 5 mg/ml	t: white
Bromocriptine	Parlodel	Sandoz	t: 2.5 c: 5	t: white c: caramel-white
Dantrolene	Dantrium	Norwich Eaton	c: 25/50/100	c: orange-light brown/orange-dark brown/orange-light brown
Diazepam	Valium	Roche	t: 2/5/10; p: 5 mg/ml	t: white/yellow/blue
Diphenhydramine†	Benadryl	Parke-Davis	c: 25/50; p: 10/50 mg/ml	c: all pink-white
Lorazepam	Ativan	Wyeth-Ayerst	t: 0.5/1/2; p: 2/4 mg/ml	t: all white
Procyclidine	Kemadrin	Burroughs Wellcome	t: 5	t: white
Propranolol	Inderal	Wyeth-Ayerst	t: 10/20/40/60/80; p: 1 mg/ml	t: orange/blue/green/pink/yellow
Trihexyphenidyl	Artane	Lederle	t: 2/5; SR: 5 mg; e: 2 mg/5 ml	t: all white SR: blue

* Drug forms: c = capsules; e = elixir; p = parenteral; s = syrup; SR = sustained release sequels; t = tablets;
† Can be purchased over the counter only in 25 mg.

PHARMACOLOGY

The basal ganglia, which mediate involuntary movements, have a critical ratio of

$$\frac{Dopamine}{Acetylcholine}$$

When neuroleptics block these dopamine receptors, they lower this ratio and generate EPS.

By reducing acetylcholine, ACAs help to restore this balance.

DOSES

General Names	Oral Doses (mg)	IM/IV Doses (mg)	Major Chemical Group
Amantadine	100 bid-tid	—	Dopaminergic agent
Benztropine	1–3 bid	1–2	ACA
Biperiden	2 bid-qid	2	ACA
Diazepam	5 tid	5–10	Benzodiazepine
Diphenhydramine	25–50 tid-qid	25–50	Antihistamine
Lorazepam	1–2 tid	—	Benzodiazepine
Procyclidine	2.5–5 tid	—	ACA
Propranolol	10–20 tid; up to 40 qid	—	β blocker
Trihexyphenidyl*	2–5 tid	—	ACA

* Start with trihexyphenidyl tablets or elixir; only later transfer to sustained-released sequels (capsules). Use sequels as a single dose after breakfast or one dose q12h. For akathisia, give trihexyphenidyl 6–10 mg qd; other EPS, provide 2–6 mg qd.

CLINICAL INDICATIONS AND USE

ACAs effects depend on the symptom.

*Influence on Extrapyramidal Symptoms**

Generic Names	Akathisia	Akinesia	Dystonia	Rabbit	Rigidity	Tremor
Amantadine	2	3	2	2	3	2
Benztropine	2	2	3	2	3	2
Biperiden	1	2	1	2	2	1
Diazepam	2	0	3	2	2	0
Diphenhydramine	2	1	2–3	2	1	2
Lorazepam	2	0	0	0	0	0
Procyclidine	1	2	2	2	2	1
Propranolol	3	0	0	2	0	0
Trihexyphenidyl	2	2	2	2	2	1

* 0 No effect
  1 Some effect (20% response)
  2 Moderate effect (20–40% response)
  3 Good effect (> 40% response)

Therefore, when should one use ACAs?

- The *pro* arguments include
  √ EPS are uncomfortable.
  √ EPS can induce patients to stop taking neuroleptics.
  √ High-potency neuroleptics often bring on EPS.

ANTICHOLINERGIC DRUGS

- √ ACAs help patients especially under 45.
- √ ACAs clearly relieve some EPS (a.k.a. dystonia, akinesia).
- The *con* arguments include
  - √ Low-potency antipsychotics infrequently produce EPS.
  - √ Patients without EPS at first can always receive ACAs if EPS arise later.
  - √ ACAs yield side effects, which may compound neuroleptic side effects (e.g., dry mouth, confusion).
  - √ Some (including the World Health Organization) contend that ACAs foster or worsen TD.
  - √ TCAs may diminish EPS, rendering ACAs unnecessary.
  - √ ACAs do not clearly relieve other EPS (a.k.a. akathisias).
  - √ Avoid ACAs in children under 3.
- In general, ACAs are indicated for patients who are
  - √ Young males,
  - √ Dystonic (or have h/o dystonia),
  - √ Taking high-potency neuroleptics (e.g., haloperidol).
- When depot antipsychotics peak after 2–7 days, patient may need ACA.
- Whether to use them in other circumstances depends on the seriousness of symptoms and the preferences of patients.

After 1–6 months of long-term maintenance antipsychotic therapy, most ACAs can be withdrawn.

- About 15% of patients will re-experience clear neurological side effects, whereas 30% will feel "better"—less anxious, depressed, and sleepy—on continued ACAs.
- Because antipsychotics have longer half-lives than ACAs, prescribe ACAs for several days *after* stopping neuroleptics.

Starting Oral Doses of Antiparkinsonian Drugs

Symptom	Medication
Dystonia	Diphenhydramine 25–50 mg IV/IM as first choice; often provides complete relief in minutes. Benztropine 1–2 mg IV/IM is the second choice; works quickly. Dystonia may disappear before injection is completed. If patient does not respond to the above, question the diagnosis. Prevent future dystonias with any ACA.
Akathisia	Propranolol preferred. Diazepam or lorazepam are second choices. If patient has not improved, double-check the diagnosis.
Parkinsonism (Akinesia)	Reduce neuroleptics to lowest effective dose. Try any ACA. Prescribe amantadine with troublesome anticholinergic symptoms.
Rabbit Syndrome	Responds well to ACAs.

SIDE EFFECTS

ACAs' and amantadine's side effects are listed below.

The side effects of diazepam, lorazepam, and propranolol are listed in the anti-anxiety chapter (see pages 193–99).

Since ACAs' side effects are anticholinergic, deal with them by

* First, eliminating the ACA,
* Second, changing to a less anticholinergic antipsychotic, (see pages 12–13) and
* Third, substituting the nonanticholinergic amantadine for the ACA.

Cardiovascular Effects

Palpitations, tachycardia
Dizziness

Gastrointestinal Effects

Dry mouth

* Management (see page 13).

Nausea, vomiting

* Reduce ACA.

Constipation

* Management (see page 14).

Paralytic ileus

Renal Effects

Urinary hesitancy or *retention* (see page 14).

Endocrine and Sexual Effects

Amantadine may reduce galactorrhea provoked by neuroleptic-induced increased prolactin.

ANTICHOLINERGIC DRUGS

Eyes, Ears, Nose, and Throat Effects

Blurred vision (see page 16).
Photophobia

* From dilated pupils

Dry eyes (see page 17).
Narrow-angle glaucoma

* ACAs can trigger narrow-angle glaucoma.
* If narrow-angle glaucoma becomes a problem, stop all ACAs and neuroleptics.
* If patient has anything like a h/o glaucoma, test before giving ACAs, TCAs, or neuroleptics (see page 17).

Nasal congestion, dry throat
Dry bronchial secretions and *strained breathing* aggravate patients with respiratory ailments.

Skin, Allergies, and Temperature

Diminished sweating (see page 18).
Skin flushing
Rashes

* Stop ACA.

Fever

* Ice bags.

Central Nervous System Effects

Confusion, delirium, disturbed concentration, disorientation (see page 25)
Restlessness, tremors, ataxia
Weakness, lethargy
Numb fingers, inability to move particular muscles, slurred speech, incoherence

* More common in the elderly and in high doses.

Stimulation, nervous excitement, insomnia, depression

* All more common with trihexyphenidyl (see precautions).

Psychosis

* This occurs especially with amantadine. Before changing a neuroleptic in a psychotic patient, make sure the patient is not on amantadine.

PERCENTAGES OF SIDE EFFECTS

Side Effects	Anticholinergics	Amantadine	Diphenhydramine
CARDIOVASCULAR EFFECTS			
Dizziness	<1	7.5	20
Hypotension	—	3	—
Tachycardia	—	—	<1
Congestive heart failure	—	0.5 (0.1–1)	—
GASTROINTESTINAL EFFECTS			
Dry mouth	20	3	20
Anorexia	—	3	5.5
Nausea	20	7.5	20
Vomiting	20	0.5 (0.1–1)	—
Constipation	20	5.5	—
Sore mouth	<1	—	—
Edema	—	3	—
RENAL EFFECTS			
Urinary hesitancy	20	0.5 (0.1–1)	—
Painful or difficult urination	—	—	5.5
HEMATOLOGIC EFFECTS			
Easy bruising	—	—	<1
EYES, EARS, NOSE, AND THROAT EFFECTS			
Blurred vision	20	—	—
Light sensitivity	20	—	—
Narrow-angle glaucoma	<1	—	—
Visual disturbance	—	0.5	5.5
Oculogyric episode	—	<0.1	—
Less tolerance for contact lenses	—	—	5.5
Dry nose and throat	20	—	20
Sore throat	—	—	<1
Dyspnea	—	0.5	—
SKIN, ALLERGIES, AND TEMPERATURE			
Rash	<1	0.5	—
Eczematoid dermatitis	—	<0.1	—
Fever	—	—	<1
CENTRAL NERVOUS SYSTEM EFFECTS			
Confusion	<1	3	—
Drowsiness	—	—	20
Muscle cramps	<1	—	—
Numbness	<1	—	—
Weakness in limbs	<1	0.5	<1

ANTICHOLINERGIC DRUGS

Side Effects	Anticholinergics	Amantadine	Diphenhydramine
Fatigue	—	0.5	<1
Headache	—	3	—
Ataxia	—	3	—
Seizures	—	<0.1	—
Slurred speech	—	0.5	—
Insomnia	—	7.5	—
Nightmares	—	—	<1
Anxiety	—	3	—
Agitation	—	—	<1
Irritability	—	3	—
Hallucinations	—	3	—
Depression	—	3	—
Psychosis	—	0.5	—

— No report

PREGNANCY AND LACTATION

Teratogenicity (1st trimester)	• No apparent fetal risk from trihexyphenidyl.
	• No reports on biperiden.
	• A few cases of amantadine-induced cardiovascular anomalies exist, but relationship to drug is unknown.
Direct Effect on Newborn (3rd trimester)	• A few cases of paralytic ileus with mother on chlorpromazine and benztropine.
Lactation	• No data.
	• Amantadine secreted in milk.

DRUG-DRUG INTERACTIONS*

Drugs (X) Interact with:	Anticholinergics (A)	Comments
Acetaminophen	X ↓	May abuse acetaminophen.
Amantadine	X ↑	Increased amantadine effects.
Antihistamines	A ↑	Increased anticholinergic effects.
*Antipsychotics	X ↓ A ↑	ACAs may slow antipsychotic actions and promote tardive dyskinesia; ACAs enhance anticholinergic effects.

Drugs (X) Interact with:	Anticholinergics (A)	Comments
Atenolol	X ↑	May increase atenolol's concentration.
*Cocaine	A ↓	Decreased anticholinergic effects.
Levodopa (L-dopa)	X ↓	May reduce L-dopa's availability; when ACAs stopped, L-dopa's toxicity may erupt.
Meperidine	A ↑	Increased anticholinergic effects.
*Methotrimeprazine	A ↓	Combination may increase EPS.
MAOIs	A ↑	May increase anticholinergic effects.
Nitrofurantoin	X ↑	ACA may increase nitrofurantoin effects.
Orphenadrine	A ↑	Increased antiparkinsonian effects.
Primidone	X ↑	Excessive sedation.
Procainamide	X ↑	Increased procainamide effect.
Propranolol	X ↓	ACAs can block β-blocker's bradycardia.
Quinidine	A ↑	Increased anticholinergic effects.
*TCAs	A ↑	May diminish EPS.

Drugs (X) Interact with:	Amantadine (A)	Comments
Alcohol	X ↑	Increased alcohol effect; possible fainting.
*Cocaine	X ↑	Major overstimulation.
Sympathomimetics	X ↑	Increased stimulation and agitation.

Codes: * Moderately important reaction; ↑ Increases; ↓ Decreases.

ANTICHOLINERGIC DRUGS

EFFECTS ON LABORATORY TESTS

Generic Names	Blood/Serum Tests	Results	Urine Tests	Results
Amantadine	WBC, Leukocytes	↓ ↓	?	
Benztropine	None		None	
Biperiden	?		?	
Diphenhydramine	WBC, RBC, Platelets	↓ ↓ ↓	?	
Procyclidine	?		?	
Trihexyphenidyl	None		None	

↑ Increases; ↓ Decreases.
? = Undetermined

WITHDRAWAL

ACAs do not cause

- Dependence
- Tolerance
  √ Some tolerance with amantadine occurs after 8 weeks.
- Addiction
- Withdrawal

Yet, even more than with antipsychotic agents, abruptly stopping ACAs can induce in 2–4 (up to 7) days

- Nausea, vomiting, diarrhea
- Hypersalivation
- Headaches
- Insomnia
- Nightmares

Less often develop

- Rhinorrhea
- Increased appetite
- Giddiness
- Dizziness
- Tremors
- Warmth or cold sensations

These symptoms

- May persist 2 weeks,
- Are not life-threatening,
- Can diminish substantially by more gradually tapering off neuroleptics and ACAs.
- This approach also decreases risk of EPS.

OVERDOSE: TOXICITY, SUICIDE, AND TREATMENT

As overdoses, ACAs' side effects escalate.

Treatments as listed above.

For general management of overdoses (see page 37)

PRECAUTIONS

Be alert to growing reports of ACA abuse.

- Arises in 0 → 17.5% of patients taking ACAs.
- Occurs with all ACAs.

- Most common with trihexyphenidyl, which alleviates EPS, but is more likely to
  - √ Energize,
  - √ Induce euphoria,
  - √ Sedate,
  - √ Induce hyperactivity, and to
  - √ Afford psychedelic and psychotogenic experiences.

ACAs contraindicated in patients with

- Urinary retention, prostatic hypertrophy
- Paralytic ileus, bowel obstruction, megacolon
- Hyperthermia, heat stroke
- Congestive heart failure
- Peripheral edema
- Narrow-angle (i.e., acute angle-closure) glaucoma
- Hypersensitivity to ACAs
- Dry bronchial secretions, especially in the elderly
- Delirium and dementia
- Cardiac patients with hypertension placed on trihexyphenidyl

NURSES' DATA

EPS are tough. These tips, especially for TD patients, might help

- Teach patients to explain to others about EPS, especially TD.
  - √ Have patient role-play explanations. It is good practice for real life and insures that patients have accurate information.
- Patients should put on loose, lightweight clothing with garments closing in front and fastening with velcro instead of with buttons or zippers.
  - √ If one side of the body is stiffer, recommend patient change clothes from the other side first.
  - √ Shoes—slip-on or those that fasten with elastic laces or velcro— are preferable to standard laced or zipped shoes.
    - □ Long-handled shoe horn might assist.
    - □ Avoid high-heeled shoes or other styles that make walking difficult.
- Prevent bathing accidents
  - √ Use no-slip rubber mat.
  - √ Insert grab-bars.
  - √ Remove glass tub or shower doors.
  - √ Install a shower chair.
  - √ Attach soap to a rope and place conveniently in bath or shower.

ANTICHOLINERGIC DRUGS

- Walking can be complicated and too fast, especially when people walk on the balls of their feet and with raised heels.
  - √ To discourage shuffling, teach patients to stop their usual walking and
    - □ Place their feet at least 8 inches apart,
    - □ Correct their posture,
    - □ Take a large step, and
    - □ Bring their foot higher in a "marching fashion."
- Because patients may fall on turns, show them how to walk (not pivot or swing) into turns.
- For patients with a problem getting out of bed at night because of stiffness or rigidity, suggest
  - √ First lie (and then sit) on the bed's side.
  - √ Slowly drop one leg over the bed's edge while pushing down with the elbow on the bed with the opposite hand.

Dentures can rub and ulcerate gums as well as imitate tardive dyskinesia.

Make referrals for physical, occupational, or speech therapy as TD or other EPS problems arise.

Apply elastic stockings to reduce swelling from orthostatic hypotension.

PATIENT AND FAMILY NOTES

Take ACAs with meals. This timing reduces dry mouth or gastric irritation.

When starting ACAs, patients should carefully drive cars, work around machines, or cross streets. Patients should initially check "reflexes" to ensure their "timing" is okay; it may be a split-second off.

One may consume alcohol on ACAs, although "one drink often feels like 2 drinks."

To prevent or relieve constipation, increase bulk-forming foods, water (2500–3000 ml/day), and exercise.

For dry mouth, avoid calorie-laden beverages and sweet candy; they foster caries and weight gain.

Do not keep medication at bedside to avoid accidental ingestion; keep it safely away from eager children.

May take oral dose up to 2 hours late.

- If dose is more than 2 hours later, skip dose; do not double the dose.

- Benztropine's relatively long action may allow for a single bedtime dose.

Make sure not to stop ACAs until a week after antipsychotic agents are stopped.

COST INDEX

Generic Names	Brand Names	Equivalent Dosage (mg)	Dose Assessed (mg)	Cost Rating*
Amantadine	Symmetrel	100	100	189
	generics	100	100	>119
Benztropine	Cogentin	1	1	4
Biperiden	Akineton	2	2	8
Diphenhydramine†	Benadryl	25 (po)	25	83
	generics	50 (IM)	50	158
			25	>9
			50	>22
Procyclidine	Kemadrin	5	5	2
Trihexyphenidyl	Artane	5	5	5
	generics	5	5	>1

* The higher the number, the more costly the drug.
† Can be purchased over the counter, which means it may, or may not, be cheaper.

ANTICHOLINERGIC DRUGS

3. Antidepressants

INTRODUCTION

Antidepressants are of 3 types

- Tricyclic antidepressants (TCAs)
- Heterocyclic antidepressants (HCAs)
- Monoamine-oxidase inhibitors (MAOIs)

This chapter discusses TCAs and HCAs; the next chapter, MAOIs.

Because of the many similarities between TCAs and HCAs, this book will always refer to both groups as TCAs. Fluoxetine, although not a TCA, will be discussed as a TCA.

This chapter focuses on

- Major depression (see pages 64–70)
- Chronic physical pain disorders (see page 70)
- Anorexia nervosa (see page 70)
- Bulimia (see page 70–71)
- Pseudodementia (see page 71)
- Adult physical disorders (see pages 71–72)
  - √ Cardiac conduction problems
  - √ Cataplexy
  - √ Congestive heart failure
  - √ Constipation (chronic)
  - √ Diarrhea (chronic)
  - √ Epilepsy
  - √ Impotence (organic)
  - √ Irritable bowel syndrome
  - √ Migraine
  - √ Narrow-angle glaucoma
  - √ Neurogenic bladder
  - √ Parkinson's disease
  - √ Peptic ulcer

√ Sleep apnea
√ Tardive dyskinesia
• Childhood stage-4 sleep disorders (see pages 72–73)
√ Enuresis
√ Night terrors
√ Sleepwalking

As detailed elsewhere, TCAs treat

• Agoraphobia (Anti-anxiety, pages 190–91)
• Attention-deficit hyperactivity disorder (Stimulants, pages 248–49)
• Atypical depression (MAOIs, pages 105–106)
• Borderline personality disorder (Lithium, page 136)
• Dysthymic disorder (MAOIs, page 106)
• Narcolepsy (Stimulants, page 250)
• Obsessive-compulsive disorder (Anti-anxiety, pages 191–92)
• Panic disorders (Anti-anxiety, page 188)
• Schizoaffective disorders (Lithium, page 135)
• Treatment-resistant depression (Stimulants, page 249)

NAMES, CLASSES, MANUFACTURERS, DOSE FORMS, AND COLORS

Generic Names	Brand Names	Manufacturers	Dose Forms (mg)*	Colors
		TRICYCLICS		
Tertiary				
Amitriptyline	Elavil	Merck Sharp & Dohme	t: 10/25/50/ 75/100/150; p: 10 mg/ml	t: blue/yellow/ beige/orange mauve/blue
	Endep	Roche	t: 10/25/50/ 75/100/150	t: orange/orange/ orange/yellow/ peach/salmon
Clomipramine	Anafranil	CIBA	c: 25/50/75	c: ivory-melon- yellow/ivory- aqua-blue/ivory- yellow
Doxepin	Sinequan	Roerig	c: 10/25/50/ 75/100/150; o: 10 mg/ml	c: red-pink/blue- pink/peach-off white/pale pink- light pink/blue- white/blue
	Adapin	Fisons	c: 10/25/50/ 75/100/150	c: orange/green-orange/ green/orange-white/ green-white/brown-tan

Generic Names	Brand Names	Manufacturers	Dose Forms (mg)*	Colors
Imipramine	Tofranil	Geigy	t: 10/25/50; p: 25 mg/2 ml	t: triangular coral/round, biconvex coral/round, biconvex, coral
	Janimine	Abbott	t: 10/25/50	t: orange/yellow/peach
Imipramine pamoate	Tofranil-PM (sustained) release)	Geigy	c: 75/100/125/150	c: coral/dark yellow-coral/light yellow-coral/coral
Trimipramine	Surmontil	Wyeth-Ayerst	c: 25/50/100	c: blue-yellow/blue-orange/blue-white
Secondary Desipramine	Norpramin	Merrell Dow	t: 10/25/50/75/100/150	t: blue/yellow/green/orange/peach/white
	Pertofrane	Rorer	c: 25/50	c: pink/maroon-pink
Nortriptyline	Pamelor	Sandoz	c: 10/25/50/75; o: 10 mg/5 ml	c: orange-white/orange-white/white/orange
	Aventyl	Lilly	c: 10/25	c: cream-gold
Protriptyline	Vivactil	Merck Sharp & Dohme	t: 5/10	t: orange/yellow

BICYCLIC

Fluoxetine	Prozac	Dista/Lilly	c: 20	c: green off-white

DIBENZOXAZEPINE

Amoxapine	Asendin	Lederle	t: 25/50/100/150	t: white/orange/blue/peach

MONOCYCLIC

Bupropion	Wellbutrin	Burroughs Wellcome	t: 75/100	t: yellow-gold/red

TETRACYCLIC

Maprotiline	Ludiomil	CIBA	t: 25/50/75	t: oval orange/round orange/white

TRIAZOLOPYRIDINE

Trazodone	Desyrel	Mead Johnson	t: 50/100/150/300	t: orange/white/orange/yellow

* c = capsule, t = tablet, o = oral, p = parenteral

PHARMACOLOGY

TCAs are divided into tertiary and secondary amines.

- Tertiary TCAs have 2 CH_3 groups on a side chain, whereas secondary TCAs have one CH_3 on a side chain.
- Tertiary TCAs are more potent blockers of serotonin re-uptake, whereas secondary TCAs are more potent blockers of norepinephrine re-uptake.
- Tertiary TCAs tend to be more anticholinergic than secondary TCAs.

Norepinephrine (NE) and serotonin (5-HT) reuptake blocking may account for their activating (NE) and sedative (5-HT) properties.

Sedation is also attributed to anticholinergic (ACH) and antihistaminic (H_1 receptor) actions.

TCAs are completely absorbed from the gastrointestinal tract and largely metabolized by first-pass effect.

- These highly lipophilic compounds are concentrated in the heart and brain.

Peak concentrations are reached at 2–8 hours, but may extend to 10–12 hours.

*TCA Amine Types and Reuptake Blockade of Major Neurotransmitters**

Generic Names	Amine Levels†	Norepinephrine	Serotonin	Potency ratio Norepinephrine: Serotonin
Amitriptyline	3	6	3	10
Amoxapine	A	3	5	5
Bupropion	A	11	12	9
Clomipramine	3	7	2	12
Desipramine	2	1	8	2
Doxepin	3	8	9	6
Fluoxetine	A	9	1	13
Imipramine	3	5	4	8
Maprotiline	2	3	11	1
Nortriptyline	2	2	7	3
Protriptyline	2	2	7	3
Trazodone	A	12	6	7
Trimipramine	3	10	10	11

* The lower the number, the stronger the blockade.
† Amine levels are 2 = secondary; 3 = tertiary; A = atypical.

*Rank Order of Other TCA Receptor Blockage**

Receptor:	Histaminic-1	Dopaminergic	Cholinergic (Muscarinic)	α_1-Adrenergic	α_2-Adrenergic
Potential results from blockade:	• Sedation • Weight gain • Hypotension	• EPS • Prolactin elevation	• Blurred vision • Dry mouth • Memory loss	• Postural hypotension • Dizziness • Tachycardia	• Block clonidine's antihypertensive effects
Generic Names	H_1	DA	ACH	α_1	α_2
Amitriptyline	2	6	1	1	1
Amoxapine	—	1	9	5	5
Bupropion	—	2	12	13	11
Clomipramine	—	3	6	4	6
Desipramine	6	9	10	10	8
Doxepin	1	8	4	2	2
Fluoxetine	—	11	11	12	10
Imipramine	3	12	5	8	6
Maprotiline	—	10	8	9	9
Nortriptyline	4	5	7	6	4
Protriptyline	5	4	2	11	7
Trazodone	7	13	13	7	2
Trimipramine	2	7	3	3	3

* The lower the numbers, the stronger the blockage.

Pharmacology of TCAs

Generic Names	Bio-availability (%)	Plasma-Bound (%)	Half-Life* (hours) Mean	Half-Life* (hours) Range	Excretion† (%)
Amitriptyline	48 ± 11	94.8 ± 0.8	21	6–44	98 R
Amoxapine	—	90	8	8–30	69 R 18 F
Bupropion	—	>80	9.8	3.9–24	87 R 10 F
Clomipramine	—	97	20	18–37	51–60 R 24–32 F
Desipramine	33–51	87 ± 3	22	12–36	70 R
Doxepin	27 ± 10	90	17	8–68	98 R
Fluoxetine	—	94 ± 1	60	48–216	60 R 30 F
Imipramine	27 ± 8	93 ± 1.5	25	15–34	98 R 2 B/F
Maprotiline	—	88	40	27–58	60 R 30 F
Nortriptyline	51 ± 5	92 ± 2	32	18–93	67 R 10 F
Protriptyline	—	92	78	55–127	50 R ? F
Trazodone	—	93 ± 2	5	3–9	70–75 R 20–25 F
Trimipramine	—	95	10	9–30	80 R 10 F

* Increased half-lives of active agents; active metabolites have different half-lives and are reflected in range.
† B = bile; F = fecal; R = renal; ? = unavailable or inconsistent.

Children:

- TCAs function a bit differently in children.
  - √ Children have less fat/muscle ratio,
  - √ Decreased volume distribution, and
  - √ Larger liver for faster metabolism.
- Therefore, a few children are
  - √ Not as protected from large doses as adults,
  - √ Have a quicker absorption, and
  - √ Display a lower protein binding.
- Because prepubertal children have more fluctuating serum TCAs, ineffectiveness and toxicity often result; more frequent doses (e.g., tid rather than qd) provide more stable therapy.

DOSES

General Doses

Generic Names	Equivalent Doses (mg)	Therapeutic Doses (mg/day)	Extreme Doses* (mg/day)	Geriatric Doses (mg/day)
Amitriptyline	100	150–300	25–450	30–100
Amoxapine	100	200–400	50–600	100–150
Bupropion	200	225–450	100–450	75–150
Clomipramine	93	125–300	25–500	50–150
Desipramine	100	150–300	25–400	20–100
Doxepin	100	150–300	25–350	30–150
Fluoxetine	20	20	20–80	5–40
Imipramine	100	150–300	25–450	30–100
Maprotiline	70	150–225	25–225	50–75
Nortriptyline	58	75–150	20–200	10–50
Protriptyline	20	30–60	10–80	10–20
Trazodone	155	200–600	50–600	50–150
Trimipramine	100	150–300	25–350	25–350

* The low doses are used for children.

Specific Antidepressant Doses

Generic Names	Starting Dose (mg/day)	Days to Reach Steady State Levels	Therapeutic Plasma Levels (ng/ml)	Active Metabolite	Reliability of Plasma Level
Amitriptyline	25–75	4–10	>100–250*	Nortriptyline	Maybe
Amoxapine	50–150	2–7	150–500*	8-hydroxyamoxapine	No
Bupropion	200–225	14(8–24)	50–100		No
Clomipramine	75–225	7–14	72–300*	Desmethylclomipramine	No
Desipramine	25–75	2–11	>125	–	Maybe
Doxepin	25–75	2–8	100–250	Desmethyldoxepin	No
Fluoxetine	20	21–35	72–300*	Norfluoxetine	No
Imipramine	25–75	2–5	>200–250	Desipramine	Maybe
Maprotiline	25–75	6–10	200–300	Desmethylmaprotiline	No
Nortriptyline†	20–40	4–19	50–150		Yes
Protriptyline	10–20	10	100–240		No
Trazodone	50–100	7–14	800–1600	Oxotriazolo-pyridinpropionic acid	No
Trimipramine	25–75	2–6	200–300		No

* Parent compound plus active metabolite.
† Only TCA with a definite therapeutic window.

CLINICAL INDICATIONS AND USE

General Information

TCAs typically require 10–14 days on a therapeutic dose to start working. Their full effect may take a full 6 weeks.

Two major mistakes in prescribing TCAs are inadequate dose and time.

Some symptoms improve before 10–14 days.

- Insomnia abates after 3–4 days.
- Appetite returns after 5–7 days.
- Diurnal mood variation (worse in A.M., better in P.M.) recedes around 8 days.
- Libido revives in 9–10 days.
- Anhedonia, hopelessness, and helplessness fade after 10–14 days.
- Dysthymia, excessive guilt, and suicidal thoughts dwindle by 12–16 days.

TCAs benefit about 65–80% of patients with nondelusional, unipolar depressions, but TCAs help a mere one-third of delusional depressions.

Initiating Therapy

Given the many clinical similarities among TCAs, consider the following.

- If patient is "slowed down," he may do best with stimulating TCAs (e.g., desipramine) that inhibit norepinephrine reuptake.
- If patient is agitated, he might do better with sedative TCAs (e.g., doxepin) that block serotonin reuptake.
- If patient is agitated or anxious, he might benefit from adding
  - √ Low doses of neuroleptics (e.g., trifluoperazine 2 mg, perphenazine 1 mg) tid-qid, but if prolonged, risks TD.
  - √ Low doses of benzodiazepines (e.g., alprazolam ½ mg, lorazepam 1 mg) tid.
- If a TCA previously aided the patient or a close blood relative, use it with the patient.
- If depressed patient exhibits paranoid or delusional thinking, adding a neuroleptic (e.g., haloperidol or trifluoperazine) might work.
  - √ Amoxapine, a dopaminergic blocker, may diminish the need for a neuroleptic.
  - √ Amitriptyline with perphenazine found slightly superior to amoxapine, but the latter had fewer EPS.
  - √ Avoid low-potency neuroleptics (e.g., chlorpromazine) because they aggravate the TCA's high anticholinergic action.

√ To reduce seizure risk with bupropion, give at least 3 doses per day, increase total daily dose no faster than 75–100 mg every 3 days, and do not exceed 450 mg/qd.

√ To reduce seizure risk with maprotiline, do not exceed 225 mg/qd.

Delusional depressed patients respond poorly to TCAs, especially when TCAs are the sole treatment.

* For instance, under 33% of delusional-depressed patients improve with amitriptyline.
* TCAs can trigger psychoses, suicide attempts, and hospitalization.
* Treat delusional-depressed patients with
  √ ECT—1st choice
  √ TCAs with neuroleptics—2nd choice
  √ TCAs alone—3rd choice

Relative predictors of a good TCA response are

* Insidious onset
* Anorexia
* Middle or late insomnia
* Psychomotor change
* Emotional withdrawal
* Anhedonia (inability to experience pleasure)
* Past success with TCAs

Relative predictors of a bad TCA response are

* Delusions
* Hypochondria
* "Overemotional," hysterical style
* Anxiety
* Childhood depression

The dexamethasone suppression test (DST) may diagnose depression.

* When a healthy person receives dexamethasone, blood cortisol is usually suppressed for over 24 hours. However,
  √ Sensitivity (accurately identifies depression) is 45%.
  √ Specificity (accurately excludes nondepression) is 90%, but
    □ Statistically significant responses in nondepressed patients, such as schizophrenia, panic attacks, obsessive-compulsive disorders, anorexia nervosa.
    □ DST interfered with by weight loss, uncontrolled diabetes, steroids, and carbamazepine.
* DST might possibly help initial diagnosis and predict relapse.
* DST protocol

✓ On day 1, give 1 mg dexamethasone po at 11 P.M.
✓ On day 2, draw venous blood for a cortisol assay at 8 A.M., 4 P.M.
and 11 P.M.
✓ DST is positive if any value is equal to or above 5 μg/dl.

Give TCAs in 2 ways

- Prescribed bid-qid, or
- Dispensed in a single, easier-to-remember bedtime dose to minimize side effects experienced during the day.

When starting TCA (e.g., imipramine), begin at 25 mg on night one and increase around 25 mg/day to reach a therapeutic dose of 150 mg qd by days 6–10.

- If patient does not improve after one week at 150 mg, escalate by 25 mg/day until reaching 250–300 mg/day.
- If patient is not better by 6th week, obtain plasma level from a trusted laboratory.
- If plasma level suggests changing the dose, do so by 25–50 mg q 2–3 days.

Most patients do *not* need TCA *plasma levels*.

Plasma levels most useful for patients who

- Have not responded to adequate trials of nortriptyline, and possibly to desipramine, imipramine, or amitriptyline.
- Are at high risk from age or medical illness, and thus, benefit from low doses.
- To monitor overdoses.
- Display medication noncompliance.
- Require documentation of TCA plasma levels for future treatment.
  ✓ (Example: patients attain therapeutic plasma level on small TCA doses, e.g., imipramine 50 mg/day.)
- Have a potential for unexpected raised or lowered TCA levels because of drug interactions.

Measured plasma levels may be

- The drug only (e.g., desipramine), or
- The drug and its chief metabolites (e.g., imipramine → imipramine + desipramine).

There may be a 30-fold difference in TCA levels after a single fixed dose.

- Slow metabolizers (e.g., elderly) at higher risk for toxicity.
- Fast metabolizers have trouble reaching adequate levels.

Patients have one of 2 types of plasma-level curves

- *Linear*
  - ✓ A direct, straight-line (linear) relationship exists between plasma level and clinical response. A specific plasma level yields a favorable response.
  - ✓ An example is imipramine (with metabolite desipramine), which collectively must surpass 200–250 ng/ml to be effective.
  - ✓ If the patient's plasma level is low, raise the dose.
- *Curvilinear*
  - ✓ A curvilinear response appears as a ∩ curve.
  - ✓ This curve shows an unfavorable response on the 2 vertical axes, but a therapeutic action on the horizontal plane.
  - ✓ Nortriptyline has a curvilinear response, also known as a "therapeutic window," which is 50–150 ng/ml.
  - ✓ Nonresponding nortriptyline patients with plasma levels of above 150 ng/ml improve by *lowering* the dose into the therapeutic window.
  - ✓ Nonresponding nortriptyline patients with plasma levels below 50 ng/ml may improve by *raising* the dose into the therapeutic window.

To obtain plasma levels

- Wait until TCAs have reached a steady-state level, which is usually 5–7 days.
- Draw blood 10–14 hours after last dose.
- Make sure tube is free of the contaminant tris-butoxyethyl.
  - ✓ Can use Venoject or glass syringes.
  - ✓ Do not use rubber stoppers.
  - ✓ Promptly centrifuge.

In treating depressed children

- Use desipramine, imipramine, or amitriptyline.
- Start at doses of 1½ mg/kg/day.
  - ✓ Escalate q4d by 1 mg/kg/day to a maximum of 3 mg/kg/day.

In treating the depressed elderly

- TCAs efficacy is 70%.
- The NIMH recommends secondary amine TCAs (e.g., nortriptyline, desipramine) for the elderly.
  - ✓ Trazodone is the NIMH's second choice.
- Initiate about one-half (or less) the starting doses in adults, but for people weighing < 70 kg, 10 mg/day of nortriptyline might suffice.

- Increase dose slowly until
  √ Clinical response noted,
  √ Sufficient plasma levels attained, or
  √ Intolerable side effects arise.
- Tertiary amines tend to show twice the plasma levels of younger patients on the same dose.

Treatment-Resistant Patients

About 30% of unipolar depressed patients are unresponsive to sufficient doses of TCAs, fluoxetine, or MAOIs after 4–6 weeks.

Lithium augmentation is preferred for these patients.

- In one study, about 30% of lithium-augmented patients (300 mg tid) improved markedly; 25% improved partially.
- Most patients recovered in 19–24 days while only 3.6% in 2 days.
- Clinical response does not correlate with serum lithium levels.
- Melancholic patients reacted better than nonmelancholic patients.
- Another approach is to *add* another drug to the TCA.
  √ Triiodothyronine (T_3) 25 μg/day lifts mood after several days in uncontrolled reports.
    □ May be stopped after 2–3 weeks without harm. Benefits euthyroid patients.
    □ May help females more than males.
  √ Neuroleptic (e.g., trifluoperazine 2–6 mg/day, perphenazine 4–8 mg/day) in delusional or severely agitated.
    □ Use briefly to avoid tardive dyskinesia.
  √ MAOI
    □ Do *not* add a TCA to ongoing MAOI! (see pages 104–105).
    □ May start MAOI and TCA together, both in low doses initially; or
    □ May add MAOI to ongoing TCAs (see pages 104–105).
    □ Safer to add MAOI to amitriptyline, doxepin, or trimipramine.
    □ Avoid adding MAOI to imipramine, desipramine, or fluoxetine; must stop fluoxetine 5–6 weeks before starting MAOI.
  √ Stimulants
    □ Methylphenidate 10–40 mg/day or dextroamphetamine 5–30 mg/day (see page 249).
    □ Probably a temporary boost.
  √ Alprazolam
    □ Alprazolam is a benzodiazepine that may treat mild to moderate depressions (see page 189).
    □ Start alprazolam at 1–1½ mg/day divided tid-qid.

- Increase by ½ mg every 3 days,
- Until reach 4 mg/day, and
- Range is 1½–10 mg/day.

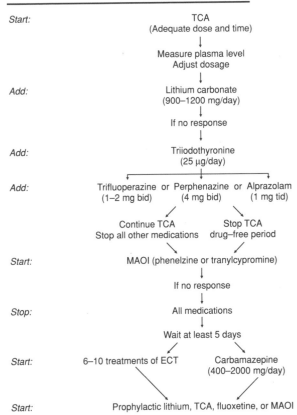

Flow Chart for Treating TCA-Resistant Patients

Start: TCA
(Adequate dose and time)
↓
Measure plasma level
Adjust dosage
↓
Add: Lithium carbonate
(900–1200 mg/day)
↓
If no response
↓
Add: Triiodothyronine
(25 µg/day)
↓
Add: Trifluoperazine or Perphenazine or Alprazolam
(1–2 mg bid)   (4 mg bid)   (1 mg tid)

Continue TCA   Stop TCA
Stop all other medications   drug–free period

Start: MAOI (phenelzine or tranylcypromine)
↓
If no response
↓
Stop: All medications
↓
Wait at least 5 days

Start: 6–10 treatments of ECT   Carbamazepine
(400–2000 mg/day)

Start: Prophylactic lithium, TCA, fluoxetine, or MAOI

Maintaining Therapy

Major depressive episodes usually persist for 6–12 months.

After 6 months of treating acute depression, maintenance therapy can begin.

- If the patient is symptom-free, continue the same TCA dose.
- If the patient has annoying TCA side effects, slowly lower the TCA dose.

After the initial 6 months of TCAs, if there has been at least 4 consecutive symptom-free months, may taper TCA dose no faster than 25 mg q 2–3 days.

- If symptoms flicker (with or without stress), maintain acute doses.

Can adjust above schedules as follows

- If this is the patient's first depression *and* his family's first depression, slowly discontinue TCA at 3 months.
- If the patient has had repeated depressions *or* his family has a h/o depression, do not lower TCAs until 9–12 months.

Chronic Physical Pain Disorders

TCAs may alleviate pain.

- TCAs work by themselves or by rendering narcotics more effective.
- Use the same or a lower TCA dose as in treating depression.
- Preferred TCAs are amitriptyline, desipramine, and doxepin.

Anorexia Nervosa

No single drug is clearly effective by itself or as an adjunct for treating anorexia nervosa. Nevertheless,

- Amitriptyline, a serotonin reuptake inhibitor, may help anorectics gain weight.
- Chlorpromazine assists severely obsessional anorectics.
  √ A possible BP drop could be dangerous in malnourished patients.
- Cyproheptadine, an antihistamine and serotonin antagonist, enables patients in gaining weight while exerting an antidepressant effect.
  √ Free of TCA's cardiovascular effects.
- Suggested trial involves
  √ Imipramine or desipramine 25 mg @ hs.
  √ Increase dose by 25 mg q2d up to 75 mg qd.
  √ If this does not work, consider cyproheptadine (12–32 mg qd), fluoxetine (60 mg qd superior to 20 mg qd), MAOI, or an opiate antagonist (e.g., naltrexone).

Bulimia

Recommended for bulimics is

- Imipramine or desipramine 25 mg @ hs.
- Escalate dose by 25 mg q2d up to 200 mg qd for normal-weight bulimics.

- If this trial does not work, consider fluoxetine (60 mg qd superior to 20 mg qd), lithium, MAOI (preferably phenelzine), an opiate antagonist (e.g., naltrexone), or pemoline.

Avoid amitriptyline, since it may stimulate appetite.

Cyproheptadine does *not* help bulimics, which may help to distinguish patients with bulimia from those with anorexia nervosa.

"Pseudodementia"

A depression in the elderly that mimics dementia.

- Treat as regular depression.

Other Adult Physical Disorders

These TCAs and MAOIs have been recommended for treating major depression coexisting with these physical disorders

Disorder	Might Help	Avoid
Cardiac conduction problem	Maprotiline Trazodone Nortriptyline Bupropion Fluoxetine	
Cataplexy	Clomipra- mine Desipramine Imipramine Fluoxetine Phenelzine	
Congestive heart failure	Nortriptyline	Trazodone
Constipation (chronic)	Amoxapine Desipramine Fluoxetine Maprotiline Trazodone	
Diarrhea (chronic)	Amitriptyline Imipramine Protriptyline Trimipramine	
Epilepsy	Desipramine Fluoxetine	Amoxapine Bupropion Maprotiline Trimipramine
Impotence (organic)	Amoxapine Bupropion Desipramine Fluoxetine Maprotiline Trazodone	

Disorder	Might Help	Avoid
Irritable bowel syndrome	Amitriptyline Desipramine Doxepin Nortriptyline Trazodone Phenelzine	
Migraine headache	Amitriptyline Doxepin Trazodone Trimipramine Phenelzine Tranylcy- promine	
Narrow-angle glaucoma	Amoxapine Bupropion Desipramine Fluoxetine Maprotiline Trazodone	
Neurogenic bladder	Amoxapine Bupropion Desipramine Fluoxetine Maprotiline Trazodone	
Parkinson's disease	Amitriptyline Doxepin Imipramine Protriptyline Trimipramine	Amoxapine
Peptic ulcers	Amitriptyline Doxepin Imipramine Trimipramine	
Sleep apnea	Protriptyline	
Tardive dyskinesia	Desipramine Imipramine Trazodone Trimipramine	Amoxapine

Childhood Stage-4 Sleep Disorders

In children, common difficulties in stage 4 sleep include

- Enuresis
- Sleepwalking
- Night terrors

For childhood enuresis, the following TCAs seem equally effective

- Imipramine
- Desipramine
- Amitriptyline
- Nortriptyline

Often require smaller doses than in treating depression in childhood. For instance,

- Start imipramine at 10–25 mg at hs.
  - √ Increase each week by increments of 10–25 mg,
  - √ Until reaching 50–75 mg/day.
- If necessary, maximum dose is $2\frac{1}{2}$ mg/kg/day.

Eighty percent of children will reduce bedwetting in less than one week with TCAs.

- Yet total remission is $< 50\%$.

Wetting often returns when drug is stopped.

TCAs are especially useful for short-term treatment, as during summer camp.

TCAs might assist in children with

- Sleepwalking and
- Severe night terrors.
  - √ Adults with night terrors might be helped by diazepam 5–20 mg.

SIDE EFFECTS

Clinicians should select a TCA considering its anticholinergic side effects.

POTENCY		ANTICHOLINERGIC
Protriptyline	MOST	Amitriptyline
Fluoxetine		Protriptyline
Nortriptyline		Trimipramine
Maprotiline		Doxepin
Clomipramine		Imipramine
Amitriptyline		Clomipramine
Amoxapine		Nortriptyline
Desipramine		Maprotiline
Doxepin		Amoxapine
Imipramine		Desipramine
Trimipramine		Fluoxetine
Trazodone	LEAST	Bupropion
Bupropion		Trazodone

TCAs are generally much more anticholinergic than neuroleptics.

- Enormous anticholinergic differences among TCAs themselves, such as amitriptyline being $> 18,000$ times more anticholinergic than trazodone.

Anticholinergic actions occur frequently, especially in the elderly.

Most anticholinergic symptoms taper off in 1–2 weeks.

Anticholinergic actions arise in many systems, and include

- Hypotension
- Dry mouth
- Constipation
- Paralytic ileus
- Urinary hesitancy or retention
- Blurred vision
- Dry eyes
- Narrow-angle glaucoma
- Photophobia
- Nasal congestion

These anticholinergic effects are discussed with their respective organ systems.

Cardiovascular Effects

Patients should be carefully checked for TCA-cardiac interactions.

Cardiac problems with TCAs are of 4 general types

- Blood pressure
- Heart rate
- Cardiac conduction
- Heart failure

Blood pressure

- *Hypotension* with *dizziness*

Most Hypotensive	Medium Hypotensive	Least Hypotensive
Doxepin	Amoxapine	Nortriptyline
Clomipramine	Protriptyline	Fluoxetine
Trimipramine	Maprotiline	Bupropion
Imipramine	Trazodone	
Amitriptyline	Desipramine	

√ TCAs generate considerable hypotension, but MAOIs cause more hypotension than TCAs.
√ Hypotension more common in
  □ Cardiac patients (14–24%) than in medically well patients (0–7%).

□ The elderly report a 4% injury rate (e.g., fractures, lacerations).
√ Measure BPs reclining and standing, before and during, the first few days of TCA treatment.
√ Tell patient to deal with hypotension by
  □ Sitting a full 60 seconds—or longer—if at all lightheaded,
  □ Standing slowly while holding onto stable object (e.g., bed), and
  □ Waiting at least 30 seconds before walking.
  □ Consider support stockings or corsets.
√ Other management
  □ Increase dose more slowly.
  □ Try less hypotensive TCA, even though hypotension may not be dose dependent.
  □ Nortriptyline produces hypotension above its therapeutic window.
  □ If BP problems threaten continued TCA use in patients without a cardiac illness, may add sodium chloride (500–650 mg bid-tid) or yohimbine (5 mg tid).
  □ Hydrate with about 8 glasses of fluid a day.
  □ Greater BP drops may be treated with fludrocortisone (0.1 mg qd-bid).

Increased heart rate

• *Tachycardia*
  √ Patients may be frightened (unduly) or distracted by tachycardia, and benefit from reassurance.
  √ More common with more anticholinergic TCAs.
• *Arrhythmias*
  √ After several weeks of TCAs (especially imipramine)—or thio-ridazine—a quinidinelike action may ensue, which can cut down premature beats.

Cardiac conduction

• *ECG changes* include
  √ Nonspecific ST and T wave changes
  √ Prolongation of PR interval
  √ Widening QRS complex
• TCA doses, and not cardiac disease, incite these ECG alterations.
• Avoid giving TCAs to patients with pre-existing bundle-branch block, especially with left- and right- sided bundle-branch block.
  √ If patient has a mild first-degree bundle branch block, TCAs might help.
  √ TCAs can produce fatalities in patients with second-degree and third-degree heart block.

- Causing fewer cardiac-condition problems are probably
  - √ Trazodone
  - √ Nortriptyline
  - √ Bupropion
  - √ Fluoxetine
  - √ Maprotiline

Heart failure

- *Myocardial depression, decreased cardiac output, congestive heart failure*
- *Pedal edema* frequently induced by
  - √ Amitriptyline
  - √ Imipramine
  - √ Trazodone

Sudden death occurs unexpectedly; supposedly due to cardiac arrhythmias.

- More common after TCA overdose: about 0.4%.

Gastrointestinal Effects

Dry mouth (see page 13)
Anorexia, nausea, vomiting, dyspepsia

- Common with fluoxetine.
- Reduce TCAs.

Diarrhea
Peculiar taste, "black tongue," glossitis
Constipation (see page 14)
Paralytic ileus

- Rare, but potentially fatal.
- Stop TCAs.

Weight gain

- TCAs increase appetite and food intake.
- More common with
  - √ Amitriptyline
  - √ Imipramine
  - √ Doxepin
  - √ Clomipramine

Weight loss

- More frequent with
  - √ Bupropion
  - √ Desipramine

√ Fluoxetine
√ Trazodone

Renal Effects

Urinary hesitancy or *retention* (see page 14)

Endocrine and Sexual Effects

Distinguish effects caused by

* Depression,
* Medication, or
* Other causes.

Increased or decreased libido, impotence, diminished sexual arousal, impaired orgasms

* Management
  √ Lower TCA dose may bring marked improvement.
  √ Cyproheptadine 4 mg/day may alleviate anorgasmia.
  √ Yohimbine (5 mg tid) or bethanechol (10 mg tid) may reduce impotence.
  √ A pure noradrenergic drug may relieve some sexual dysfunctions.

Priapism

* A rare persistent, painful erection most often from trazodone.
  √ Chlorpromazine, thioridazine, and antihypertensives cause other cases.
  √ Most common in trazodone doses < 150 mg, although it can arise on doses from 50–400 mg.
  √ Occurs primarily during 1st month of treatment, but it can erupt anywhere from 3 days to 18 months after drug initiated.
* If sexual ability is to be retained, intervention with 4–6 hours is mandatory. If caught too late, condition will be irreversible.
* All patients on trazodone must be warned in advance about priapism.
* Management
  √ May require surgery.
  √ Medications, ice packs, enemas provide inconsistent results.
  √ These medications include
    □ Neostigmine 7½–15 mg ½–1 hour before intercourse, or
    □ Metaraminol 10 mg injected into penis.
  √ In emergencies, clinicians can call Bristol-Myers at 1-800-321-1335.

Testicular swelling (rare)

- Reported from desipramine.
  - √ Stop drug.

Breast engorgement (males and females)

Appetite stimulation, carbohydrate craving (except fluoxetine)

Eyes, Ears, Nose, and Throat

Blurred vision (see page 16)

Photophobia

- From dilated pupils.

Dry eyes (see page 17)
Narrow-angle glaucoma

- Virtually all TCAs, but especially the most anticholinergic, can precipitate a painful narrow-angle glaucoma.
- If patient might have this type of glaucoma, postpone all anticholinergic agents, including TCAs, until diagnosis is clear (see page 17).

Nasal congestion
Dry bronchial secretions and *strained breathing* for patients with respiratory difficulty

Skin, Allergies, and Temperature

Increased, and occasionally *decreased, sweating*

Fluoxetine especially increases sweating.

- Management
  - √ Daily showering,
  - √ Talcum powder,
  - √ Place patients on less anticholinergic TCAs.

Skin flushing

Allergies rare, and display

- *Rashes*
  - √ Cease TCAs.
- *Jaundice, hepatitis*
- *Urticaria, pruritus*
- *Photosensitivity*

Central Nervous System Effects

Sedation, drowsiness

Most Sedative	Medium Sedative	Least (or not) Sedative
Doxepin	Amoxapine	Bupropion (not)
Amitriptyline	Imipramine	Fluoxetine (not)
Clomipramine	Maprotiline	Desipramine
Trimipramine	Nortriptyline	Protriptyline
Trazodone		

- Sedation, especially fatigue, during first 2 weeks of therapy.
- Management
  - √ Prescribe less sedating TCAs during the day.
  - √ Give all TCAs in single hs dose.
  - √ Switch to less sedating TCA.

Confusion, disturbed concentration, disorientation (see page 25)

Effect of Increasing Age on Risk
of Confusional States with TCAs

Age (years)	Risk Rate (%)
10–29	0
30–39	4
40–49	25
50–59	43
60–69	33
70–79	50
Overall risk	13

- Switch to a less anticholinergic TCA, in particularly fluoxetine or trazodone. Also consider amoxapine, desipramine, or nortriptyline.

Delirium

- Dose dependent; in 6% of tertiary TCA-treated patients.
- Occurs with plasma levels of >450 ng/ml.
- May begin with greater depression or psychosis.
  - √ Increased TCAs or adding neuroleptics may worsen toxicity.

Memory impaired

- Especially in the elderly,
- Determine cause carefully. May be

√ Depression,
√ Organic brain syndrome,
√ Endocrine problem, or
√ Medication-induced toxicity.

* If patient tries to remember something and can't, the culprit is more organically based: if the person doesn't try at all, depression is more likely.

Weakness, lethargy, fatigue
Muscle tremors, twitches, jitters (occasional)
Speech blockage, stuttering
Seizures

* Afflict 0.1–0.9% of TCA-treated patients.
  √ 3% for clomipramine and imipramine.
* More recent reports of seizures with
  √ Maprotiline when
    □ Given in high doses (200–400 mg qd),
    □ Rapidly escalated to 150 mg/day in 7 days, and
    □ Patients have pre-existing seizures.
  √ Bupropion given > 450 mg/day.

Agent	Frequency of Use (%)	Seizures Reported (N)
Maprotiline	3.6	112
Amitriptyline	34.2	35
Imipramine	13.5	15
Nortriptyline	2.2	11

* With TCAs, seizures erupt with
  √ Overdose,
  √ Pre-existing seizures (including alcohol withdrawal), and
  √ Pre-existing organic brain disorder.
* Higher TCA plasma levels (>450 ng/ml) risk, but are insufficient to cause, seizures.
  √ Weeks of high TCA plasma levels may occur before seizures.
  √ High chronic levels typically have no prodromal phase; they generate a single, tonic-clonic, sometimes fatal, grand mal seizure.
* Acute TCA overdose triggers multiple seizures and status epilepticus.

"Spaciness," depersonalization

* Management
  √ Escalate dose more slowly.
  √ If side effect persists, switch to another TCA.

Paresthesias (infrequent)
Ataxia
Extrapyramidal side effects

- Rarely seen with TCAs.
- Most often with amoxapine
  √ Parkinsonian reactions
  √ Akathisia (doses from 50–200 mg/day)
    □ Reported with fluoxetine.
  √ Dyskinesia
    □ Uncommon.
    □ Arises with reduced dose.
    □ Disappears quickly.
  √ Tardive dyskinesia
- *Neuroleptic malignant syndrome* (NMS) (see pages 20–22).
  √ Amoxapine is the only antidepressant to cause NMS.

Tremors

- High-frequency tremors commonly seen, especially with noradrenergic TCAs or lithium.
- Management of persistent tremor can involve
  √ Lower TCA doses,
  √ Propranolol 10–20 mg bid-qid, or
  √ Low doses of benzodiazepines (e.g., alprazolam ¼ mg bid).

Insomnia

- Prescribe more sedating TCAs at hs.
- Most common with fluoxetine and bupropion.
  √ Then with protriptyline and amoxapine.

Weird dreams, such as *nightmares, hypnagogic hallucinations*, and *vivid dreams*

- Usually emerge when full dose of TCAs consumed at hs.
- May reduce by
  √ Changing TCA or
  √ Spreading dose throughout day.

Excitement, restlessness
Precipitation of

- *Hypomania, mania,*
- *Panic reactions,*
- *Anxiety,* or
- *Emotional instability.*

Delusions, visual or auditory hallucinations
"Serotonin syndrome"

- With more potent serotonin re-uptake inhibitors, including clomipramine and fluoxetine.
- Patients may experience one, several, or all of these symptoms
  - √ Restlessness
  - √ Diaphoresis
  - √ Hyperreflexia
  - √ Myoclonus
  - √ Nausea, abdominal cramps
  - √ Diarrhea
  - √ Insomnia
- Management
  - √ Cyproheptadine, the serotonin antagonist, can alleviate the serotonin syndrome.
  - √ Stop any tryptophan the patient might have been taking.
  - √ Select less serotonergic-type antidepressant.

PERCENTAGES OF SIDE EFFECTS

Part I

Side Effects	Amitriptyline	Amoxapine	Bupropion	Clomipramine	Desipramine
CARDIOVASCULAR EFFECTS					
Hypotension	32 (10–44)	36 (30–42)	4.3 (2.5–10)	13 (6–30)	6
Hypertension	—	—	1.6	—	—
Dizziness, lightheadedness	42.5 (10–65)	>30	28.3 (2–22.3)	37 (10–54)	6
Fainting, syncope	—	—	1.2	0.0	—
Tachycardia	20	20	6.4 (<2–10.8)	14.7 (4–30)	6
Palpitations	5	—	3.7	4	—
ECG abnormalities	20	<2	<2	20	6
Cardiac arrhythmias	6	<2	3.7	6	6
Sweating	22.5 (10–30)	6	14.2 (2–22.3)	21 (10–30)	—
GASTROINTESTINAL EFFECTS					
Dry mouth and throat	58.5 (30–90)	29.3 (14–30)	30.5 (10–44)	52.7 (>30–84)	20
Anorexia, lower appetite	0.0	—	18.3	12	—
Increased appetite	5	—	3.7	11	—

Side Effects	Amitri-ptyline	Amoxa-pine	Bupro-pion	Clomipr-amine	Desipr-amine
Nausea, vomiting	5.5	—	14.4 (2–22.9)	19.5 (2–33)	6
Taste changes	—	—	3.1	—	—
Dyspepsia, upset stomach	5	—	3.1	16 (6–22)	—
Diarrhea	—	—	6.8	13	—
Constipation	29.4 (10–38.2)	27 (12–>30)	20.7 (2–30)	33.5 (10–47)	6
Salivation	—	—	3.4	—	—
Weight gain	>30	<2	11.2 (<2–18)	19 (10–30)	6
Weight loss	—	—	23.2	—	—
Edema	1	—	—	—	2
RENAL EFFECTS					
Urinary hesitancy or retention	10.5 (2–15)	20	3.9 (1.9–10)	11 (2–30)	—
ENDOCRINE AND SEXUAL EFFECTS					
Menstrual changes	—	—	4.7	12	—
Breast swelling	—	—	—	2	—
Lactation	—	—	—	4	—
Priapism	0.0	0.0	0.0	0.0	0.0
Disturbed sexual function	4.3 (0–10)	—	3.2	16.3 (8–30)	7 (2–10)
EYES, EARS, NOSE, AND THROAT EFFECTS					
Blurred vision	35.2 (10–55.7)	6.5 (2–10)	18.3 (2–34.3)	20	6
Tinnitus	10	—	—	—	—
Sore throat, flu	—	—	5	10	—
SKIN, ALLERGIES, AND TEMPERATURE					
Rashes	6	11.5 (3–30)	7 (2–10)	7 (2–10)	6
Abnormal skin pigment	—	—	2.2	4	—
Fever, hyperthermia	—	0.5	1.6	4	—
CENTRAL NERVOUS SYSTEM EFFECTS					
Parkinsonism	—	—	1.5	—	—
Akinesia	—	—	8	—	—
Akathisia	—	—	1.5	—	—
Weakness, fatigue	20	5.5 (2–10)	9.7 (2–18)	30 (2–54)	6
Muscle cramps	5	—	1.9	13	—
Seizures	<2	<2	2 (0.3–2.2)	2.1 (0.5–3)	<2
Headache	10.5 (2–15)	6	15.9 (2–25.7)	6	<2
Slurred speech	—	—	—	3	—

Side Effects	Amitri- ptyline	Amoxa- pine	Bupro- pion	Clomipr- amine	Desipr- amine
Tremor	25 (5–40)	9 (2–12)	13.6 (2–21.1)	16.3 (6–33)	6
Drowsiness, sedation	39.6 (30–58.8)	16 (14–30)	9.7 (2–19.8)	30 (2–54)	6
Insomnia	10.5 (2–15)	20	12.3 (2–18.6)	8.5 (1.5–30)	6
Confusion, disorientation	11.3 (0–30)	6	7.2 (2–10)	4.5 (2–10)	—
Anxiety, nervousness (i.e., mental)	—	—	3.1	15.8 (9–18)	—
Agitation, restlessness (i.e., motoric)	—	—	31.9	3	—
Excitement, hypomania	5.7 (<2–15)	6	3.6 (1.2–10)	<2	6
Depression	—	—	—	5	—

Part II

Side Effects	Doxepin	Fluoxetine	Imipramine	Maprotiline
CARDIOVASCULAR EFFECTS				
Hypotension	20	10.5 (<1–30)	37 (>30–40)	6
Hypertension	—	<1	—	—
Dizziness, sedation	20	9.2 (1.6–30)	26.3 (15–30)	7 (2–10)
Tachycardia	20	1.2	20	6
Palpitations	—	1.3	5	—
ECG abnormalities	6	<2	20	<2
Cardiac arrhythmias	6	1.5	6	<2
GASTROINTESTINAL EFFECTS				
Dry mouth and throat	43 (>30–56)	37 (2–95)	30	26 (22–>30)
Anorexia, lower appetite	—	9	—	—
Increased appetite	—	1	—	—
Nausea, vomiting	<2	20.7	20	4
Taste changes	—	2.2 (1.8–3)	—	—
Dyspepsia, stomach upset	—	6.2	—	—
Diarrhea	—	12.2	—	—

Side Effects	Doxepin	Fluoxetine	Imipramine	Maprotiline
Constipation	31.5 (10–43)	7.6 (2–30)	20	13 (6–30)
Jaundice	—	1	—	—
Weight gain	6	1	20	20
Weight loss	—	13	—	—
Edema	—	<1	—	—
RENAL EFFECTS				
Urinary hesitancy or retention	4.5 (<2–10)	1.5 (<1–<2)	20	6
ENDOCRINE AND SEXUAL EFFECTS				
Menstrual changes	—	1.7	—	—
Breast swelling	—	<1	—	—
Priapism	0.0	0.0	0.0	0.0
Disturbed sexual function	6	1.5	2.5	—
Hypothyroidism	—	<1	—	—
HEMATOLOGIC EFFECTS				
Blood dyscrasias	—	<1	—	—
EYES, EARS, NOSE, AND THROAT EFFECTS				
Blurred vision	20	4.5 (2–10)	16.7 (10–30)	12 (4–30)
Nasal stuffiness	—	2.3	—	—
Sore throat, flu	—	7.8	—	—
SKIN, ALLERGIES, AND TEMPERATURE				
Allergies	—	1.1	—	—
Rashes	<2	4.2 (2.7–10)	6	20
Abnormal skin pigment	—	2	—	—
Sweating	20	7.5 (2–8.4)	20	6
Fever, hyperthermia	—	1.2	—	—
CENTRAL NERVOUS SYSTEM EFFECTS				
Akathisia	—	17.4 (9.8–25)	—	—
Weakness, fatigue	6	4.2	20	4
Muscle cramps	—	1.4	—	—
Rigidity	—	<1	—	—
Seizures	<2	1.1 (0.2–<2)	>3 (0.6–>3)	>3 (0.2–>3)
Headache	<2	20.1 (10–30)	20	3
Slurred speech	—	—	6	—

Side Effects	Doxepin	Fluoxetine	Imipramine	Maprotiline
Tremor	6	13.9 (7.9–30)	20	11.5 (3–30)
Drowsiness, sedation	34.5 (30–39)	15.8 (10–30)	26 (20–32)	18 (10–30)
Insomnia	6	16.9 (10–30)	20	2
Disorientation, confusion	<2	10.8 1.5–30	4.3 0–10	6
Restlessness, agitation (i.e., motoric)	—	25.5 (14.9–36)	—	2
Anxiety, nervousness (i.e., mental)	—	10.9 (9.4–15)	—	4.5
Excitement, hypomania	<2	7.3 (1–30)	15 (5–30)	6

Part III

Side Effects	Nortriptyline	Protriptyline	Trazodone	Trimipramine
CARDIOVASCULAR EFFECTS				
Hypotension	6	20	10.1 (3.8–30)	20
Hypertension	—	—	1.7	—
Dizziness, sedation	5.5	20	21.9 (10–30)	20
Fainting, syncope	—	—	3.7 (2.8–4.5)	—
Tachycardia	6	6	3.2 (0.0–10)	6
Palpitations	—	—	0.0–0.7	—
Shortness of breath	—	—	1.2	—
ECG abnormalities	6	20	<2	20
Cardiac arrhythmias	6	6	<2	6
GASTROINTESTINAL EFFECTS				
Dry mouth and throat	20	2	17.7 (2–33.8)	20
Anorexia, lower appetite	—	—	1.7 (0.0–3.5)	—
Nausea, vomiting	2.3	—	15.7 (9.9–30)	<2
Taste changes	—	—	0.7	—
Dyspepsia, indigestion	—	—	4.6	—

Side Effects	Nortriptyline	Protriptyline	Trazodone	Trimipramine
Diarrhea	—	—	2.2 (0.0–4.5)	—
Constipation	8.6	20	13.6 (7–30)	20
Weight gain	6	—	4.5 (1.4–10)	20
Weight loss	—	—	3.4 (1–5.7)	—
Edema	—	—	4.9	—
RENAL EFFECTS				
Urinary hesitancy or retention	<2	<2	4.8 (<2–10)	<2
ENDOCRINE AND SEXUAL EFFECTS				
Priapism	0.0	0.0	(0.01–0.001)	0.0
Disturbed sexual function	<2	<2	1.4	—
EYES, EARS, NOSE, AND THROAT EFFECTS				
Blurred vision	5.5	20	8.3 (2–14.7)	6
Nasal stuffiness	—	—	4.3 (2.8–5.7)	—
SKIN, ALLERGIES, AND TEMPERATURE				
Rashes	<2	<2	<2	<2
Sweating	2.5	20	1.2	6
CENTRAL NERVOUS SYSTEM EFFECTS				
Weakness, fatigue	20	20	6.6 (<2–11.3)	6
Muscle cramps	—	—	5.4	—
Seizures	<2	<2	<2	<2
Headache	<2	—	10.4 (2–19.8)	6
Incoordination	—	—	3.4 (1.9–4.9)	—
Tremor	11.3 (0–30)	6	4.9 (2 –10)	20
Drowsiness, sedation	6.8 (0–15)	<2	29.1 (20–50)	>30
Insomnia	<2	20	5.1 (<2–9.9)	6
Disorientation, confusion	11.3 (0–30)	—	3.7 (<2–5.7)	20
Anxiety, nervousness (i.e., mental)	—	—	10.6 (6.4–14.8)	—
Excitement, hypomania	8 (2–15)	20	3.3 (1.4–5.1)	<2

A N T I D E P R E S S A N T S

PREGNANCY AND LACTATION

Teratogenicity
(1st trimester)

- Little evidence of teratogenicity.

- Limb abnormalities have developed in children from mothers taking amitriptyline, imipramine, or nortriptyline; the role of drugs is unclear.

- Clomipramine in 3 women caused 3 toxic newborns, with lethargy, hypotonia, cyanosis, jitters, irregular breathing, respiratory acidosis, and hypothermia.

- Best to avoid these 4 TCAs during pregnancy.

Direct Effect
on Newborn
(3rd trimester)

- Tachycardia, autonomic lability, respiratory distress, muscle spasms, and congestive heart failure has occurred in infants if large TCA doses taken prior to delivery.

- Imipramine and desipramine have produced neonatal withdrawal, with colic, diaphoresis, weight loss, cyanosis, rapid breathing, and irritability.

- Infants developed urinary retention from mothers on nortriptyline.

Lactation

- Present in breast milk.

Drug Dosage in Mother's Milk

Generic Names	Milk/ Plasma Ratio	Time of Peak Concentration in Milk (hours)	Infant Dose (μg/kg/day)	Maternal Dose (%)	Safety Rating*
Amitriptyline	?	?	16.0	0.90	A
Amoxapine	?	?	<3 mg	<0.07	A
Desipramine	?	?	18–40.2	0.5–1.0	B
Doxepin	?	?	0.25	0.01	A
Imipramine	?	1	4.4	0.13	A
Maprotiline	?	?	39.0	1.60	B
Nortriptyline	?	?	8.3–27.0	0.53–1.30	B
Trazodone	0.14	2	9.0	1.10	B

* A: Safe throughout infancy; B: Reasonably unsafe before 34 weeks, but safe after 34 weeks.

DRUG-DRUG INTERACTIONS

Drugs (X) Interact with:	Tricyclic Antidepressants (T)	Comments
Acetaminophen	X ↓	May abuse acetaminophen.
Acetazolamide	T ↑	Reduces TCA's excretion; clinical importance unclear.
*Alcohol	X ↑ A ↑	CNS depression.
Ammonium chloride	T ↓	May increase TCA's excretion; clinical importance unclear.
Anticholinergics	X ↑	Increased anticholinergic actions.
Antihistamines	X ↑	Increased drowsiness; use nonsedating antihistamine, such as terfenadine.
*Antipsychotics	X? T ↑	Potentiate each other. Toxicity. More anticholinergic TCAs may diminish EPS.
*Barbiturates	X ↑ T ↑	CNS depression.
Benzodiazepines	X ↑ T ↑	CNS depression.
Birth control pills	T ↓	May diminish TCA effects.
Carbamazepine	X ↓ T ↓	Decreased TCA effect; may lower seizure control. Monitor serum levels.
Chlordiazepoxide	X ↑	Few cases of more sedation.
Chlorothiazide	T ↑	Thiazide diuretics increase TCA actions.
*Cimetidine	T ↑	Triggers anticholinergic toxicity; give patient less TCA or substitute ranitidine or famotidine for cimetidine.
*Clonidine	X ↓	Inhibit clonidine's antihypertensive actions. Methyldopa, bupropion, fluoxetine, maprotiline are safer.
Cocaine	X ↑	Cardiac arrhythmias.
Cyclobenzaprine	T ↑	Cyclobenzaprine, which is chemically similar to TCAs, may produce cardiac problems.
Debrisoquin	X ↓	Hypotension.
*Dextroamphetamine	X ↑ T ↑	TCAs may increase amphetamine's effects, while dextroamphetamine augments TCAs.
Dicumarol	X ↓	Increased bleeding time.
Disopyramide	X? T?	See quinidine.
Disulfiram	T ↑	May increase TCA level.
†Epinephrine	X ↑	TCAs and direct-acting sympathomimetics (e.g., epinephrine) increase arrhythmias, hypertension, and tachycardia. TCAs inhibit pressor effects of indirect-acting sympathomimetics (e.g., ephedrine). Because TCAs block the reuptake of direct-acting sympathomimetics, their concentration increases at receptor sites. Since indirect-acting sympathomimetics require uptake into the adrenergic neuron to induce their effects, TCAs block them. The cardiovascular result

Drugs (X) Interact with:	Tricyclic Antidepressants (T)	Comments
		from the mixed-acting sympathomimetics depends on the % of each group. Avoid TCAs with direct-acting sympathomimetics.
Fenfluramine	T↑	Raises TCA effects.
*Fluoxetine	T↑	TCA toxicity.
†Guanethidine	X↓	Severe hypertension. Doxepin, bupropion, fluoxetine, maprotiline, trazodone, trimipramine, and methyldopa may be safer.
Insulin	X↑	TCA enhances hypoglycemia in diabetics.
Levodopa	X↓	TCAs may diminish levodopa's absorption.
Lidocaine	X? T?	See quinidine.
Liothyronine	T↑	Liothyronine potentiates TCAs' effects, especially in women; arrhythmias.
Lithium	T↑	May augment TCAs.
Meperidine	X↑ T↑	Potentiate each other. Use lower doses of meperidine or another narcotic.
Methyldopa	X↓	Hypotension. Amitriptyline biggest problem.
Methylphenidate	X↑ T↑	TCAs may increase methylphenidate's effects, while methylphenidate may augment TCAs.
Molindone	X↑	Greater molindone effect.
*MAOIs	X↑	*Never* add TCAs to MAOIs; this risks hypertensive crisis, mania, muscular rigidity, convulsions, high fever, coma, and death. If TCAs are to be used, first taper MAOI, keep patient off MAOI for 10–14 days, maintain MAOI diet during this interval, and then slowly begin TCA. If combine TCAs and MAOIs, start both drugs together or stop TCAs for 2–3 days before adding an MAOI. Best to *not* give (1) large doses, (2) IM/IV drugs, (3) imipramine with tranylcypromine, and (4) a MAOI to patients recently on fluoxetine or clomipramine. (See page 105)
Morphine	X↑ T↓	CNS depression; May decrease TCA levels. Common with amitriptyline and desipramine.
Phenylbutazone	X↓	TCAs may delay absorption of phenylbutazone.
*Phenytoin	X↓	Lower seizure control.
Prazosin	X↓	Hypertension. Safer to use bupropion, fluoxetine, desipramine, and protriptyline.
Procainamide	X? T?	See quinidine.

Drugs (X) Interact with:	Tricyclic Antidepressants (T)	Comments
Propranolol	X ↓ T ↓	Patients may become more depressed on β blockers. Desipramine's low anticholinergic action may interfere with β blockers' cardiac actions.
Quinidine	X? T?	Because of TCA's quinidinelike effects, there can occur myocardial depression, diminished contractility, and dysrhythmias, which can lead to congestive heart failure. Quinidine and TCAs may yield irregular heartbeat early on.
Reserpine	X ↑ T ↑	Although reserpine alleviates depression, patients may develop hypotension, flushing, diarrhea, and mania.
Sulfonylureas	X ↑	TCA enhances hypoglycemia in diabetics.
Tobacco smoking	T ↓	Smokers may lower TCA plasma levels; importance unclear.
Warfarin	X ↓	Increased bleeding time.

Drugs (X) Interact with:	Amitriptyline (A)	Comments
Disulfiram	X ↑	Two cases of organic brain syndrome. Cleared when both drugs stopped.
Ethchlorvynol	X ↑	Transient delirium.

Drugs (X) Interact with:	Clomipramine (C)	Comments
Haloperidol	C ↑	Increases clomipramine levels.
*MAOI	X ↑ C ↑	Prompts serotonin syndrome.

Drugs (X) Interact with:	Desipramine (D)	Comments
Methadone	D ↑	Desipramine reported to increase by 108%; use together carefully.

Drugs (X) Interact with:	Doxepin (D)	Comments
Propoxyphene	D ↑	Propoxyphene doubles doxepin levels, inducing lethargy. Five days after stopping propoxyphene, patient's mental status returns to normal.

Drugs (X) Interact with:	Fluoxetine (F)	Comments
Digitoxin	X ↓	Diminishes digitoxin's effect.
Lithium	X ↑ ↓	Lithium toxicity may occur or lithium level may decrease.

A N T I D E P R E S S A N T S

*MAOI	X↑ F↑	Prompts serotonin syndrome.	
Tryptophan	F↑	Prompts agitation, restlessness, and GI distress.	

Drugs (X) Interact with:	Maprotiline (M)	Comments
Propranolol	M↑	Maprotiline toxicity.

Drugs (X) Interact with:	Trazodone (T)	Comments
*Barbiturates	T↑	BP drop; avoid.
Digitalis	X↑	Increases digitalis.

Codes: * Moderately important interaction; † Extremely important interaction; ↑ Increases, ↓ Decreases, ↑↓ Increases and decreases; ? Unsure.

EFFECTS OF LABORATORY TESTS

Generic Names	Blood/Serum Tests	Results	Urine Tests	Results
Amitriptyline	Glucose	↑↓	None	
Amoxapine	WBC, LFT	↓↑	None	
Desipramine	Glucose	↑↓	None	
Doxepin	Glucose	↑↓	None	
Fluoxetine	ESR, Bleeding time	↑↑	Albuminuria	↑
	Glucose	↓		
	Cholesterol, Lipids	↑↑		
	Potassium, Sodium	↓↓		
	Iron	↓		
	LFT	↑↓		
Imipramine	Glucose	↑↓	None	
Maprotiline	Glucose	↑↓	None	
Nortriptyline	Glucose	↑↓	None	
Trazodone	WBC, LFT	↓↑	None	

Codes: LFT are liver function tests: SGOT, SGPT, LDH, bilirubin, alkaline phosphatase. ↑ Increases; ↓ Decreases; ↑↓ Increases and decreases.

WITHDRAWAL

TCAs do not provoke

- Dependence
- Tolerance
- Addiction
- Withdrawal

Yet, because of cholinergic rebound, abruptly stopping TCAs can result in

- "GI psychosomatic" syndrome
  √ Anorexia, nausea, vomiting, diarrhea, queasy stomach, cramps
  √ Increased salivation
  √ Anxiety, agitation, irritability
  √ Cold sweat
  √ Tachycardia
  √ Headache, neck pains
  √ Chills, coryza, malaise, rhinorrhea, dizziness
- Sleep disturbances
  √ Insomnia
  √ Hypersomnia
  √ "Excessive" dreaming, or
  √ Nightmares
- Hypomanic or manic symptoms

These symptoms

- Begin 2–4 (and up to 7) days after suddenly stopping TCAs.
- Withdrawal-like symptoms may persist 1–2 weeks.
- Are not life-threatening.
- Can diminish, or not exist, by withdrawing TCAs more gradually, no faster than (imipramine) 25 mg q 2–3 days.

Three major studies have shown

- Somatic, GI symptoms happened in 21–55% of adults withdrawn from imipramine.
- 80% adults developed symptoms within 2 weeks of being withdrawn from amitriptyline.
- Children are more susceptible than adults.

Amoxapine, if stopped after 6 months or prescribed in low doses for a long time, can generate tardive dyskinesia (see pages 22–24).

OVERDOSE: TOXICITY, SUICIDE, AND TREATMENT

A 10-day therapeutic dose of TCAs can be lethal, making suicide far more likely than with antipsychotic agents.

- 10–20 mg/kg of TCAs yield moderate to severe toxicity.
- 30–40 mg/kg of TCAs are often fatal for adults.
- Children have died from 20 mg/kg of imipramine.

There may be a latent period of 1–12 hours between drug-taking and toxicity.

ANTIDEPRESSANTS

Attempted and completed suicides seem to *decline* with increased TCA doses

Daily Dose (mg)	Prevalence of Suicidal Behavior (%)
0–74	30.4
75–149	10.1
150–249	5.1
>250	0.5

The general management of TCA overdoses (see page 37).

In addition

* For cardiorespiratory problems
  √ Hypotension, dizziness (see pages 74–75)
  √ Cardiac arrhythmias
    ▫ When QRS is < 0.10, ventricular arrhythmias are less frequent.
    ▫ Treat ventricular arrhythmias with phenytoin, lidocaine, or propranolol.
  √ Supraventricular arrhythmias
  √ Cardiac conduction problems
    ▫ Give IV sodium bicarbonate to achieve pH of 7.4–7.5.
    ▫ Quinidine, procainamide, and disopyramide should be avoided in managing conduction problems and arrhythmias, since they further depress cardiac function.
  √ Cardiac failure: use digitalis.
* For severe urinary retention
  √ Acid-base problems are quite severe for TCA overdoses.
  √ Acidosis is usually most severe.
  √ Dialysis is fairly useless because of low drug concentrations.
  √ Void patient by catheter if no recent voiding.
* For seizures (see page 80)

Toxicity and Suicide Data

Generic Names	Toxicity Doses Average (Highest) (g)	Mortality Doses Average (Lowest) (g)	Toxic Levels (μg/ml)	Lethal Supplies (days)
Amitriptyline	1.343 (2.0)	2.166 (0.50)	≥ 1	10
Desipramine	—	—	≥ 1	12
Imipramine	3.1 (5.375)	3.619 (0.50)	≥ 1	10
Nortriptyline	—	—	≥ 1	15
Fluoxetine	3	1.8	2461 ng/ml	—

PRECAUTIONS

TCAs contraindicated in patients with h/o

- Cardiovascular problems, hypertension, and acute myocardial infarction
  √ Taking thyroid might foster cardiovascular toxicity, including arrhythmias.
- Using MAOIs, or having consumed them within past 14 days
- Hypersensitivity to TCAs
- Narrow-angle glaucoma
- Increased intraocular pressure
- Seizures
  √ Avoid bupropion in patients with h/o anorexia nervosa and bulimia because they are prone to develop seizures.
  √ Avoid clomipramine > 250 mg qd in adults and 3 mg/kg (or 200 mg) in children and adolescents.

TCAs may precipitate mania in 50% of bipolar patients.

- It is common for patients recovering from depression to undergo a "switch phase" into a "high" *before* returning to normality.
  √ This "high" might last a day, and is not worth "overtreating," yet if a true switch has uncovered a manic process, it is best to treat this with
    □ Reducing or stopping TCA dose or
    □ Adding or pretreating with lithium.

Fluoxetine can increase plasma levels of TCAs and cause toxicity.

Although TCA abuse is rare, amitriptyline abuse, with doses up to 2000 mg/day can intoxicate, prolong sleep, and induce retrograde amnesia. Halting amitriptyline can be difficult and needs active treatment.

NURSES' DATA

Depressed patients are suicidal, and therefore

- Monitor for "cheeking," hoarding, or suicidal indications.
- A sudden disappearance of a side effect (e.g., dry mouth) suggests hiding medication.

Remind patient (and family) about a 7–28 day lag on a full therapeutic dose before TCAs fully work.

- Tell patient about this *frequently* (1–3 times a day), since depressed patients often have trouble remembering and need ongoing reassurance.

For constipation, have patient, especially the elderly, ingest fluids and foods.

Reassure patient that drowsiness, dizziness, and hypotension usually subside after first few weeks.

- Hypotension is more common among cardiac patients.
- √ Hypotensives often injure themselves.
- For dizzy patients, review hypotension instructions (see pages 74–75).

Avoid extreme heat and humidity, as TCAs alter temperature regulation.

Tell male patients about trazodone's rare, but dangerous, tendency to cause a painful, persistent erection.

PATIENT AND FAMILY NOTES

When starting TCAs, patients should be careful driving cars, working around machines, and crossing streets. When first on TCAs, drive briefly in a safe place, since reflexes might be a tad off.

TCAs potentiate alcohol: "One drink feels like 2 drinks."

Patients may take TCAs at any time; food does not interfere.

- Trazodone poses the only exception; trazodone's absorption is increased by 20% with food on an empty stomach. Take trazodone an hour before meals or all at bedtime.

Keep TCAs away from bedside or any readily accessible place, where they might be taken by "accident." Store safely away from eager children.

If possible, ingest full dose at bedtime to reduce experience of side effects. But if one forgets bedtime (or once-a-day dose), consume it within 3 hours; otherwise

- Wait for next dose and
- Do not double the dose.

Suddenly stopping TCA can trigger nausea, bad dreams, altered heart beat, and cold in 2–4 days.

- If this happens, call doctor.
- If cannot reach doctor, take one TCA tablet until contacting physician.

COST INDEX

Generic Names	Brand Names	Equivalent Dosage (mg)	Dose Assessed (mg)	Cost Rating*
Amitriptyline	Elavil	75	75	24
	Endep	75	75	19
Amoxapine	Asendin	150	150	55
Bupropion	Wellbutrin	100	100	24
Clomipramine	Anafranil	25	25	18
Desipramine	Norpramin	75	75	31
	Pertofrane	75	50 tab	59
Doxepin	Sinequan	75	75	22
	Adapin	75	75	18
	generics	75	75	12
Fluoxetine	Prozac	20	20	108
Imipramine	Tofranil	50	50	30
	Janimine	50	50	8
	SK-Pramine	50	50	6
	generics	50	50	>2
Imipramine pamoate	Tofranil PM	75	75	28
Maprotiline	Ludiomil	75	75	17
Nortriptyline	Pamelor	75	75	33
	Aventyl	75	34	84
Protriptyline	Vivactil	15	10	26
Trazodone	Desyrel	100	100	58
	generics	100	100	>10
Trimipramine	Surmontil	75	50 tab	32

* The higher the number, the higher the cost.

4. Monoamine-Oxidase Inhibitors

INTRODUCTION

This chapter discusses monoamine-oxidase inhibitor (MAOI) treatment of

- Major depression (see pages 101–103)
- Atypical depression (see page 103)
- Dysthymic disorder (see page 104)

Other chapters examine the MAOI treatment of

- Anorexia nervosa (Antidepressants, page 70)
- Bipolar depression (Lithium, pages 132–33)
- Borderline personality disorder (Lithium, page 136)
- Bulimia (Antidepressants, pages 70–71)
- Cataplexy (Antidepressants, page 71)
- Irritable bowel syndrome (Antidepressants, page 72)
- Migraines (Antidepressants, page 72)
- Obsessive-compulsive disorder (Anti-anxiety, pages 191–92)
- Narcolepsy (Stimulants, page 250)
- Panic disorders (Anti-anxiety, page 188)

NAMES, CLASSES, MANUFACTURERS, DOSE FORMS, AND COLORS

Generic Names	Brand Names	Manufacturers	Dose Forms (mg)*	Colors
		HYDRAZINES		
Isocarboxazid	Marplan	Roche	t: 10	t: peach
Phenelzine	Nardil	Parke-Davis	t: 15	t: orange
		NONHYDRAZINE		
Tranylcypromine	Parnate	SmithKline Beecham	t: 10	t: rose-red
		OTHERS		
Pargyline†	Eutonyl	Abbott	t: 10/25	t: pink/orange
Selegiline‡	Eldepryl	Somerset	t: 5	t: white

*t = tablets
† Pargyline primarily for hypertension.
‡ Selegline (formerly called deprenyl) primarily for Parkinson's disease.

PHARMACOLOGY

MAOIs best treat depression, when at least 80% of platelet MAO levels are inhibited.

* Platelets and neurons are similar because both have a
  √ Membrane pump that concentrates serotonin
  √ Vesicles containing excessive serotonin and MAO
* Eighty percent of platelet MAOI levels are usually inhibited by 60 mg/day of phenelzine.

MAO is found mainly in nerve tissue, the liver, and the lungs.

* MAOIs interfere with hepatic metabolism of many drugs (e.g., barbiturates, atropine).

MAOIs are hydrazines or nonhydrazines.

* Hydrazines (e.g., phenelzine, isocarboxazid) irreversibly inhibit MAO.
  √ Their actions persist after stopping the drug and resume when enzyme resynthesis occurs.
* Nonhydrazines (e.g., tranylcypromine) reversibly inhibit MAO.
  √ Their effects begin sooner and end faster.

Half-lives in hours

- Phenelzine: 2.8 (1½–4)
- Isocarboxazid: similar to phenelzine
- Tranylcypromine: 2.4 (1.54–3.15)

DOSES

Generic Names	Equivalent Doses (mg)	Usual Doses (mg/day)	Dosage Range (mg/day)	Starting Doses (mg/day)	Geriatric Doses (mg/day)
Isocarboxazid	10	10–30	10–50	30	5–15
Phenelzine	15	45–60	45–90	15	15–45
Tranylcypromine	10	20–40	10–50	10	10–20

CLINICAL INDICATIONS AND USE

Studies indicate that

- Overall, TCAs and MAOIs yield the same improvement rates.
- TCAs are equal to MAOIs in treating the nonpsychotic depressions (i.e., major depression, dysthymic disorder).
- TCAs are superior to MAOIs in treating psychotic depression, although ECT may be better than either drug.
- MAOIs may be superior to TCAs in treating atypical depression (see page 103).

In elderly patients

- MAOIs may help more than TCAs because they are less anticholinergic; yet, since the elderly are at a greater risk for hypotension, MAOIs pose a risk; tranylcypromine may be preferred.
- MAOIs may alleviate depression in demented patients.

To start therapy

- Begin with one tablet on first day.
- Boost by one tablet q 1–2 days.
- Until reach 60 mg of phenelzine, 40 mg of tranylcypromine, or 30 mg of isocarboxazid.
- May note some improvement after 2–3 days.
- If patient has insomnia with MAOIs, give the last dose before 6 P.M., or at lunch.
- Tranylcypromine is the most stimulating MAOI.
- Phenelzine exerts a mild to moderate sedative effect.

MONOAMINE OXIDASE INHIBITORS

To hasten MAOI effects may wish to *add*

- Lithium or
- Tryptophan 2–6 grams/day
  - √ (Currently [1/1/91] off the American market.)
  - √ May prompt the serotonin syndrome (see page 104).

T$_3$ does *not* speed MAOI response.
Negative results from early MAOI studies arose partly from too low a
MAOI dose.
Platelet MAO levels may indicate therapeutic effects, but they are still
very expensive, and not always reliable.

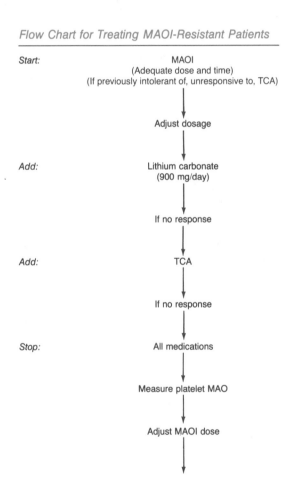

Flow Chart for Treating MAOI-Resistant Patients

Start: MAOI
                    (Adequate dose and time)
       (If previously intolerant of, unresponsive to, TCA)

                            ↓

                      Adjust dosage

                            ↓

Add: Lithium carbonate
                        (900 mg/day)

                            ↓

                      If no response

                            ↓

Add: TCA

                            ↓

                      If no response

                            ↓

Stop: All medications

                            ↓

                  Measure platelet MAO

                            ↓

                    Adjust MAOI dose

                            ↓

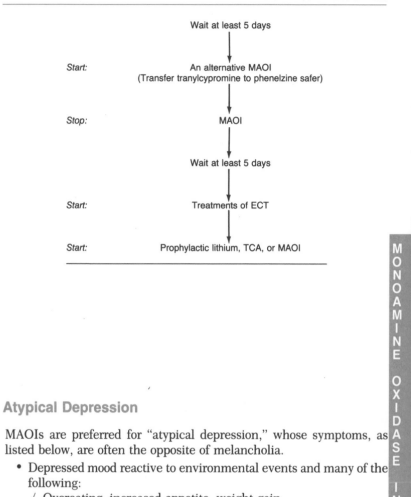

Wait at least 5 days

↓

Start: An alternative MAOI
(Transfer tranylcypromine to phenelzine safer)

Stop: MAOI

↓

Wait at least 5 days

↓

Start: Treatments of ECT

Start: Prophylactic lithium, TCA, or MAOI

Atypical Depression

MAOIs are preferred for "atypical depression," whose symptoms, as listed below, are often the opposite of melancholia.

- Depressed mood reactive to environmental events and many of the following:
  - √ Overeating, increased appetite, weight gain
  - √ Carbohydrate or sweet craving
  - √ Hypersomnia, more time in bed, or initial insomnia
  - √ "Rejection-sensitivity" (consistently perceiving minor slights as major insults or rebuffs)
  - √ More "reactive" mood
  - √ Feeling better in the morning and worse as the day proceeds (a reverse diurnal mood variation)
  - √ Phobic-anxiety
  - √ Panic attacks
  - √ Hypochondriasis
- Patients with TCA-responsive depressions have trouble participating or initiating tasks, whereas those with MAOI-responsive depressions function in events, but avoid starting them.

MONOAMINE OXIDASE INHIBITORS

Dysthymic Disorder

Dysthymic disorder is similar to major depression, but dysthymia is

* Less episodic, more constant,
* No distinct onset
* Rapidly changing or vague neurovegetative signs,
* Emptiness more than guilt or true sadness.

Treatment of dysthymic disorder is controversial.

* If it more closely resembles a major depression, TCAs are the drug of choice.
* If it more closely resembles an atypical depression, MAOIs are the drug of choice.

Serotonergic and Noradrenergic Interactions

Adding or substituting MAOIs and TCAs can generate 2 major problems

* *Serotonergic crisis* (hyperthermic reaction)
* *Noradrenergic crisis* (hypertensive reaction)

Serotonergic Crises Characterized by	Noradrenergic Crises Characterized by
Elevated temperature, fever	Hypertension (BP increases 20–30 points),
Abnormal muscle movements, such as fasciculations, twitches, myoclonic jerking, hyperreflexia, and (rarely) generalized seizures	Occipital headaches (often radiate frontally; can be violent),
(May see)	Stiff or sore neck,
Hypotension,	Flushing, sweating, cold and clammy skin,
Anxiety, Agitation,	Tachycardia > bradycardia,
Shivering,	Nausea, vomiting,
Enhanced startle response,	(If severe, may see)
Insomnia,	Sudden unexplained nosebleeds,
Confusion, Delirium,	Dilated pupils, Visual disturbances, Photophobia,
Seizures, Shock,	Constricting chest pains,
Death	Stroke or coma,
	Death

Serotonergic Crises Caused by	Noradrenergic Crises Caused by
TCAs	Tyramine-containing foods
Fluoxetine/clomipramine	Stimulants
Meperidine	Ephedrine
Tryptophan	Pseudoephedrine
Dextromethorphan	Phenylephrine
Diphenoxylate ?	Phenylpropanolamine

Serotonergic and noradrenergic crises are escalated by

* Dose
* Sequence of medication.

Adding or Replacing MAOIs and TCAs

Start With	Add/ Substitute	Risks and Instructions
TCA	MAOI	Low risk of hyperthermic reaction; reduce TCA dose by 50%, slowly add MAOI, taper TCA over 2 weeks.
MAOI	TCA	High risk of hyperthermic reaction; wait 2–4 weeks between stopping MAOI and starting TCA.
MAOI + TCA together		Low risk of hyperthermic reaction; raise doses slowly.
Fluoxetine/clomipramine	MAOI	High risk; hyperthermic reaction; do not start MAOI until fluoxetine (or clomipramine) stopped for 5 weeks or negative in serum.
MAOI	Fluoxetine/clomipramine	High risk of hyperthermic reaction; do not overlap; wait at least 2 weeks between stopping MAOI and starting fluoxetine (or clomipramine).
MAOI (Hydrazine)	MAOI (Nonhydrazine)	High risk of hypertensive reaction; wait 2–4 weeks before substituting nonhydrazine.
MAOI (Nonhydrazine)	MAOI (Hydrazine)	Moderate risk of hypertensive reaction; wait 2–4 weeks before replacing with hydrazine.
MAOI	Surgery/ECT	Direct-acting pressor agents (e.g., epinephrine and norepinephrine) may cause fewer hypertensive reactions than indirect-acting pressor agents (including tyramine); medically and legally best to stop MAOI 2 weeks before surgery or ECT; regional block is an alternative.
MAOI	Dental work	Local anesthetics with epinephrine may pose a risk; either stop MAOI for 2 weeks, avoid epinephrine, or pretreat 1 hour before dental work with chlorpromazine (25 mg) or nifedipine (10 mg).

MONOAMINE OXIDASE INHIBITORS

Trimipramine may cause fewer noradrenergic reactions.
Sleep problems with MAOIs may be relieved by adding small doses of

* Trazodone
* Doxepine

- Amitriptyline
- Imipramine

Give patients

- A wallet card describing the MAOI regimen (obtained from Parke-Davis at 1–800–223–0432).
- MAOI diet and drug information (see below).
- (If "responsible") medication to treat a throbbing, severe headache if they cannot get to an emergency room in 15–30 minutes.
  √ Chlorpromazine 25–50 mg or preferrably
  √ Nifedipine 20 mg
    □ Chew capsule and then
    □ Place under tongue.

Emergency room interventions for hypertensive crisis include

- Chlorpromazine or nifedipine (as above)
- Phentolamine 5–10 mg IV slowly
- If severe reaction, sodium nitroprusside IV slowly.

Potentially Dangerous Over-the-Counter Drug Products

Ephedrine

Bronkaid
Bronkolixer
Primatene
Vicks Vatronel nose drops

Phenylephrine	Phenylpropanolamine	Pseudoephedrine
Cerose—DM	Alka-Seltzer plus cold and night-time cold medicine	Actifed
Congespirin for children	A. R. M. allergy relief	AllerAct
Dimetane decongestant	Acutrim appetite pills	Allerest no drowsy formula
Dristan decongestant	Allerest allergy, headache	Benadryl combinations
Dristan nasal spray	BC cold powder	CoAdvil
4-Way Fast acting nasal spray	Bayer children's cough and cold remedies	Comtrex allergy sinus
Neo-Synephrine nasal spray and nose drops	Cheracol plus head cold/cough formula	Comtrex cough formula
Nostril nasal decongestant	Contac decongestants	Contac cold and sinus
Novahistine elixir	Coricidin "D" decongestant	Dimacol
Prefrin liquifilm	Coricidin maximum strength	Dorcol cough and decongestant
Relief eye drops	Dexatrim appetite pills	Dristan maximum strength
Robitussin night relief	Dimetapp	Excedrin sinus
St. Joseph's nasal congestant	4-Way cold tablets	Fedahist
Vicks sinex decongestant nasal spray and ultra fine mist	Naldecon CX, DX, EX	Isoclor
	Robitussin-CF	Novahistine DMX
	Sinarest	Ornex
		Pediacare

Phenylephrine	Phenylpropanolamine	Pseudoephedrine
	Sine-off sinus	Robitussin-PE
	Snaplets-DM, EX	Ryna, C, CX
	St. Joseph's cold tablets	Sinarest, no drowsiness
	Triaminic	Sine-Off, no drowsiness
	Triaminicin	Sinutab
	Triaminicol	Sudafed
		Thera-Flu
		Triaminic night light
		Tylenol allergy sinus and cold
		Vicks daycare daytime cold
		Vicks 44-D, 44M
		Vicks NyQuil
		Vicks pediatric

- Prescription pills
  - √ Anti-asthma drugs (bronchodilators)
    - ▫ Avoid epinephrine, ephedrine.
    - ▫ Beclomethasone inhaler is safer than inhaler containing isoproterenol or another β-adrenergic bronchodilator.
  - √ Antihypertensive drugs, especially
    - ▫ Guanethidine
    - ▫ Reserpine
  - √ Narcotics, especially meperidine (can be lethal)
  - √ Amphetamines, "pep-pills," appetite suppressants
  - √ Cocaine, crack
  - √ Anesthetics (general and local)
  - √ Dopa (dihydroxyphenylalanine), dopamine, levodopa
  - √ Buspirone (elevated BPs seen)

Foods to be avoided fall into 4 major groups

- Aged cheeses
- Air-dried sausages
- Fava beans
- Sauerkraut
- Foods to *definitely avoid*
  - √ Aged cheeses (English stilton, blue cheese, old cheddar, Danish blue, brick, mozzarella, parmesan, gruyère, brie, swiss, camembert, etc.)
    - ▫ Because 80% of all hypertensive crises are secondary to aged cheeses—explaining why hypertensive crises are called

MONOAMINE OXIDASE INHIBITORS

"cheese reactions"—even some of the more moderate tyramine cheeses (e.g., brie, emmentaler, and gruyère) are included.
  □ Some cheeses are allowed: cottage, processed cheese slices, ricotta, and cream cheeses are safe.
  √ Chianti wine should probably still be avoided, despite questionable findings.
  √ Fava (Italian, broad) beans (because of dopa content)
  √ Concentrated yeast extracts, especially Marmite
    □ Brewer's yeast is safe.
  √ Pickled herring brine should be avoided, but other fish is safe.
  √ Sausage: salami, mortadella, air-dried sausage, 5-day chicken liver must be avoided. Bologna, salami, pepperoni, summer sausage, fresh chicken liver, corned beef, and liverwurst are safe.
  √ Sauerkraut should be avoided.
  √ Chinese foods, oriental soup stocks (e.g, miso) should be dodged until more evidence becomes available.
  √ Aspartame, the artificial sweetener, may cause a hypertensive reaction.
    □ Consume less than 1 gram of aspartame-sweetener in beverages per day.
  √ If uncertain, avoid protein food fermented at any time.
• Foods *no longer at risk*
  √ Chocolate (has phenethylamine)
  √ Figs, raisins, overripe fruit, avocadoes
  √ Tea, coffee, cola, and other caffeine-containing beverages (some experts limit these to 3 cups/glasses a day)
  √ White and red wine, other spirits (assuming wine kept under 3 ounces/day)
  √ Yogurt
  √ Caviar, snails, tinned fish
  √ Canned and packaged soup
• A summary of studies shows:

Tyramine Content of Beer

Beer	Brewer	Tyramine Concentration µg/ml	Tyramine Content per Serving (mg)*
Amstel	Amstel	4.52	1.54
Export Draft	Molson	3.79	1.29
Blue Light	Labatts	3.42	1.16
Guinness Extra Stout	Labatts	3.37	1.15
Old Vienna	Carling	3.32	1.13
Canadian	Molson	3.01	1.03

Beer	Brewer	Tyramine Concentration μg/ml	Tyramine Content per Serving (mg)*
Miller Light	Miller	2.91	0.99
Export	Molson	2.78	0.95
Heineken	Heineken	1.81	0.62
Blue	Labatts	1.80	0.61
Coors Light	Coors	1.45	0.49
Carlsberg Light	Carling	1.15	0.39
Michelob	Anheuser-Busch	0.98	0.33
Genesee Cream	Genesee	0.86	0.29
Stroh's	Stroh's	0.78	0.27

* Based on a 341 ml serving (one bottle).

Tyramine Content of Wines

Wine	Color	Type	Country	Tyramine Concentration (μg/ml)	Tyramine Content per Serving (mg)*
Rioja (Siglo)	Red		Spain	4.41	0.53
Sherry	Red			3.60	—
Ruffino	Red	Chianti	Italy	3.04	0.36
Blue Nun	White		Germany	2.70	0.32
Retsina	White		Greece	1.79	0.21
La Colombaia	Red	Chianti	Italy	0.63	0.08
Riesling				0.60	—
Brolio	Red	Chianti	Italy	0.44	0.05
Sauterne	White			0.40	
Beau-Rivage	White	Bordeaux	France	0.39	0.05
Beau-Rivage	Red	Bordeaux	France	0.35	0.04
Maria Christina	Red		Canada	0.20	0.20
Port	Red			0.20	—
Cinzano	Red	Vermouth	Italy	†	†
LePiazze	Red	Chianti	Italy	†	†

* Based on a 120 ml (4 ounce) serving.
† Nil.

Tyramine Content of Other Alcohol

Type	Tyramine Concentration (μg/ml)	Tyramine Content per Serving (mg)
Ale	8.8	—
Harvey's Bristol Cream	2.65	0.32 mg/4 ounces
Dubonnet	1.59	0.19 mg/4 ounces
Vermouth	high	high
Bourbon	†	†
London distilled dry gin (Beefeater)	†	†

Type	Tyramine Concentration (μg/ml)	Tyramine Content per Serving (mg)
Gin	†	†
Vodka	†	†
Rum	†	†
Scotch	†	†

† Nil.

Tyramine Content of Cheeses

Type	Tyramine Content (μg/g)	Tyramine Content per Serving (mg)*
Liederkranz	1454.50	—
Cheddar (New York State)	1416.00	—
English Stilton	1235.96	17.3
Cheddar, old center (Canadian)	1013.95	7.5
Blue cheese	997.79	15.0
Swiss	925.00	—
3-year-old white	779.74	11.7
Camembert (Danish)	681.50	—
Emmentaler	612.50	—
Extra-old	608.19	9.1
Gruyère (British)	597.50	—
Brick (Canadian)	524.00	—
Gruyère (American)	516.00	—
Cheddar (25 samples)	384.00	—
Gouda	345.00	—
Edam	310.00	—
Colby	285.00	—
Mozzarella	284.04	2.4
Roquefort (French)	273.50	—
Danish blue	256.48	5.5
D'Oka (imported)	234.00	—
Limberger	204.00	—
Cheddar, center cut (Canadian)	192.00	—
Argenti (imported)	168.00	—
Romano	159.00	—
Cheese spread, Handisnack	133.81	2.0
Gruyère (Swiss)	125.17	1.9
Cheddar, fresh (Canadian)	120.00	—
Muenster	105.00	1.5
Provolone	94.00	—
Camembert (American)	86.00	—
Parmesan, grated (American)	81.01	0.2
Old Coloured (Canadian)	77.47	1.2
Feta	75.78	1.1
Parmesan, grated (Italian)	69.79	1.1

Type	Tyramine Content (μg/g)	Tyramine Content per Serving (mg)*
Gorgonzola	55.94	0.8
Processed (American)	50.00	—
Blue cheese dressing	39.20	0.6
Medium (Black Diamond)	34.75	0.5
Processed (Canadian)	26.00	—
Swiss Emmentaler	23.99	0.4
Brie (M-C) with rind	21.19	0.3
Cambozola Blue Vein (germ)	18.31	0.3
Brie (d'OKA) without rind	14.65	0.2
Farmers, Canadian plain	11.05	0.2
Cheez Whiz (Kraft)	8.46	0.1
Brie (d'OKA) with rind	5.71	0.1
Cream cheese (plain)	4.62	0.1
Brie (M-C) without rind	2.82	<0.1
Sour cream (Astro)	1.23	<0.1
Boursin	0.98	<0.1
Cottage cheese	<0.20	—
Cream cheese	<0.20	†
Havarti (Canadian)	†	†
Ricotta	†	†
Bonbel	†	†

* Based on a 15-gram (single slice) serving.
† Nil.

Tyramine Content in Fish

Type	Tyramine Concentration (μg/g)	Tyramine Content per Serving (mg)
Pickled herring*	Up to 3030	
Pickled herring brine	15.1 μg/ml	—
Lump fish roe	4.4	0.2 mg/50 g
Sliced schmaltz herring in oil	4.0	0.2 mg/50 g
Smoked carp	†	—
Smoked salmon	†	—
Smoked white fish	†	—

* Other reports indicate that the tyramine content of pickled herring is nil.
† Nil.

MONOAMINE OXIDASE INHIBITORS

*Tyramine Content in Meat and Sausage**

Type	Tyramine Concentration (μg/g)	Tyramine Content per Serving (mg)
Sausage, Belgian dry-fermented	803.9	—
Liver, beef, spoiled	274	—
Sausage, dry-fermented	244	—
Salami	188	5.6
Mortadella	184	5.5
Air-dried sausage	125	3.8
Sausage, semi-dried fermented	85.5	—
Chicken liver (day 5)	77.25	1.5
Bologna	33	1.0
Aged sausage	29	0.9
Smoked meat	18	0.5
Corned beef	11	0.3
Kolbasa sausage	6	0.2
Liver, beef, fresh	5.4	—
Liverwurst	2	0.1
Smoked sausage	1	<0.1
Sweet Italian sausage	1	<0.1
Pepperoni sausage	†	†
Chicken liver (day 1)	†	†

* Based on 30 g serving.
† Nil.

*Tyramine Content in Paté**

Type	Tyramine Concentration (μg/g)	Tyramine Content per Serving (mg)
Salmon mousse paté	22	0.7
Country style paté	3	0.1
Peppercorn paté	2	0.1

* Based on 30 g serving.

Tyramine Content in Fruits and Vegetables

Type	Tyramine Concentration (μg/g)	Tyramine Content per Serving (mg)
Banana peel*	58.35	1.424 mg/peel
Raspberries	54.15	—
Raspberry jam	<38.0	—
Avocado, fresh ‡	23.0	†
Orange	10.00	—
Plum (red)	6.00	—

Type	Tyramine Concentration (μg/g)	Tyramine Content per Serving (mg)
Tomato	4.00	—
Banana pulp	4.00	1.0
Eggplant	3.00	—
Potato	1.0	—
Spinach	1.00	—
Grapes	†	†
Figs, California-Blue Ribbon	†	†
Raisins (California seedless)	†	†
Fava (Italian) (broad) bean pods * **	†	†

* The peel of the banana and the pod of the fava contain considerable dopamine; the banana pulp and the actual fava carry no risk.
† Nil.
‡ Some claim fresh avocado is nil.
** Dopamine = 700 μg/g

Tyramine Content in Yeast Extracts

Type	Tyramine Concentration (μg/g)	Tyramine Content per Serving (mg)
Marmite concentrated yeast extract	1184	6.45 mg/10 g
Yeast extracts	2156	—
Brewer's yeast tablets (Drug Trade Co.)	—	191.27 g/400 mg
Brewer's yeast tablets (Jamieson)	—	66.72 g/400 mg
Brewer's yeast flakes (Vegetrates)	—	9.36 g/15 g
Brewer's yeast debittered (Maximum Nutrition)	—	†

† Nil.

Tyramine Content in Other Foods

Type	Tyramine Concentration (μg/g)	Tyramine Content per Serving (mg)
Soy Sauce (Japanese)	509.30	—
Soy Sauce (Tamari)	466.00	—
Meat extracts (soup, gravy, bases)	199.50	—
Soybean paste	84.85	—
Sauerkraut (Krakus)	56.49	13.87
Beef bouillon mix (Bovril)	—	231.25 μg/package
Beef bouillon (Oetker)	—	102.00 μg/cube
Soy sauce	18.72 μg/ml	0.2 mg/10 ml
Soy sauce, chemically hydrolyzed	1.8	—
Cocoa powder	1.45	—
Beef gravy (Franco American)	0.858 μg/ml	<0.1 mg/30 ml

Type	Tyramine Concentration (μg/g)	Tyramine Content per Serving (mg)
Chicken gravy (Franco American)	0.46 μg/ml	<0.1 mg/30 ml
Chicken bouillon mix (Maggi)	†	†
Vegetable bouillon mix	†	†
Yogurt	<0.2	†

† Nil.

SIDE EFFECTS

MAOIs are less anticholinergic than TCAs.

* Almost no clinical anticholinergic actions from tranylcypromine.
* Phenelzine can generate anticholinergic episodes over 20% of the time.

Most anticholinergic symptoms taper off in 1–2 weeks (see page 12); they are discussed with their respective organ systems.

Cardiovascular Effects

Hypotension

* This can be MAOI's most critical side effect.
* MAOIs produce more orthostatic hypotension than TCAs.
  √ Afflicts 50% of patients on MAOIs.
  √ Over 10% of patients on MAOIs develop severe injuries (e.g., passing out, fractures).
  √ Especially frequent in the elderly.
  √ Common with congestive heart failure.
  √ Hypotension happens more in people with pre-existing hypertension, although it still affects the normotensive.
* Symptoms include
  √ Dizziness, lightheadedness
  √ Coldness
  √ Headaches
  √ Fainting, especially with salt or fluid restriction
* Management (see pages 74–75)
* Avoid adding chlorpromazine or thioridazine to MAOIs because they aggravate hypotension.

Except for BP problems, MAOIs have fewer cardiovascular side effects than TCAs.

* MAOIs cause less myocardial toxicity,
* Exert little effect on heart rate, cardiac conduction, and myocardial function,
* May be preferable for some cardiac patients.

Gastrointestinal Effects

Dry mouth (see page 13)
Constipation (see page 14)
Hepatotoxicity

- Incidence between 1/3,000–1/10,000.
- Frequency: isocarboxazid > phenelzine > tranylcypromine.
- Tranylcypromine is the preferred MAOI for patients with liver disease.
- Hepatotoxicity displays
  √ Weakness, malaise
  √ Rash
  √ Nausea, anorexia
  √ Jaundice
  √ Eosinophilia
  √ Elevated enzymes

Flatus (rare)

- Giving oral lactose may help.

Weight gain

- Phenelzine > tranylcypromine.
- Amitriptyline generates more weight gain than phenelzine.
- In one year, whereas phenelzine can add > 20 pounds, typical weight gain is 5–10 pounds.

Peripheral edema

- Uncommon.
- Phenelzine and isocarboxazid produce edema more than tranylcypromine.
- Reduce dose; prescribe a diuretic.

Renal Effects

Urinary hesitancy or *retention* (see page 14)

Endocrine and Sexual Effects

More common with MAOIs than with TCAs, especially

- *Anorgasmia*
- *Impotence*

Also see

- *Decreased libido, difficulties achieving and maintaining erection, slowed or impaired ability to ejaculate*

MONOAMINE OXIDASE INHIBITORS

Management

- Reduce dose or
- Add cyproheptadine 2–4 mg qd-qid to alleviate anorgasmia in both sexes.
  - √ Cyproheptadine may introduce drowsiness, stimulate appetite, or increase carbohydrate craving.
- Methyltestosterone po or by monthly depot injections may improve male sexual dysfunction.
- Bethanechol 10 mg tid may facilitate erectile functioning.

Carbohydrate craving
Falling blood sugar

- More frequent with phenelzine and isocarboxazid.

Eyes, Ears, Nose, and Throat

Narrow-angle glaucoma (see page 17)
Blurred vision (see page 16)
Dry eyes (see page 17)
Nasal congestion

Skin, Allergies, and Temperature

Decreased sweating
Fever, chills

Central Nervous System Effects

Myoclonic twitches

- MAOIs cause more often than TCAs.
- Management
  - √ Reduce or stop MAOIs,
  - √ Change to another MAOI, or
  - √ Add clonazepam, carbamazepine, or valproic acid.

Speech blockage

- Lower or stop MAOI.

Pyridoxine deficiency

- Isocarboxazid and phenelzine lead to a pyridoxine (vitamin B_6) deficiency with primarily
  - √ Peripheral neuropathy or
  - √ Muscle spasms, pains, and paresthesias.

- Also see
  √ Stomatitis
  √ Anemia
  √ Hyperacusis (or buzzing in the ear)
  √ Hyperirritability
  √ Depression
  √ Carpal tunnel syndrome
  √ "Electric shocks" or jumping movements of the extremities
  √ Ataxia
  √ Hyperactive deep tendon reflexes, clonus (possibly)
  √ Convulsions and coma (rarely)
- Treat with pyridoxine 100–300 mg/day po.

Seizures

- MAOIs may alter the seizure threshold of patients with epilepsy.

Toxicity

- *"Drunk," ataxic, confused*
- Reduce dose.

Sedation

- Insomnia often generates daytime sedation.

Decreased sleep (sometimes without fatigue), *insomnia*

- Tranylcypromine causes initial insomnia most often.
- Switch to phenelzine, or
- Move dose(s) to earlier time in day, perhaps before noon.

Nightmares, hypnagogic phenomena, vivid dreams

- Occur more often if MAOIs provided at hs.
- Sleep disturbances more common with MAOIs than with TCAs.

Psychosis, behavioral problems

- *Stimulation*
  √ May arise day or night.
  √ Generally manifests more with TCAs than with MAOIs. This happens even though tranylcypromine, with its amphetamine-like effects, can stimulate considerably.
- Management
  √ Reduce dose or transfer to another drug.
- *Paranoid outbursts, delusions*
  √ Reduce or stop MAOI.

MONOAMINE OXIDASE INHIBITORS

- *Manic responses*
  - √ Erupts on MAOIs, with or without TCAs.
  - √ May stimulate so that the patient may feel unusual or jittery.
  - √ Management
    - □ Reduce, or stop, this MAOI.
    - □ Add lithium to restrain the "high."

PERCENTAGES OF SIDE EFFECTS

Side Effects	Isocarboxazid	Phenelzine	Tranylcypromine
CARDIOVASCULAR EFFECTS			
Hypotension	15	20	15
Hypertensive crises	3.5	3.4	5.8
		(0.8–8)	(2–9.9)
Dizziness, lightheadedness	18.6	17.5	28.3
			(5–52.4)
Tachycardia	—	17.5	20
Palpitations	5	5	7.3
			(0–10)
Cardiac arrhythmias	4	—	<2
GASTROINTESTINAL EFFECTS			
Dry mouth and throat	20	30	25.9
			(10–47.6)
Anorexia, lower appetite	—	—	4.8
Increased appetite	—	—	0.0
Nausea, vomiting	10	10	6
			(0–10)
Dyspepsia, upset stomach	20	20	12.5
			(2–19)
Constipation	9.3	9.3	10
	(2–20)	(2–20)	(5–19)
Hepatitis	0.02	<0.01	<0.001
Weight gain	20	20	6
Edema	7.5	7.5	—
RENAL EFFECTS			
Urinary hesitancy or retention	6.6	6.6	2.5
ENDOCRINE AND SEXUAL EFFECTS			
Disturbed sexual function	6.5	10	6
	(0–10)	(0–30)	
EYES, EARS, NOSE, AND THROAT EFFECTS			
Blurred vision	10.5	17.5	8.5
			(2–10)
Tinnitus	—	—	4.8

Side Effects	Isocarboxazid	Phenelzine	Tranylcypromine
SKIN, ALLERGIES, AND TEMPERATURE EFFECTS			
Rashes	6	<2	6
Sweating	8.5 (2–20)	8 (2–20)	—
CENTRAL NERVOUS SYSTEM EFFECTS			
Weakness, fatigue	6	<2	<2
Seizures	—	1	0.0
Paresthesias	—	—	4.8
Headache	20	6	14.3
Tremor	5.5	12.5	9.5
Drowsiness, sedation	8 (2–20)	12.5 (0–30)	18.9 (0–47.6)
Insomnia	6	20	18.6 (10–23.8)
Confusion, disorientation	4.3	4.3	10.2 (2–14.3)
Anxiety, nervousness (i.e., mental)	—	—	2
Agitation, restlessness (i.e., motoric)	4	—	5
Excitement, hypomania	9.3 (2–20)	13.8 (5–30)	17.1 (10–30)

PREGNANCY AND LACTATION

Teratogenicity (1st trimester)
- Some increased malformations have been found in phenelzine and tranylcypromine; significance unclear.

Direct Effect on Newborn (3rd trimester)
- No data

Lactation
- In breast milk; safety data are unclear.

DRUG-DRUG INTERACTIONS

Drugs (X) Interacts with:	Monoamine-Oxidase Inhibitors (M)	Comments
Acebutolol	X ↑	If an MAOI is stopped, BP of patients on acebutolol may rise.
*Alcohol	M ↑	Drowsiness
Anesthetics	X ↑	Potentiate CNS depression or excitement, muscle (general) stiffness or hyperpyrexia.

MONOAMINE OXIDASE INHIBITORS

Drugs (X) Interacts with:	Monoamine- Oxidase Inhibitors (M)	Comments
Anticholinergics	X ↑	Increased atropine-like effects.
Antipsychotics	X ↑ M ↑	Hypotension. May increase EPS.
*Barbiturates	X ↑	CNS depression.
Benzodiazepines	X ↑	Increased benzodiazepine effect. Edema.
Buspirone	M ↑	Case reports of elevated BP. May insert 10 days between buspirone and MAOI.
Caffeine	X ↑	Irregular heartbeat or high BP. Avoid in high quantities because of reports of hypertensive crisis.
*Carbamazepine	X ↓	Seizures in epileptics.
*Clomipramine	X ↑	Serotonergic crisis. Do not combine.
Clonidine	M ↑	May potentiate MAOIs.
*Cocaine	M ↑	Hypertensive crisis. See sympathomimetics.
Codeine	X ↑	Increased analgesia.
*Cyclobenzaprine	X ↑ M ↑	Fever, seizures, and death reported. Cyclobenzaprine is chemically similar to TCAs. Avoid until more data.
†Dextroamphetamine	M ↑	Hypertensive crisis. Tranylcypromine most dangerous. See sympathomimetics.
Dextromethorphan	M ↑	A few reports of serotonergic crisis.
Disulfiram	X ↑	Severe CNS reactions. Unclear.
Diuretics (Thiazides)	X ↑	BP drop.
Doxapram	X ↑	CNS stimulation, agitation, and hypertension; MAOI may lower doxapram's cardiovascular effect. Until more evidence exists, avoid combination.
Enflurane	X ↑	See anesthetics.
†Ephedrine	M ↑	Hypertensive crisis. See sympathomimetics.
†Fenfluramine		Serotonergic crisis. See sympathomimetics.
*Fluoxetine	X ↑	Serotonergic crisis. Some deaths. Wait > 2 weeks after halting MAOI before starting fluoxetine, and > 5 weeks after stopping fluoxetine to launch MAOI.
*Guanadrel	X ↑	Initial hypertension followed by hypotension. Wait 10–14 days between drugs.
*Guanethidine	X ↑	Initial hypertension followed by hypotension. Wait 10–14 days between drugs.
Halothane	X ↑	See anesthetics general.
Hydralazine	X ↑	Tachycardia; may increase BP.
*Hypoglycemics (oral)	X ↑	May lower blood sugar.
*Insulin	X ↑	May lower blood sugar.
†Levodopa (L-dopa)	X ↑ M ↑	Hypertensive crisis and CNS stimulation. Adding MAOI to L-dopa may also induce akinesia and tremor. Use TCA instead. See sympthomimetics.
†Meperidine	M ↑	Serotonergic crisis. Other opiates safer.
†Metaraminol	M ↑	Hypertensive crisis. See sympathomimetics.
Methyldopa	M ↑	Hypertensive reaction may occur in theory.

Drugs (X) Interacts with:	Monoamine- Oxidase Inhibitors (M)	Comments
*Methylphenidate	M ↑	Hypertensive crisis. See sympthomimetics.
Morphine	X ↑	Increased analgesia.
†Phenylephrine	M ↑	Hypertensive crisis. See sympathomimetics.
†Phenylpropanolamine	M ↑	Hypertensive crisis. See sympathomimetics.
†Pseudoephedrine	M ↑	Hypertensive crisis. See sympathomimetics.
*Reserpine	X ↑	Initial hypertension followed by hypotension. Wait 10–14 days between drugs.
*Succinylcholine	X ↑	Prolonged muscle relaxation or paralysis.
Sympathomimetics: †Amphetamines, *Cocaine, †Ephedrine, †Fenfluramine, †Levodopa, †Metaraminol, †Methylphenidate, †Phenylephrine, †Phenylpropanolamine, †Pseudoephedrine, †Tyramine	M ↑	Hypertensive crisis generated with indirect-acting sympathomimetics, but not by direct-acting sympathomimetics (e.g., epinephrine). Most common with tranylcypromine. (See pages 102–103).
Terfenadine	M ↑	Increased MAOI side effects.
*TCAs	M ↑	*Never* add TCAs to MAOIs; this risks serotonergic crisis. Best to *not* give (1) large doses, (2) IM/IV drugs, (3) imipramine with tranylcypromine, and (4) a MAOI to patients recently on fluoxetine or clomipramine. (see pages 102–103).
*Tryptophan	X ↑	Serotonergic crisis. Tryptophan off American market, but old bottles exist.
Tubocurarine	X ↑	Prolonged muscle relaxation or paralysis.
†Tyramine	M ↑	Hypertensive crisis. See sympathomimetics.

Codes: * Moderately important interaction; † Extremely important interaction; ↑ Increases; ↓ Decreases.

EFFECTS ON LABORATORY TESTS

Generic Names	Blood/Serum Tests	Results	Urine Tests	Results
Isocarboxazid	LFT	↑	?	
Phenelzine	Glucose	↓	5-HIAA, VMA	—
	LFT	↑		
Tranylcypromine	Glucose	↓	5-HIAA, VMA	—

Codes: LFT = SGOT, SGPT, LDH, alkaline phosphatase, bilirubin; ↑ Increases; ↓ Decreases; ? Undetermined.

MONOAMINE OXIDASE INHIBITORS

WITHDRAWAL

MAOIs do not cause

* Dependence
* Tolerance
* Addiction
* Definite withdrawal

Although MAOIs are less anticholinergic than TCAs, a milder episodic withdrawal might still arise 2–4 days after suddenly stopping MAOIs. This withdrawal from phenelzine, and possibly from isocarboxazid, may exhibit
   √ Agitation
   √ Nightmares
   √ Psychosis
* Symptoms decline by re-introducing a low MAOI dose.
* Gradually withdrawing MAOIs one tablet every 3–4 days is safer.

Because tranylcypromine resembles amphetamine, a quick withdrawal from tranylcypromine resembles an acute withdrawal from dextroamphetamine.

* Tranylcypromine withdrawal exhibits
   √ Prominent insomnia, disrupted sleep, hypersomnia
   √ Restlessness, anxiety, depression
   √ Diarrhea
   √ Headache
   √ Weakness
   √ Confusion, delirium
   √ Hallucinations, psychosis
* These patients often have a h/o tranylcypromine abuse.
* Patients on long-term tranylcypromine *may* have greater risk.
* Prevalence of tranylcypromine withdrawal is probably low.

Withdrawal from MAOIs is not life-threatening.

MAOI diet and drug regimen should persist for at least 2 weeks after the last MAOI dose.

OVERDOSE: TOXICITY, SUICIDE, AND TREATMENT

A 10-day supply of MAOIs taken at once can be lethal.

Overdose symptoms

* May develop in 4–12 hours,
* Maximize at 24–48 hours,

- Usually resolve in 3–4 days,
- But may persist for 12–14 days.

Most acute MAOI overdoses exaggerate side effects.

- Early to mild symptoms include
  - √ Drowsiness
  - √ Dizziness (can be severe)
  - √ Headache (can be severe)
  - √ Insomnia
  - √ Restlessness, anxiety, irritability
  - √ Ataxia
- More severe symptoms include
  - √ Confusion, incoherence
  - √ Tachycardia, rapid and irregular pulse
  - √ Hypotension
  - √ Seizures
  - √ Hallucinations
  - √ Hyperreflexia
  - √ Fever
  - √ Respiratory depression
  - √ Increased or decreased temperature
  - √ Hyperactivity
  - √ Spasm of masticatory muscles
  - √ Opisthotonos
  - √ Sweating
  - √ Rigidity
  - √ Coma

The general management of MAOI overdoses include (see page 37).

- Remember that diet and drug interactions may also occur during overdose.

Most overdoses accentuate side effects. Additional problems include

- For hypotension
  - √ May lead to shock, coma, cardiovascular insufficiency, myocardial infarction, and arrhythmias.
  - √ Push fluids.
  - √ Pressor amines (e.g., norepinephrine) may help, but the hypertensive effects of these agents may potentiate MAOI-toxicity.
  - √ Avoid CNS stimulants and contraindicated drugs.
- For seizures (see page 80).
- For increased temperature, apply external cooling.
- For hepatotoxicity, evaluate liver function tests about 4–6 weeks after MAOI overdose.

MONOAMINE OXIDASE INHIBITORS

Carefully observe patient for at least one week after the overdose.

Toxicity and Suicide Data

Generic Names	Toxicity Doses Average (Highest) (g)	Mortality Doses Average (Lowest) (g)	Lethal Supply of MAOIs (days)
Isocarboxazid	(0.5)		10–12
Phenelzine	(0.750)	1.012 (0.375)	6–10
Tranylcypromine	(0.750)		10–12

PRECAUTIONS

MAOIs contraindicated in
* Cerebrovascular disease and congestive heart failure
* Pheochromocytoma
* Food with tyramine, tryptophan, dopamine (see pages 102–14)
* Medications listed before (see pages 102–107)
* Patients to have elective surgery in 10–14 days (see pages 102–103)
* Recurrent or severe headache
* Hypersensitivity to MAOIs
* Myelography
   √ Stop MAOI at least 48 hours before myelography.
   √ Resume MAOI at least 24 hours after myelography.
* Liver disease or abnormal liver function
* Children under 16

Tranylcypromine addiction has been reported in a few cases.
* Partly arises from tranylcypromine's stimulating properties.
* A few cases of tolerance without addiction have occurred.
* Maximum doses for each patient ranged from 120–700 mg/day with an average being 267 mg/day.
* Patients typically presented with delirium and agitation.
* After MAOI is stopped, patients treated best with TCA.

MAOIs may suppress anginal pain, which means that patients should be warned about overexertion.

MAOIs may increase symptoms of Parkinson's disease.

Use MAOIs cautiously in patients with
* Hyperthyroidism
* Diabetes
* Renal impairment
* Epilepsy

NURSES' DATA

Monitor suicidal patients for "cheeking" or hoarding MAOIs.

Remind patient about a 4–6 week lag on a therapeutic dose before MAOIs fully work.

Tell patients about MAOI diet, stressing its importance without overdoing its seriousness.

* Review the patient's use of
  √ Specific favorite foods, including cooking methods with wine
  √ Over-the-counter medications (especially nose sprays, cold tablets, diet pills)
  √ Prescription drugs (e.g., TCAs)
  √ Recreational substances (e.g., wine, cocaine)
* Insure patient knows differences between hypertensive crisis and hypotensive reaction (see pages 74–75, 102, 114).

MAOIs produce insomnia and overstimulation.

* Excessively caffeinated beverages (e.g., Coke, Mountain Dew) may accelerate anxiety, agitation, and confuse diagnosis.
* If patient experiences insomnia on MAOIs, doctor can change timing and/or dosage of MAOI.

PATIENT AND FAMILY NOTES

Be familiar with MAOI diet and drugs.

MAOIs may impair patient's performance of potentially hazardous tasks (e.g., driving a car, working near machinery, crossing streets). When a patient starts MAOIs, he should drive briefly in a safe place to check reflexes.

No MAOIs should be at bedside or at any other quickly accessible place.

Keep safely from children.
For dizzy patients, review hypotension instructions (see pages 74–75, 114).

Carry a Medic Alert card to inform emergency room doctors about MAOIs.

* Inform every physician, surgeon, dentist, and pharmacist about using an MAOI.
* Before buying any over-the-counter drug, check the label, or ask the pharmacist, about the drug's compatibility with MAOIs.

MONOAMINE OXIDASE INHIBITORS

May take MAOIs with regular meals.

- If forget dose, can consume it within 2 hours.
- Otherwise wait for next regular dose.
- Do not double dose.

Must remain on MAOI regimen for 10–14 days after stopping MAOIs.

Do not abruptly halt MAOIs because a few patients develop GI upset and bad dreams 1–3 days after doing so.

- Call physician instead.
- If cannot reach a physician, take one more pill until contacing him.

COST INDEX

Generic Names	Brand Names	Equivalent Dosage (mg)	Dose Assessed (mg)	Cost Rating*
Isocarboxazid	Marplan	10	10	11
Phenelzine	Nardil	15	15	5
Tranylcypromine	Parnate	10	10	6

* The higher the number, the higher the cost.

INTRODUCTION

As a salt, lithium prevents and treats manic and depressive swings in bipolar disorders.[1]
Drugs modulating "highs" and "lows" are called "mood stabilizers."

- Mood stabilizers are lithium and some anticonvulsants.
- This chapter considers lithium; the next, anticonvulsants.

This chapter examines lithium for

- Bipolar disorder (see pages 130–34)
- Unipolar depression (see pages 134–35)
- Schizoaffective episode (see page 135)
- Emotionally unstable character disorder (see pages 135–36)
- Borderline personality disorder (see page 136)
- Premenstrual dysphoria (see page 136)
- Alcoholism (see page 136)

Discussed in other chapters, lithium helps

- Aggression: (Anticonvulsants, pages 158–60)
- Uncontrolled rage reaction: (Anticonvulsants, page 159)

---

[1] Clinicians seeking information on lithium may call the Lithium Information Center at the University of Wisconsin: 608-263-6171.

NAMES, MANUFACTURERS, DOSE FORMS, AND COLORS

Generic Names	Brand Names	Manufacturers	Dose Forms (mg)*	Colors
Lithium carbonate	Eskalith	SmithKline Beecham	t: 300; c: 300	t: gray; c: gray-yellow
	Eskalith CR †	SmithKline Beecham	t: 450	t: yellow
	Lithane	Miles	t: 300	t: green
	Lithobid †	CIBA	t: 300	t: peach
Lithium citrate	Cibalith-S	CIBA	s: 8 mEq/5 ml	s: raspberry

* c = capsules; s = syrup; † = sustained release; t = tablets.

PHARMACOLOGY

Lithium's intracellular functions include

- Delays norepinephrine-sensitive adenylate cyclase.
- Reverses or balances calcium-mediated processes.
- Passes through sodium channels.
- At high concentrations, passes through potassium channels.
- Diminishes sensitivity to neurotransmitter receptors.

The GI tract completely absorbs lithium in 6 hours.
Lithium's bioavailability is 100%.
Cerebral concentration is 40% of plasma concentration.
Peak plasma levels occur at $\frac{1}{2}$–2 hours; steady-state plasma levels at 4–5 days.
Lithium's average half-life is 20–24 hours, and ranges from 8–35 hours.
Sustained-release lithium

- Has delayed GI absorption (60–90%), which may slow fluctuations in plasma lithium.
- Peaks at 4–6 hours.
- Releases less lithium in the stomach.
- Delivers more lithium in the small intestine.

Lithium citrate is the most rapidly absorbed, usually within $\frac{1}{4}$–1 hour.
The kidneys excrete 95% of lithium.

- The feces excrete 1%,
- Sweat excretes 4–5%.
- 33–67% of lithium excreted in 6–12 hours,
- The rest excreted over 10–14 days.

Sodium depletion significantly increases lithium retention.

LABORATORY INVESTIGATIONS

With lithium treatment, obtain the following tests.

	Before Starting Lithium	Every 6 Months	Every 12 Months
ECG*	Yes	—	Yes
Electrolytes	Yes	—	—
CBC, differential, ESR	Yes	—	Yes
BUN, creatinine, creatinine clearance	Yes	Yes	—
Urinalysis	Yes	—	—
Fasting blood sugar	Yes	—	Yes
T₃RU, T₄RIA, T₄I†	Yes	—	Yes
TSH	Yes	Yes	—
Antithyroid antibodies	Yes	Yes	—
Calcium‡	Yes	—	Yes
Side effect check list	Yes	Yes	—

* For patients over 40 or with h/o cardiac disease; these patients should also take another ECG one month after obtaining steady-state plasma level.
† RU = resin uptake; RIA = radio immunoassay; I = free thyroxin index.
‡ Re-obtain serum calcium 2–6 weeks after lithium begins.

DOSES

Lithium plasma levels determine the most effective dose.

Always base lithium dosage on clinical state and side effects, not on plasma level.

Tests for calculating lithium's initial dose are not particularly informative; nevertheless, one generally can predict the total daily effective lithium dose by giving the patient 600 mg of lithium, checking the lithium level 24 hours later, and prescribing the corresponding dose from this table.

24-Hour Lithium Level (mEq./l.)	Total Daily Dose (mg)
0.05–0.09	3600
0.10–0.14	2700
0.15–0.19	1800
0.20–0.23	900
0.24–0.30	600
> 0.30	300

Lithium plasma levels are

Condition	Usual Plasma Level (mEq./l.)	Plasma Level Range (mEq./l.)	Elderly Plasma Level (mEq./l.)
Acute mania	0.80–1.2	0.5–1.5	0.6–0.8
Maintenance	0.60–1.0	0.46–1.2	0.3–0.6

Saliva lithium levels can assist if drawing blood becomes difficult.

- Therapeutic lithium saliva levels (1.6–2.5 mEq./l.) are twice as high as plasma levels.
- Saliva levels are 1–3 (usually 2) times the plasma level.
- To calculate this ratio, determine several plasma and saliva levels and note their ratio.

Lithium often given bid, but a single, bedtime dose may produce less polyuria and renal structural abnormalities.

Slow (sustained) release lithium may lower side effects (e.g., tremor, nausea) at peak levels.

- May cause more diarrhea than standard lithium.
- Less dose fluctuation than standard lithium.
- Twice daily dosing with slow-release lithium may generate 10% higher 12-hour serum levels than same dose of standard lithium.

CLINICAL INDICATIONS AND USE

General Information

Lithium carbonate and lithium citrate have no major clinical differences.
Predictors for a good initial lithium response include

- H/o of mania or hypomania associated with grandiosity or elation
- No atypical (schizoaffective) symptoms
- Depressive episodes (past or present) with anergia, hypersomnia, increased appetite
- Less than 4 cycles/year
- Previous compliance with treatment
- First-degree relative with bipolar disorder

Other factors that might predict a good initial lithium response are

- H/o "switch" to mania on TCAs or spontaneously
- High calcium:magnesium ratio
- Low MHPG (while depressed)
- Augmented TSH response to TRH in depressed bipolar patients
- Any periodic, fully-remitting psychopathology

Initiating Therapy

Mania

Lithium aborts 60–80% of acute manic and hypomanic episodes in 10–21 days.

Lithium is particularly effective in reducing affective and ideational signs of mania, especially

- Elation, grandiosity, expansiveness
- Flight of ideas
- Irritability, manipulativeness
- Anxiety

To a lesser extent, lithium diminishes

- Pressured speech
- Suspicious feelings
- Insomnia
- Psychomotor agitation
- Threatening or assaultive behavior
- Hypersexuality
- Distractibility

Although lithium and neuroleptics can both calm acute manic symptoms (e.g., grandiosity, pressured speech), treatment may begin with

- Lithium by itself,
- Lithium together with antipsychotics, or
- Neuroleptics followed by lithium.

If *lithium alone* is started

- Obtain blood tests (see above).
- Therapeutic and toxic lithium plasma levels are close.
- Treat patients with the lowest effective dose, which typically produces lithium levels from 0.8–1.2 mEq./l (1 mEq = 1 mmol).
- Start lithium in a healthy adult at 300 mg bid.
  - √ Increase dose by 300 mg q 3–4 days.
  - √ Raise dose until
    - □ Clear therapeutic results, or
    - □ Plasma level reaches 1.5 mEq./l., or
    - □ Side effects emerge.
- Measure lithium level around day 4–5 to determine plasma level.
  - √ Draw lithium 12 hours after the last dose.
  - √ Get further lithium levels at the same post-lithium dose time each week to confirm therapeutic plasma level.
  - √ Obtain levels every month for the next 6 months, and then
  - √ Every 2–3 months.

- Lithium may work in 7–10 days or may require 3–5 weeks.
- During manic episodes, patients may need increased lithium.
- Reduce above doses by 50% in patients over 60 or in patients with a renal disorder.
- If lithium does not induce improvement in 3 weeks, add an antipsychotic.

If starting *lithium and antipsychotic jointly*

- Initially, highly manic (especially agitated) patients are best treated with an antipsychotic (e.g., haloperidol, chlorpromazine) *and* lithium.
- Prescribe lithium (as above).
- Initiate a neuroleptic.
  √ Begin with haloperidol 5 mg po or IM bid-qid, since it acts rapidly and sedates minimally.
  √ Raise neuroleptics qod, such as haloperidol elevated 5 mg qod.
  √ If dystonia occurs, add ACA.
  √ Chlorpromazine 50–100 mg po or 25–50 mg IM is roughly equivalent to haloperidol.
- After controlling mania, taper patient off neuroleptic.

If *antipsychotic is followed by lithium*

- Start neuroleptic (as above).
- Launch lithium (as above) after mania diminishes.
- Taper patient off antipsychotic after acute mania ends.

In treating the elderly

- Start lithium in lower doses (e.g., 300–600 mg/day).
- Monitor lithium q 3–4 days.
- Increase lithium by 300 mg until reach a therapeutic level between 0.6–0.8 mEq./l.
- Doses over 900 mg/day are often unnecessary and toxic.

If patient develops EPS on antipsychotic agents, may replace with clonazepam or carbamazepine.

- Anticonvulsants do not increase depressions.
- Act as quickly as antipsychotics and possibly faster than lithium.
- Seem especially useful in rapidly-cycling patients.
- Do not increase lithium toxicity.
- Clonazepam produces sedation; carbamazepine does not.

Bipolar Depression

Lithium is more effective in bipolar than in major depressions.

General indications

- For moderate to moderately severe bipolar depression, lithium is preferred.
- For severe bipolar depressions, start a TCA *and* lithium together.

TCAs have two disadvantages when added to lithium.

- TCAs may decrease cycle length, thereby increasing manic and/or depressive episodes.
  √ In one study, patients off TCA had a bipolar period every 150 days, whereas on TCAs, they had one every 50 days.
- TCAs (and MAOIs) can propel depressed patients to "switch" into mania or hypomania.
  √ If this occurs, reduce antidepressant dosage or pretreat with lithium.
- About 25–35% of patients benefit at some time from adding a TCA during a depression.

Rapid-cycling patients.

- Have more than 3 recurrences in a single year.
- Respond less well to lithium than patients with fewer episodes.
- Often require a full year to respond to lithium.
  If rapid cycling occurs,

- Check (and treat) for hypothyroidism.
- Prescribe carbamazepine, or perhaps, valproic acid (see pages 155–57).
- TCAs may trigger rapid cycling.
- MAOIs preferred over TCAs.
- Use neuroleptics briefly to avoid tardive dyskinesia.

Patients with less severe bipolar illness, such as cyclothymia or bipolar II (hypomania and major depression) may improve on lithium.

Maintaining Therapy

Frequency of bipolar relapses in 2 years

- In 20–40% of patients on lithium,
- In 65–90% of patients without lithium.

Although lithium prevents manic and depressive episodes, < 50% achieve complete relief.

- When patients halt lithium, relapse usually springs up in several weeks.

After onset of initial symptoms, maintain bipolar patients on lithium for 9–12 months. If manic episode breaks out, decreased sleep is often the first sign.

Manage a recurring manic episode by

- Increasing lithium plasma level
- Adding a neuroleptic, clonazepam, or carbamazepine

If a depressive episode breaks out

- Check lithium level and thyroid function.
  √ Correct, if needed.
- Raise lithium to 1.2 mEq./l. or higher, since depression may improve in 7–10 days.
- If depression is severe, add TCA, but reluctantly, because they may aggravate condition.
- Some experts suspect that adding a MAOI might be safer than adding a TCA.

If a patient is on a combination of lithium and TCA/MAOI, it is probably best to discontinue the TCA/MAOI after 1–2 months of remission to minimize the effect of these drugs on the mood cycle.

"Lifelong" lithium prophylaxis would be favored when

- Male
- Sudden onset
- More frequent manic and depressive episodes
- More than 3 previous (high or low) episodes
- Disorder begins past age 30
- First episode *not* precipitated by environmental event
- Poor family and/or social supports

Before stopping lithium

- Discuss pros and cons with patient and family.
- Detail the first signs of mania or depression.
- Instruct everyone about what to do if symptoms emerge.

If patient stops and must return to lithium, and if he has previously tolerated a particular lithium dose well, the patient may restart on this full dose without titrating the dose upwards.

Taper lithium 300 mg/month.

Unipolar Depression (see pages 564–70)

TCAs treat major (unipolar) depression better than lithium.
Patients unresponsive to a TCA or MAOI after 3–6 weeks may benefit from lithium's addition.

- Lithium may aid patients on imipramine more than patients on amitriptyline.
- Lithium is favored over TCAs in more cyclic (frequent) unipolar depressions—that is, an episode every 12–24 months.

- If a depression emerges with "reverse biological signs"—hypersomnia, anergia, overeating—this might be the first glimpse of a bipolar disorder possibly helped by lithium.

Schizoaffective Disorder

Lithium at 0.8–1.1 mEq./l. combined with an antipsychotic reduces affective symptoms in schizoaffective disorders.

- Lithium might help schizoaffective patients, who have not responded to other treatments in 6 months.

Lithium is best for

- Overactivity, excitement
- Posturing, mannerisms
- Confusion
- Insomnia
- Pressured speech
- Irritability
- Episodic timing of symptoms

TCAs *and* neuroleptics are best for

- Schizodepressive symptoms.
- Combination is superior to either drug alone

Schizoaffective patients may be diagnosed as having "atypical bipolar disorder" with characteristics of

- Chronic psychoses between episodes, or alternatively,
- Reasonably good adjustment between episodes, but with marked, non-affect-consonant delusions and hallucinations during euphoric or hyperactive periods.

Anticonvulsants, such as carbamazepine, may treat schizoaffective disorders. Valproic acid combined with other agents improved 42–57% of schizoaffective patients.

Emotionally Unstable Character Disorder (EUCD)

EUCDs show depressive or hypomanic mood swings, which last from a few hours to several days, and are usually not environmentally triggered.

EUCD patients also have at least one of the following

- Drug and medication abuse
- Delinquent behavior, problems with authority
- Poor school/work performance
- Sexual promiscuity
- Malingering

LITHIUM

- Childhoods with impulsiveness, low frustration tolerance, and hyperactivity

Patients are often women in their late teens to early thirties. These patients have mood shifts like the cyclothymic personality, but whereas the cyclothymics tend to have responsible adult goals, the EUCD patients are immature, young, hedonistic, without goals, and confused "wise-guys." EUCD mood swings are often missed.

Lithium (as in treating acute mania) appears to decrease frequency and severity of

- Depression
- Impulsiveness
- Antisocial behavior

Thioridazine (about 300–600 mg/day) might help.

Borderline Personality Disorder

No drug effectively treats borderline personality disorder.

If any agent is prescribed, target specific symptoms.

These agents often include

- Antipsychotics for cognitive problems
- Lithium for mood swings
- Benzodiazepines for chronic anxiety
- TCAs for depression
- MAOIs if dysphoria arises from interpersonal rejection
- Carbamazepine to decrease behavioral outbursts

Overall, borderlines do better with lithium and a low-dose, high-potency neuroleptic.

Always be alert to potential for overdose.

Premenstrual Dysphoria

Lithium may inhibit irritability, elation, or depression in women with premenstrual difficulties; efficacy is low.

Alcoholism

In alcoholic patients, lithium may diminish alcohol consumption, but not depression.

Moderate quantities of alcohol can trigger hypomania.

SIDE EFFECTS

Among 237 patients on lithium, only 10% were without side effects, whereas 25% had 3 or more side effects.

Lithium's side effects arise from

- Peak blood levels or
- Steady-state levels.

Peak plasma levels

- Occur 1–2 hours after the dose.
- Most commonly generate lethargy, transient nausea, stomach discomfort, urinary frequency, and fine tremor.
- Can reduce peak plasma level side effects by
  √ Substituting sustained-release lithium,
  √ Giving less lithium in morning and larger dose at hs.
  √ Starting lithium at lower doses, or
  √ Changing brands.

Steady-state levels

- Achieved by 4–5, and sometimes up to 7, days.
- Reduce by lowering lithium.

Salt-restricted diets and diuretics diminish sodium, allowing lithium to replace sodium and accumulate in the cell.

- Thus, normal plasma lithium can induce toxicity.
- Avoid diuretics or salt-restricted diets; if they are required, determine the lithium dose based on the patient's clinical state and not on lithium level.

Hypokalemia can intensify lithium side effects.

Cardiovascular Effects

At therapeutic lithium levels, the most common ECG changes are

- *T wave flattening or inversion* in 20% of patients
- *Widening of QRS complex*

These changes are

- Benign.
- Poorly correlated with serum lithium level.
- Stopped readily by discontinuing lithium.
- Should not be confused with more serious problems (e.g., hypokalemia).

Arrhythmias

- Usually in patients with pre-existing cardiac disease.
- Common in sino-atrial node dysfunction with fainting, dizziness, palpitations, or without symptoms.
- Reversed by halting lithium.
- Ventricular arrhythmias reported rarely.

Sudden death

- Have occurred on lithium, usually in patients with pre-existing heart disease.
- A cardiologist's consultation might help before placing a cardiac patient on lithium.

Gastrointestinal Effects

Initial nausea

- Dose-related, but may arise on normal serum lithium levels.
- Often occurs early in treatment, especially when raising doses.
- Accompanied by other GI symptoms.
- Management
  - √ Ingest lithium with meals, snacks, milk, and if necessary, antacids.
  - √ Spread out dose or diminish lithium.
  - √ Try sustained-release preparation, which might cause diarrhea.
  - √ Replace with lithium citrate syrup.
  - √ Sometimes one can raise lithium carbonate dose more slowly without causing GI symptoms.

Chronic nausea, anorexia, vomiting, dehydration, and *fever* constitute a flulike syndrome.

- Vomiting can cause more dehydration, which may elevate plasma lithium.
- Stop lithium until flulike syndrome ends.

Diarrhea

- More common in toxicity, but can occur with normal serum lithium and with sustained-release forms.
- Frequency decreases with
  - √ Conventional lithium doses
  - √ Lithium with (highly anticholinergic) TCAs
- Management
  - √ Reduce lithium dose,
  - √ Antidiarrheal medication,
  - √ Take lithium during meals, or
  - √ Switch to lithium citrate.

Weight gain, edema

- Common, often causing patients to stop lithium.
- 15 pounds gained in 60% of patients.
- 25 pounds gained in 20% of patients.

- Unclear why some patients acquire 40–60 pounds, whereas others add nothing.
- Edema may increase weight.
  □ Shortly after initiating lithium, patients often accumulate 5–7 pounds of fluid and edema.
- Management
  √ Reduce lithium dose.
  √ Diminish by ingesting lower-calorie fluids, or
  √ Cautious use of
    □ Hydrochlorothiazide 50 mg qd-qod, or
    □ Spironolactone 50 mg qd-bid.
  √ Substitute carbamazepine for lithium, since carbamazepine does not increase weight.

Renal Effects

Nephrogenic diabetes insipidus (NDI)

- Characteristics include
  √ Difficulty concentrating urine.
  √ Urine volume up to 4–8 liters/day
  √ Increased serum lithium
- NDI may exhibit
  √ Polyuria
  √ Nocturia
  √ Thirst
  √ Higher sodium
  √ Lower potassium
  √ Toxicity
  √ Dehydration
- Polyuria may affect 50–70% of patients on long-term lithium.
  √ 10% of lithium patients have renal output > 3 liters/day.
- Management
  √ Lower or stop lithium.
    □ Benefits in 1–3 weeks.
    □ Once-a-day regular lithium preferred.
  √ Increase fluid intake to dilute lithium.
  √ Paradoxically, thiazide diuretics diminish lithium-induced polyuria.
  √ Thiazides in *polyuria*
    □ May increase serum sodium,
    □ May decrease serum potassium, and
    □ May increase serum lithium by 30–50%.
  √ Cautiously treat with hydrochlorothiazide 50 mg/day and by

    □ Reducing lithium,

    □ Monitoring lithium and electrolyte levels.

   √ A newer alternative is to prescribe amiloride 5–10 mg bid.

    □ Markedly decreases polyuria.

    □ Normal diet and sodium intake.

    □ No effect on lithium level or serum potassium.

    □ To be safe, still monitor serum lithium and electrolytes.

Interstitial nephritis

- Chronic, serious, uncommon, usually reversible.
- May stem from long-term lithium therapy.
- Acute rise in serum creatinine and decline of 24-hour creatinine clearance.
- Discontinue lithium.

Endocrine and Sexual Effects

Euthyroid goiter, hypothyroidism

- 20% of lithium patients develop thyroid problems.
- 5–15% have clinical signs or altered hormone levels.
- Lithium inhibits synthesis and release of T_3 (triiodothyronine) and T_4 (thyroxine), which stimulates TSH (thyroid-stimulating hormone), which stimulates the thyroid gland to re-establish euthyroidism. During this compensatory process, the gland might become large (goiter) or hypothyroid or both.
- A euthyroid goiter shows
  - √ Anergia
  - √ Normal thyroid function tests
  - √ Increased TSH
- Hypothyroidism shows
  - √ A goiter or no goiter
  - √ Increased TSH is the most diagnostic test
  - √ Antithyroid antibodies
- Timing highly variable.
- Management
  - √ Can usually continue lithium with either thyroid disorder.
  - √ Add thyroxine 0.05–0.2 mg/day *or* start thyroxine 0.1 mg qd for 2 weeks and then 0.2 mg qd.

Hyperparathyroidism

- Serum calcium and parathyroid hormone levels enter high-to-normal range in half the patients in the first month on lithium.
- Abnormally high levels occur in 10% of patients.
- Rarely of clinical significance.

- Symptoms of hyperparathyroidism include
  - √ Mood changes, anxiety
  - √ Apathy
  - √ Aggressiveness
  - √ Psychosis
  - √ Sleep disturbance
  - √ Delirium, dementia, confusion
  - √ Convulsions

Glucose tolerance, carbohydrate craving

- Lithium may decrease glucose tolerance, but it is not diabetogenic.
- No reason to obtain glucose tests.
- Increased sugar increase leads to *dental carries.*

Hematologic Effects

Leukocytosis

- Reversible, benign, and not indicative of disease.
- WBC around 12,500–15,000/mm^3.
- May need to stop lithium.

Skin, Allergies, and Temperature

Usually idiosyncratic rather than dose-related.
Acne and psoriasis are common.

Acne

- May appear or get worse during lithium.
- May need to halt lithium.

Psoriasis

- Aggravation of pre-existing or dormant psoriasis.
- Dry noninflamed papular eruption is common.

Allergic rash

- Allergic rash may disappear by changing specific lithium product, in which case allergy is due to something other than lithium.

Maculopapular rash

- With or without psoriasis.
- Mildly annoying, erythematous rash.
- Relieve with 50:50 zinc ointment.

Alopecia

- In 12% of women; rarely in men.
- Hair disappears anywhere on body.
- Hair can regrow on or off of lithium.

Other management of skin lesions

- Antihistamines can best treat urticarial lesions.
- Topical steroids.
- Bacitracin for localized infections

Central Nervous System Effects

Tremors

- Dose-related tremor may affect half the patients.
- Tremors may disappear after the first 2–3 weeks of constant lithium dose.
- Lithium tremor is
  √ Present at rest, but worsens on intentional movement
  √ Worsens with anxiety and performance
  √ Usually confined to fingers
    □ If severe, may involve hands and wrists.
  √ Irregular in amplitude and rhythm
  √ Jerking fingers with flexion or extension
  √ Erupting in side thrusts
  √ Variable in its frequency and intensity throughout day, and from day to day
  √ Productive of jagged, irregular, and hard-to-read handwriting when severe
- Lithium tremor differs from others in that
  √ In parkinsonism (EPS) tremor, the fingers, hands, and wrist move faster and as a unit; micrographia also appears, but not in lithium tremor.
  √ In parkinson's disease, the tremor is slow and rhythmic, with prominent rotational and flexing movements.
  √ In anxiety, the tremor is fine, rapid, and rhythmic with side-to-side movements.
  √ In essential (familial) tremor, the movement is smooth, wide, and runs in families, which differs from lithium tremor.
- Lithium tremor may increase with
  √ Greater serum lithium, although it may exist with normal serum levels.
  √ Adding TCAs.
- Tremors may diminish by
  √ More frequent smaller doses.

√ Decreased total lithium dose, especially if serum concentration is > 0.8 mEq./l

√ Sustained-release lithium preparations.

√ Propranolol 10 mg qid initially.

  ▫ May escalate dose to 20 mg tid-qid.

  ▫ Before starting propranolol, r/o congestive heart failure, bronchospasm, or other contraindications to β blockers.

  ▫ Alternatives to propranolol are metoprolol (25–50 mg) or nadolol (20–40 mg) bid.

√ Move lithium doses *slowly* upwards.

√ Stop TCAs.

√ ACAs don't help.

Seizures

- Grand mal (rarely).
- Usually (but not always) in patients with epilepsy.
- Well-controlled seizure does *not* r/o the introduction of lithium.

Memory loss, "dullness of senses," reduced coordination, lethargy, ataxia, inhibited motor skills

- Confirm lithium is the cause.
  √ The absence of "highs" may account for patients' describing these problems.
  √ Hypothyroidism may be the culprit.
- Occur on > 0.8 mEq./l. of lithium.
- Management
  √ Reduce or stop dose
  √ Remedial memory training.
  √ Thyroid replacement, if necessary.

Cogwheeling, mild parkinsonism

PERCENTAGES OF SIDE EFFECTS

Side Effects	Lithium
CARDIOVASCULAR EFFECTS	
Dizziness, lightheadedness	20
T-wave changes (benign)	25
ECG abnormalities	20
GASTROINTESTINAL EFFECTS	
Dry mouth and throat	27.5 (10–50)
Anorexia, lower appetite	12.5
Nausea, vomiting	15.2

Side Effects	Lithium
Dyspepsia, upset stomach	10.3
Diarrhea	14.4
Thirst	26.7
Polydipsia	37.6
	(10–55.3)
Weight gain	29.7
	(1–60)
Edema	10.2

RENAL EFFECTS

Kidney defect	25
	(<10–50)
Polyuria	31.2
	(10–60)

ENDOCRINE AND SEXUAL EFFECTS

Menstrual changes	5.5
Hypothyroidism	8.5
	(1–20)
Goiter	4.1
	(1.7–6.1)
Disturbed sexual function	20

EYES, EARS, NOSE, AND THROAT EFFECTS

Blurred vision	<1
Vertigo	10

SKIN, ALLERGIES, AND TEMPERATURE

Rashes	6.3
Abnormal skin pigment	1
Hair loss (women only)	12

CENTRAL NERVOUS SYSTEM EFFECTS

Cogwheeling	23
	(5–75)
Weakness, fatigue	10.5
	(1–30)
Muscle cramps	5.5
Hypertonia	<15
Jerking limbs	<1
Slurred speech	5.5
Rigidity	5.0
Headache	<40
Resting tremor	37.5
	(10–50)
Drowsiness, sedation	22.8
	(1–<40)
Confusion, disorientation	22.8
	(1–<40)
Memory impairment	32.5
	(0–45)

PREGNANCY AND LACTATION

Teratogenicity
(1st trimester)

- 11–12% risk of anomalies, with figures ranging from 3.6–14.3%.

- High frequency of congenital cardiac abnormalities, especially a 400-fold increase of Ebstein's anomaly of the tricuspid valve.

- If pregnancy is planned, discontinue lithium about 1–2 months before conception, and remain off lithium until at least the first trimester's end.

- If patient on lithium becomes pregnant, get her off lithium.

- If patient exposed to lithium before week 12, consider cardiac ultrasound at week 20.

- During first trimester, avoid lithium, and if necessary, give carbamazepine to control manic episode; also consider ECT.

- Goiters observed in newborns, and so should follow mother's thyroid status during pregnancy.

Direct Effect
on Newborn
(3rd trimester)

- Lithium toxicity may develop in newborn with hypotonia, cyanosis, bradykinesia, depressed thyroid, goiter, atrial flutter, hepatomegaly, ECG changes, cardiomegaly, GI bleeding, diabetes insipidus, or shock.

- Most of these effects reverse in 1–2 weeks, which corresponds to the renal elimination of lithium in the newborn; diabetes insipidus may persist for several months.

- During second and third trimesters, consider lithium and carbamazepine equally if one drug is necessary.

- Decrease or stop lithium 2–3 days before and after delivery.

Lactation

- Lithium ranges from 10–100% of maternal level.

- Studies show 10–50%, while others suggest 33–50%.
- Average is 40%.

Drug Dosage in Mother's Milk

Generic Name	Milk/ Plasma Ratio	Time of Peak Concentration in Milk (hours)	Infant Dose (mg/kg/day)	Maternal Dose (%)	Safety Rating*
Lithium	0.42	?	0.41	1.8†	B

* B: Unsafe before 34 weeks, but safer after 34 weeks, although others believe it is safe at all times.
† Calculated assuming maternal dose of 20–25 mg/kg/day.

DRUG-DRUG INTERACTIONS

Drugs (X) Interacts with:	Lithium (L)	Comments
Acetazolamide	L ↓	Reduces serum lithium and efficacy.
Alcohol	L ↑	Alcohol may increase serum lithium.
Amiloride	L ↑	Potassium-saving diuretic may possibly increase lithium concentration and toxicity; monitor.
Ampicillin	L ↑	Increased lithium effect and toxicity.
Antipsychotics:		Infrequently, lithium and high doses of
*Haloperidol	X ↑ L ↑	haloperidol have produced toxicity, with fever,
*Thioridazine	X ↑ L ↑	lethargy, weakness, confusion, agitation,
Chlorpromazine	X ↓ L ↓	extrapyramidal symptoms, and cerebellar signs. Permanent brain damage and irreversible dyskinesias may ensue. Reactions typically arise in a few days, often at normal lithium levels. Most chronic lithium-haloperidol or lithium-thioridazine treatment appears benign. Lithium plus chlorpromazine may lower both drugs; may generate NMS.
Caffeine	L ↓	Increased lithium excretion; heavy coffee drinkers have trouble reaching therapeutic levels on even 2400 mg/day.
Captopril	L ↑	Lithium toxicity and impaired kidney function occur. May need to halt or stop lithium or captopril.
*Carbamazepine	L ↑	On normal lithium, carbamazepine may induce lithium toxicity. After ceasing one agent for a few days, neurotoxicity vanishes. Other patients improve on the combination.
Decamethonium	X ↑	Prolonged muscle paralysis.
Dextroamphetamine	X ↓	Lithium may inhibit dextroamphetamine's euphoria.
Digitalis	X ↑	Digitalis toxicity may cause cardiac arrhythmias.
*Diltiazem	L ↑	Lithium-induced neurotoxicity, nausea, weakness, ataxia, and tinnitus. Stop diltiazem or lower lithium to 300 mg/day.
Enalapril	L ↑	Lithium toxicity and impaired kidney function occur. May need to halt or stop lithium or enalapril.

Drugs (X) Interacts with:	Lithium (L)	Comments
Hydroxyzine	L ↑	Cardiac conduction disturbance.
Ketamine	L ↑	Increased lithium toxicity from sodium depletion.
Loop diuretics: Furosemide Ethacrynic acid	L ↑	Increases lithium, but safer than thiazide diuretics.
Marijuana	L ↑	Increased absorption of lithium; importance unclear.
Mazindol	L ↑	A few cases of lithium toxicity after 3 days of mazindol. Worse with inadequate salt intake.
*Methyldopa	L ↑	Lithium toxicity may develop with a normal lithium level. Toxicity ends 1–9 days after stopping methyldopa.
NSAIAs: *Indomethacin *Piroxicam Ibuprofen Phenylbutazone	L ↑	Adding indomethacin increases plasma lithium 30–61% in 3–10 days. Be careful adding all NSAIAs.
Pancuronium	X ↑	Prolonged muscle paralysis.
Phenytoin	L ↑	A few cases of lithium toxicity.
*Potassium iodide	L ↑	Sometimes Li + KI → hypothyroidism + goiter, which is no reason to halt lithium. Treat thyroid instead.
*Sodium bicarbonate	L ↓	Sodium bicarbonate may lower plasma lithium.
*Sodium chloride	L ↓	High sodium may reduce serum lithium concentration; low sodium intake may increase serum lithium and toxicity.
Spectinomycin	L ↑	Increased lithium effect and toxicity.
Spironolactone	L ↑	Potassium-saving diuretic may increase lithium concentration and toxicity.
Succinylcholine	X ↑	Prolonged neuromuscular blockade.
Sympathomimetics: Norepinephrine, Dobutamine, Epinephrine	X ↓	Lithium usually decreases pressor actions of norepinephrine and other direct-acting sympathomimetics.
*Tetracyclines	L ↑	Lithium + tetracycline may increase lithium toxicity. Unclear if other tetracyclines (e.g., doxycycline) affect lithium.
Theophylline	L ↑	Theophylline may significantly diminish lithium in 3–4 days. Stopping theophylline may yield excessive lithium.
†Thiazide diuretics: Chlorothiazide Hydrochlorothiazide	L ↑	Any diuretic that promotes sodium and potassium excretion may yield cardiotoxicity and neurotoxicity. Potassium-sparing diuretics are safer. Watch for hypercalcemia.
TCAs	L ↑	Increased tremor.
Triamterene	L ↑	Potassium-saving diuretic may increase lithium concentration and toxicity.
Tryptophan	L ↑	Increased lithium efficacy. Tryptophan off American market.
Urea	L ↓	Urea may reduce lithium; scanty clinical evidence.
*Verapamil	L ↑	Lithium-induced neurotoxicity, nausea, weakness, ataxia, and tinnitus. Symptoms ended after verapamil stopped or when lithium lowered to 300 mg/day.

Codes: * Moderately important interaction; † Extremely important interaction; ↑ Increases; ↓ Decreases.

EFFECTS ON LABORATORY TESTS

Generic Names	Blood/Serum Tests	Results	Urine Tests	Results
Lithium	^{131}I uptake	↑	Glycosuria	↑
	T_3	↓	Albuminuria	↑
	T_4	↓	VMA	↑
	Leukocytes	↑	Renal concentrating ability	↓
	Eosinophils	↑	Electrolytes	↑↓
	Platelets	↑		
	Lymphocytes	↓		
	Na^+, K^+	↑↓		
	Ca^{++}, Mg^{++}	↑↑		
	Serum phosphate	↓		
	Parathyroid hormone	↑		
	Glucose tolerance	↑↓		
	Creatinine	↑ r		

Codes: ↑ Increases; ↓ Decreases; ↑↓ Increases and decreases; r = rarely.

WITHDRAWAL

Lithium does not induce

- Dependence
- Tolerance
- Addiction
- Withdrawal

It can be stopped quickly without any apparent difficulty.

OVERDOSE: TOXICITY, SUICIDE, AND TREATMENT

Therapeutic indexes (i.e., toxic dose : effective dose) are

- Antipsychotics = about 100
- TCAs/MAOIs = about 10
- Lithium = about 3

Being a nonmetabolized salt, lithium toxicity results not only from the drug, but also from water and sodium loss based on

- Decreased fluid or food intake (during manic or depressive swings)
- Diuretics
- Fever
- Abnormal GI conditions (e.g., nausea, diarrhea, vomiting)
- Pyelonephritis

Although no clearly defined relationship exists between serum lithium and toxicity, the serum level 12 hours after the last dose roughly predicts the intoxication's severity.

Side Effects by Levels of Lithium Carbonate

Therapeutic Lithium Levels (0.6–1.5 mEq./l.)	Mild to Moderate Toxicity (1.5–2.0 mEq./l.)	Moderate to Severe Toxicity (2.0–2.5 mEq./l.)	Severe Toxicity (Over 2.5 mEq./l.)
Polydipsia	Dry mouth	Anorexia	Generalized seizures
Polyuria	Drowsiness	Chronic nausea	Oliguria
Nausea	Vomiting	Chronic vomiting	Renal failure
Mild diarrhea	Diarrhea	Blurred vision	Death
Fine hand tremor	Abdominal pain	Muscle fasciculations	
Weight gain	Dizziness	Clonic limb movements	
Edema	Vertigo	Hyperreflexia	
Hypothyroidism	Coarse hand tremor	Nystagmus	
Goiter	Dysarthria	Choreoathetoid movements	
	Muscle weakness	Convulsions	
	Sluggishness	Delirium	
	Excitement	Fainting	
	Lethargy	EEG changes	
		Stupor	
		Leg tremor	
		Cardiac arrhythmias	
		Irregular pulse	
		Coma	

Recovery of lithium-intoxicated patients

- 70–80% fully recover.
- 10% display persistent sequelae: dementia, ataxia, polyuria, dysarthria, spasticity, nystagmus, and tremor.
- 10–25% die.

The general management of lithium overdoses includes (see page 37)

- Baseline ECG (to determine arrhythmia)
- Draw
  - √ Blood lithium
  - √ Creatinine
  - √ Electrolytes
  - √ Urinalysis (look for albuminuria)
  - √ Serum glucose (before IV fluids used)
- If patient is severely intoxicated
  - √ Restore fluids and electrolyte balance; correct sodium depletion.

√ Give 0.9% infusion of IV sodium chloride when lithium intoxication appears secondary to total body sodium depletion. This sodium infusion should be 1–2 liters in first 6 hours.

√ Rapid infusion of large volumes of IV potassium diuretic does not seem to help.

√ Lithium excretion also fostered by use of IV
  □ Sodium bicarbonate,
  □ Urea,
  □ Mannitol,
  □ Acetazolamide, or
  □ Aminophylline.

• Hemodialysis for 8–12 hours when
  √ Serum lithium > 3 m Eq./l.,
  √ Serum lithium 2–3 mEq./l. and patient's condition is deteriorating,
  √ Fluid or electolyte abnormalities are unresponsive to conventional supportive measures,
  √ Creatine clearance or urine output decreases substantially or
  √ Serum lithium is not reduced by at least 20% in 6 hours.

• Serum lithium level often rebounds after hours of hemodialysis; this requires repeated hemodialysis.

• Goal of hemodialysis is to concentrate serum lithium less than 1 mEq./l. at least 8 hours after hemodialysis is completed.

• Treat convulsions with short-acting barbiturates (e.g., thiopental).

Lithium can be restarted 48 hours after the patient is clinically normal.

Toxicity and Suicide Data

Generic Name	Toxicity Dose Average (g)	Mortality Dose Average (g)	Toxic Levels (mEq./l.)	Fatal Levels (mEq./l.)
Lithium Carbonate	6	10–60	2–4	4–5

PRECAUTIONS

About 33–45% of patients on lithium stop taking the drug during the first year of treatment, because of

• Complaints of memory loss
• Miss the "highs"
• GI, CNS, thyroid, and less frequently, renal side effects
• Depressive relapse (13% stopped lithium for this reason in one study.)

Close follow-up, especially during the first year, is essential.

Contraindications

- Salt-restricted (free) diet, diuretics, vomiting, diarrhea
  - ✓ Patients should be on normal diet with adequate fluids (2500–3000 ml) at start of treatment; watch cardiac patients.
  - ✓ Infection, exercising, sweating can increase salt output.
- Severe disability or dehydration
- Hypersensitivity to lithium
- Cardiovascular disease
  - ✓ Sinus node dysfunction ("sick sinus syndrome") should *not* receive lithium.
- Brain and renal damage
- Pregnancy

Since the ability to excrete lithium dwindles with age, use reduced doses in the elderly.

NURSES' DATA

Remind patients and family about lithium's side effects and the need to consume adequate (normal) salt and sufficient fluids.

- Avoid salt-restricted diet, diuretics, vomiting, diarrhea, excessive sweating, infection, overexercise, working heavily in overheated weather.
- At least initially, patients need 2500–3000 ml/day or 10 8-oz glasses of water/day.

Importance of monitoring lithium levels

- Describe logistics and procedures for monitoring lithium.
  - ✓ Draw blood circa 12 hours after last dose or immediately before morning dose.
  - ✓ Patient should not swallow lithium on morning before blood test.

Pregnancy warnings.

Be alert to noncompliance.

Remind patients and close relatives that lithium is not an "artificial chemical," but a naturally occurring mineral in the water; some find this reassuring.

PATIENT AND FAMILY NOTES

Have a Medic Alert wallet-card or bracelet indicating lithium's use.

Tell physicians and surgeons, especially cardiologists and GI specialists, about taking lithium.

No lithium should be at bedside or at any other quickly accessible place to prevent accidents. Maintain safely away from children.

Ingest lithium when prescribed, at regular times each day as decided on with physician.

- If forget dose, can consume in 2 hours.
- Otherwise wait for next scheduled dose.
- Do not double dose.

Ingest lithium with meals, snack, or milk to diminish GI irritation.

COST INDEX

Generic Names	Brand Names	Equivalent Dosage (mg)	Dose Assessed (mg)	Cost Rating*
Lithium carbonate	Eskalith	300	300	27
	Lithonate	300	300	30
	Lithane	300	300	44
	generics	300	300	>19
	Lithobid (slow release)	300	300	55
	Eskalith-CR (controlled-release)	300	450	58
Lithium citrate	Cibalith-S	300	300 syrup	90
	generics	300	300 syrup	>47

* The higher the number, the higher the cost.

6. Anticonvulsants

INTRODUCTION

Carbamazepine, valproic acid, and clonazepam are anticonvulsants that prevent and treat bipolar disorders, especially mania.

- Carbamazepine is structurally similar to the TCA imipramine.
- Divalproex is chemically akin to valproic acid; they are discussed together.
- Clonazepam is a benzodiazepine, whose mood-stabilizing operations are examined here. Its other actions are presented in anti-anxiety agents.

This chapter discusses anticonvulsants for

- Aggression (see pages 158–60)
- Bipolar disorder (see pages 155–58)
- Unipolar depression (see page 158)

Other chapters examine anticonvulsants for

- Alcohol and hypnosedative withdrawal (Hypnotics, pages 236–37)
- Schizoaffective disorders (Lithium, page 135)
- Schizophrenia (Antipsychotics, page 11)
- Panic attacks (Anti-anxiety, pages 188–89)

NAMES, MANUFACTURERS, DOSE FORMS, AND COLORS

Generic Names	Brand Names	Manufacturers	Dose Forms (mg)*	Colors
Carbamazepine	Tegretol	Geigy	t: 100/200; su: 100 mg/5 ml	t: red-speckled/pink; su: yellow-orange
Clonazepam	Klonopin†	Roche	t: ½/1/2	t: orange/blue/white
Divalproex	Depakote	Abbott	t: 125/250/500	t: salmon-pink/peach/lavender
Valproic acid	Depakene	Abbott	c: 250; s: 250 mg/5 ml	c: orange; s: red

* c = capsules; s = syrup; su = suspension; t = tablets.
† Was called Clonopin.

PHARMACOLOGY

Carbamazepine

* Inhibits kindling, a process that accelerates behavioral and convulsive responses from a repetition of the same stimulus.
* Absorbed slowly and erratically.
* Average plasma binding is 76%.
* Since carbamazepine induces its own liver metabolism, its dose may need increasing after 3–5 weeks.
* Carbamazepine's half-life diminishes rapidly
  √ Initially after single dose at 30–65 hours.
  √ 3 weeks later to 12–20 hours.
  √ During chronic therapy about 12 hours.
* Carbamazepine produces in the liver its chief metabolite, carbamazepine 10, 11-epoxide, with a half-life of 5–8 hours.

Valproic acid

* Has anti-kindling, anticonvulsant, and GABA-ergic effects.
* Is quickly, and almost completely, absorbed.
  √ Divalproex absorption is delayed 1–4 (average 2) hours.
  √ Absorption more rapid with syrup, with peak levels reached in ¼–2 hours.
* Half-life ranges from 6–18 hours
  √ Lower half-life (≈ 9 hours) when patients take other anticonvulsants.
  √ Increased half-life in children < 18 months (≈ 10–67 hours), and in patients with cirrhosis or acute hepatitis (up to 25 hours).

- Conjugated in liver ($\approx$ 70%).
- Excreted as glucuronide, mostly in urine, and slightly in feces and air.

Pharmacology of Anticonvulsants

	Carbamazepine	Clonazepam	Valproic Acid
Bioavailability (%)	77	98	100
Plasma-Bound (%)	65–80	86 $\pm$ $\frac{1}{2}$	93 $\pm$ 1
Volume Distribution (Liters/kg)	1.4 $\pm$ 0.4	3.2 $\pm$ 1.1	4 $\pm$ 0.9
Peak Plasma Level (hours)	4–8	1–4	1–4
Half-Life (hours)	15 $\pm$ 5	23 $\pm$ 5	13 $\pm$ 3
Excretion unchanged (%)	15–25 in feces	< 1 in urine	< 3 in feces and urine

DOSES

Valproic acid comes in three clinical forms.

- Divalproex sodium (Depakote), which is an enteric-coated, stable compound with equal amounts of valproic acid and sodium valproate
- Valproic acid
- Sodium valproate (Depakene capsules and syrup)

General Anticonvulsant Doses for Treating Mania

Generic Names	Starting Doses (mg/day)	Days to Reach Steady State Level	Therapeutic Doses (mg/day)	Dosage Range (mg/day)	Therapeutic Plasma Levels (μg/ml)
Carbamazepine	400	4–6	800–1200	200–1800	6–12
Clonazepam	1–2	5–8	4–16	0.5–40	?
Valproic acid	500	3–6	1000–1500	1000–3000	50–100

CLINICAL INDICATIONS AND USE

Anticonvulsants

- Clearly control acute mania (with or without lithium),
- Often prevent mania,
- Occasionally treat and prevent unipolar or bipolar depressions,
- Aid more rapid cycling patients than does lithium,
- Relieve psychotic symptoms secondary to complex partial seizures,
- Infrequently reduce schizophrenia,

ANTICONVULSANTS

* Dampen affective swings in schizoaffective patients,
* Diminish impulsive and aggressive behavior in some nonpsychotic patients, and
* Facilitate alcohol and benzodiazepine withdrawal.
* Carbamazepine *starts* its clinical benefits in this sequence
  √ < 1 day: seizures
  √ 2 days: pain
  √ 3½ days: sleep
  √ 6 days: mania
  √ 14 days: depression
  √ (Aggression relief occurs over time, and does not fit into this sequence.)
* Carbamazepine's *full effect* is
  √ Within hours for epilepsy
  √ 2 weeks for mania
  √ 3 or more weeks for depression

Mania

Between 20–30% of bipolar patients do not respond to or tolerate lithium. *Carbamazepine*'s efficacy for mania is 55–76%.

* May help up to 60% of rapid cyclers; lithium assists 10–15%.
* For acute mania, lithium + neuroleptic is more effective than lithium + carbamazepine.
  √ But carbamazepine does not induce tardive dyskinesia and has fewer side effects: 59% for carbamazepine versus 86% for chlorpromazine.
  √ Carbamazepine may lower neuroleptic doses for agitated psychotic patients.

Clinical Profiles: Lithium and Carbamazepine

Clinical Profile	Lithium	Carbamazepine	Lithium-Carbamazepine Combination
Mania	+ +	+ +	+ + +
Dysphoric	+	+	+ +
Rapid cycling	+	+ +	+ +
Continuous cycling	+	+	+ +
Negative family history	+	+ +	+ + +
Depression	+	+	+ + +
Prophylaxis of mania and depression	+ +	+ +	+ + +

+ = effective; + + = very effective; + + + = possible synergism.

In treating or preventing mania, start carbamazepine at 200 mg bid.

- Increase dose by 200 mg/day until the patient
  √ Improves sufficiently and
  √ Is free of significant side effects.
    □ If dose raised too quickly, common side effects are nausea, vomiting, ataxia, drowsiness, dizziness, diplopia, and clumsiness.
    □ If side effects occur, lower carbamazepine dose and later raise it more slowly.
- Serum levels should not determine dosage.
  √ Draw blood levels no sooner than 5 days of a changed dose.

If lithium fails with acute mania, can add or substitute carbamazepine.

- The chief problem is triggering acute confusion.
  √ Repeat mental status testing.
  √ If possible, lower neuroleptic doses and stop ACAs.
- On lithium and carbamazepine, some patients improve whereas others worsen.
- Once carbamazepine stabilized, can taper off lithium.
- The elderly are safer on carbamazepine without lithium.

Valproic acid effectively treats mania.

- Positive results seen in patients who are
  √ Lithium non-responders or intolerant
  √ Rapid-cyclers
  √ Nonparoxysmal EEG abnormalities
  √ (To a lesser extent) h/o closed head injury antedating onset of illness
- Synergistic effect with lithium, and thus it seems safe to combine lithium with valproic acid.
- 54–71% of manic patients improve when valproic acid added to other treatments.
- Valproic acid's efficacy is greater for mania than for depression.
- Patients improve at 4–14 days after obtaining a therapeutic plasma level.
- Dose
  √ Start at 250 mg with meal.
  √ Slowly increase dose (250 mg q4d) to tolerate nausea, vomiting, and sedation.
  √ Give tid doses.
  √ Go to effective dose usually around 1800 mg/day.

Clonazepam may reduce mania, but this might only be sedation.

ANTICONVULSANTS

Depression

Carbamazepine definitely relieves a few depressed patients.

- Carbamazepine should only be used as a last resort for depression.
- Typical dose is 1000 mg/day.
- Takes at least 2–4 weeks to reduce depression.
  - √ Carbamazepine may induce depression in borderline personality disorder.

Valproic acid's antidepressant effect is questionable.

Clonazepam may treat depression.

- 84% improvement in 25 patients with major or bipolar depressions, but others doubt its efficacy, stress its addictive potential, and believe it causes depression.
  - √ May diminish agitation in depression.
  - √ Rapid onset of activity.
- Dose: 1.5–6 mg/day.

Aggression

Because aggression stems from many sources, no single agent is clearly indicated. Acute aggression differs from chronic aggression, and each requires its own treatment.

Acute aggression is medically managed by either

- Haloperidol
  - √ Initially, 1–2 mg po or 1 mg IM, q1h until control,
    - □ Half this dose in the elderly.
  - √ Then haloperidol 2–4 mg or 1 mg IM, q8h.
  - √ Do not use haloperidol for aggression for > 6 weeks.
- Lorazepam
  - √ Initially, 1–2 mg po or IM, q1h until calm,
    - □ If IV dose must be given, push slowly, and insure not to inject more than 2 mg IV to prevent respiratory depression and laryngospasm.
    - □ May repeat in ½ hour.
  - √ Maintain dose in nonagitated person at 2 mg po or IM tid.
  - √ Taper at 10% a day from the highest dose to avoid withdrawal.
  - √ Do not treat aggression with lorazepam for over 6 weeks.

Chronic aggression, the more common problem, may only diminish *after* a therapeutic dose level exists for 4–8 weeks.

- Should inform patient about this time lag.

- Drug management includes
  - √ Propranolol, detailed in anti-anxiety chapter, lowers organically-based violence in patients with
    - □ Alzheimer's disease
    - □ Huntington's disease
    - □ Schizophrenia with agitation or aggression unrelated to psychotic ideas
    - □ Stroke
  - √ Anticonvulsants, especially carbamazepine, treat violence related to temporal lobe epilepsy and to other organic ailments.
  - √ Lithium reduces manic-associated violence.
  - √ Avoid antipsychotics because aggression is often a chronic problem, and patients risk TD, hypotension, and oversedation. Neuroleptics' only role is to alleviate aggression clearly associated with psychosis.
  - √ Avoid anti-anxiety benzodiazepines, since they rarely halt chronic violence and may trigger paradoxical rage attacks.
  - √ Buspirone has the advantage over other anti-anxiety agents in being nonsedative and nonaddicting.

Psychotropic Drug Treatment of Chronic Aggression

Generic Groups	Indications	Appropriate Dose	Special Clinical Considerations
Anti-Anxiety Agents	Acute relief of violence or agitation from hypno-sedative effects.	Standard doses	Risks paradoxical rage attacks, oversedation, tolerance, and addiction.
Buspirone	Aggression and anxiety.	10–20 mg tid	Takes 4–6 weeks to work.
Carbamaz-epine	Aggression from complex partial seizures and other organic brain disorders.	1200–1600 mg/day in divided doses (serum levels at 6–12 µg/ml)	Monitor for bone-marrow suppression or blood abnormalities. Physician ratings higher than patient ratings.
Lithium	Aggression and irritability related to manic excitement. Uncontrolled rage attacks triggered by "nothing" or by minor stimuli. Lithium's efficacy is low, but danger of rage merits lithium's consideration. Lithium might block outbursts from schizophrenic patients without reducing psychosis.	300 mg tid (serum levels at 0.6–1.2 mEq./l)	Effective for violence in prisoners and mentally retarded.

(Side vertical text: ANTICONVULSANTS)

Generic Groups	Indications	Appropriate Dose	Special Clinical Considerations
	May diminish hostile outbursts from organic patients. Does not abate premeditated violence.		
Nadolol	Diminished assaultiveness in 5/6 chronic paranoid schizophrenics.	80–160 mg/day; mean was 96 mg/day	Few reports.
Neuroleptics	Aggression related to psychotic ideation.	Standard doses for schizophrenia	Oversedation and multiple side effects, such as TD, when used chronically.
	Prompt relief of violence or aggression from sedative effects.		
Propranolol	Recurrent or chronic aggression or irritability in patients with organic brain disorders or in psychotic patients whose aggression is unrelated to psychotic thought.	200–800 mg/day in divided doses; range is 40–1440 mg/day. Start at 20 mg tid; raise by 60 mg/day q 3 days until therapeutic effect or 800 mg/day.	Onset may take 4–8 weeks.

SIDE EFFECTS

General

Side effects discussed here are for carbamazepine and valproic acid. Clonzepam's side effects are outlined in the anti-anxiety chapter.

Side effects can be minimized by

- Gradually building up dose
- Using more frequent smaller doses

So far, side effects appear similar when anticonvulsants are used for

- Psychiatric and neurologic disorders
- Adults and children

Since carbamazepine and valproic acid are often alternatives, or additions, to lithium, first compare their major side effects.

Side Effects: Lithium, Carbamazepine, Valproic Acid

Clinical Profile	Lithium	Carbamazepine	Valproic Acid
Cardiovascular effects			
Hypotension	–	+	–
Fainting	+	+	–
Dizziness	+	+	(+)
Hypertension aggravated	–	+	–
Congestive heart failure	–	+	–

Clinical Profile	Lithium	Carbamazepine	Valproic Acid
Gastrointestinal effects			
Increased appetite	+	−	(+)
Anorexia	(+)	+	−
Hypersalivation	(+)	−	(+)
Dry mouth	+	+	−
Thirst	+	+	−
Nausea, vomiting	+	+	+
Abdominal cramps	+	+	+
Diarrhea	+	+	(+)
Constipation	−	+	(+)
Hepatitis	−	+	+
Jaundice	−	+	+
Edema	+	−	(+)
Weight gain	+	−	+
Weight loss	(+)	+	−
Pancreatitis	−	+	+
Renal effects			
Polyuria, polydipsia	+	−	(+)
Urinary frequency	+	+	−
Acute urinary retention	−	(+)	−
Nephrogenic diabetes insipi-dus	+	−	−
Interstitial nephritis	+	−	−
Endocrine and sexual effects			
Hypothyroidism	+	−	−
Goiter	+	−	−
Hyponatremia, water intoxi-cation	−	(+)	−
Parathyroidism	(+)	−	−
Amenorrhea	+	−	(+)
Impotence	+	+	−
Hematologic effects			
Leukopenia	−	+	(+)
Leucocytosis	+	−	−
Eosinophilia	(+)	+	(+)
Agranulocytosis	−	+	+
Anemia	−	+	(+)
Thrombocytopenia	−	+	+
Bruising	−	+	+
Petechiae	−	+	+
Eyes, ears, nose, and throat			
Blurred vision	+	+	−
Nystagmus	−	−	(+)
Diplopia	−	+	(+)
"Spots before eyes"	−	−	(+)
Vertigo	+	−	−
Hyperacusis	−	+	−
Tinnitus	−	(+)	−
Skin, allergies, and temperature			
Psoriasis	(+)	−	−
Pruritic rash (allergy)	+	+	+
Pruritus, generalized	(+)	+	+
Alopecia	+	(+)	+
Photosensitivity	−	+	+
Chills, fever	(+)	+	−
Central nervous system effects			
Parkinsonism (mild)	+	−	−
Cogwheeling	+	−	−
Weakness	+	−	+
Muscle or leg cramps	+	+	−
Rigidity	+	−	−

ANTICONVULSANTS

Clinical Profile	Lithium	Carbamazepine	Valproic Acid
Seizures	+	−	−
Jerking limbs	+	+	−
Peripheral neuritis	−	(+)	−
Headache	+	+	(+)
Paresthesias	−	(+)	(+)
Ataxia	+	+	(+)
Incoordination	+	+	(+)
Dysarthria	+	+	(+)
Tremor	+	(+)	(+)
Sedation	−	+	+
Confusion	+	+	(+)
Increased alertness	−	−	+
Memory impairment	+	−	−
Insomnia	+	−	−
Hypersomnia	+	−	−
Weird dreams	+	−	−
Anxiety	−	−	(+)
Restlessness	+	−	−
Depression	−	(+)	(+)
Hallucinations	−	+	−
Psychosis, acute	−	−	(+)

Codes: + present; − absent; (+) rare.

Carbamazepine Side Effects

Common Dose-Related Side Effects	Less Common Dose-Related Side Effects	Idiosyncratic Reactions
Dizziness	Tremor	Rash (including exfoliation)
Clumsiness	Memory impairment	
Ataxia	Confusion (especially in elderly and when combined with lithium or neuroleptics)	Lenticular opacities
Drowsiness		Hepatitis
Dysarthria		Blood dyscrasias (aplastic anemia, leukopenia, thrombocytopenia)
Diplopia	Cardiac conduction delay	
Nausea and vomiting	Inappropriate ADH secretion	
Reversible mild leukopenia		
Reversible mildly raised LFTs		

Cardiovascular Effects

Usually benign; carbamazepine only.

Dizziness from orthostatic hypotension

Decreased atrioventricular conduction times

- Carefully use carbamazepine in patients with heart block.

Gastrointestinal Effects

Dry mouth (see page 13)

Nausea, vomiting, anorexia, indigestion

- Usually transient, these GI symptoms usually occur on empty stomach.
- Valproic acid also affects 15–20% of patients.
- Management
  √ Move dosage up more slowly.
  √ Give valproic acid with meals.
  √ Divalproex sodium may cause this less than valproic acid.

Hepatitis, hepatotoxicity

Carbamazepine, and especially valproic acid (15–30%), temporarily raise LFTs slightly during first 3 months of therapy.

- Valproic acid may induce hyperammonemia, often with confusion and lethargy.
- Treat LFT elevations with diminished doses.
- High LFTs do not predict liver disease.

Carbamazepine causes a rare, occasionally fatal, hypersensitivity reaction with fever and rash during the first month.

Valproic acid generates potentially fatal hepatotoxicity, especially in patients

- Under 2 years old,
- Taking other anticonvulsants, and
- Having severe neurological disease, mental retardation, or inborn error of metabolism.

This hepatotoxicity preceded by malaise, weakness, lethargy, anorexia, vomiting, and seizures.

- Valproic acid contraindicated in patients with liver disease.

Weight gain, increased appetite from valproic acid, but not carbamazepine.

Constipation (see page 14)

Renal Effects

Few effects, and mainly with carbamazepine.

Endocrine and Sexual Effects

Water intoxication occurs with hyponatremia and confusion for patients on carbamazepine.

Hematologic Effects

Leukopenia

- Carbamazepine may lower WBC by as much as 25% initially, but this decrease is usually transitory and without adverse effects.
- In 2% of patients carbamazepine induces a persistent leukopenia (<3000 WBC/mm^3) or a *thrombocytopenia.* Valproic acid rarely produces thrombocytopenia in high doses.
- If during carbamazepine therapy WBC count drops to 4000 mm^3
  √ Obtain another WBC count in 2 weeks.
  √ If WBC count does not return to normal in 2 weeks, reduce carbamazepine.
- Consider stopping carbamazepine immediately with any of these symptoms
  √ WBC count below 3000/mm^3
  √ Neutrophil count below 1500
  √ LFTs increased three-fold
  √ Fever
  √ Infection, sore throat
  √ Petechiae, bruising
  √ Weakness
  √ Pallor

Aplastic anemia

- Severe, potentially fatal.
- Carbamazepine produces aplastic anemia in < 0.002% of patients.

Mild anemia happens in <5% of patients.

Bone marrow suppression afflicts 3% of carbamazepine users.
May also see

- *Agranulocytosis* (rare and severe)
- *Pancytopenia*
- *Eosinophilia*
- *Purpura*

Petechiae, bruising, hemorrhage, nose bleeds, and *anemia* occur occasionally on valproic acid.

Eyes, Ears, Nose, and Throat

Blurred vision (see page 16)

Nasal congestion

Skin, Allergies, and Temperature

Rash

- Allergic rash is common carbamazepine side effect.
- Seen in 3–15% of psychiatric patients.
  - √ Usually arises between 9 and 23 days after carbamazepine begun.
  - √ Stop carbamazepine if there develops
    - □ *Exfoliative reaction*
    - □ *Urticaria*
    - □ *Stevens-Johnson syndrome* (acute inflammatory skin disorder with "iris" target lesions).
- Management
  - √ Avoid sunlight.
  - √ Treat minor rashes with antihistamines.

Alopecia stems from valproic acid more than from carbamazepine.

Fever, chills, sweating, lymphadenopathy, muscle cramps, and *joint aches* may arise from carbamazepine.

Pulmonary hypersensitivity arises from carbamazepine with symptoms of hay fever, dyspnea, pneumonitis, or pneumonia.

Central Nervous System Effects

Drowsiness, sedation

- Sedation appears dose related.
- Management
  - √ Gradually increase doses from beginning.
    - □ Start carbamazepine dose as low as 100 mg/day.
    - □ Then increase 100 mg every 3 days up to 400 mg/day.
    - □ If patient accommodates to sedation at 400 mg/day, dosages can be increased 200 mg every 3 days.
    - □ Can minimize sedation by administering greater proportion of carbamazepine at bedtime.
- Valproic acid is less sedating than carbamazepine, but it can cause substantial *lethargy.*

Tremor is common valproic acid side effect.

- Reduce dose.

ANTICONVULSANTS

Confusion from carbamazepine

* May be secondary to
  √ Being on lithium and neuroleptics,
  √ Older age,
  √ Organic brain disease,
  √ *Hyponatremia,* and
  √ On rare occasions, *water intoxication.*

Severe skin reactions suggest impending blood dyscrasia.

PERCENTAGES OF SIDE EFFECTS

Side Effects	Carbamazepine	Valproic Acid
CARDIOVASCULAR EFFECTS		
Dizziness, lightheadedness	11.4 (5.9–40)	0.0
Fainting, syncope	< 1	—
Palpitations	< 1	—
Bradycardia	< 1	—
Chest pain	< 1	—
GASTROINTESTINAL EFFECTS		
Anorexia, lower appetite	—	13 (1–20)
Nausea, vomiting	> 5	13 (1–20)
Dyspepsia, upset stomach	—	5.5
Diarrhea	3	3
Constipation	—	< 1
Hepatitis	< 0.001	0.00665 (< 0.010–0.00333)
Salivation	—	3.5
Mouth sores	5.5	—
Weight gain	0.0	< 1
Weight loss	—	< 1
Edema	0.0	< 1
ENDOCRINE AND SEXUAL EFFECTS		
Menstrual changes	—	20
HEMATOLOGIC EFFECTS		
Aplastic anemia	0.00103 (0.0005–0.0020)	< 1
Anemia (mild)	5	< 1
Agranulocytosis	0.0017 (0.0001–0.0048)	< 1

Side Effects	Carbamazepine	Valproic Acid
Blood dyscrasias (all types)	3	—
Bone marrow suppression	3	< 1
Leukopenia (transient)	11 (10–12.7)	< 1
Leukopenia (permanent)	2.5 (2–3.2)	0.0
Petechia	—	5.5
Bruising easily	5.5	5.5
Thrombocytopenia	2	< 1
EYES, EARS, NOSE, AND THROAT EFFECTS		
Blurred vision	12.5 (> 5–30)	< 1
Double vision	—	< 1
Nystagmus	—	< 1
Sore throat/flu	5.5	—
SKIN, ALLERGIES, AND TEMPERATURE		
Rashes	6.6 (1–15)	5.5
Abnormal skin pigment	5.5	0.0
Hair loss	0.0	5.5
CENTRAL NERVOUS SYSTEM EFFECTS		
Weakness, fatigue	5.5	5.5
Body jerks	< 1	—
Numbness	< 1	—
Headache	5.5	5.5
Ataxia, incoordination	26.8 (10.4–≤ 50)	1.5
Slurred speech	5.3	—
Tremor	0.0	< 1
Drowsiness, sedation	35.4 (10–50)	5.5
Confusion, disorientation	5.5	—
Hallucinations	5.5	—
Depression	5.5	5.5
Switch into mania	11.8	—
Excitement, hyperactive	—	11

A
N
T
I
C
O
N
V
U
L
S
A
N
T
S

PREGNANCY AND LACTATION

Teratogenicity (1st trimester)
- Anticonvulsants have an overall 4–5% teratogenic rate when taken during the first trimester.

- Among carbamazepine's teratogenic population, 20% had developmental delay, 26% had fingernail hypoplasia, and 11% had craniofacial defects.

- Valproic acid produces a few malformations akin to the fetal hydantoin syndrome—e.g., lumbosacral meningocele, microcephaly, prolonged clotting abnormalities, cleft lip, prenatal growth deficiency.

- Valproic acid causes a 1–2% chance of neural tube defects, such as spina bifida.

- If a woman taking antiepileptics becomes pregnant, stopping the anticonvulsants risks status epilepticus and the child's life; whether to remove antiepileptics depends on the nature of the seizure, the mother's condition, etc.

- Only add anticonvulsants during pregnancy if absolutely necessary.

- During first trimester, it is best to avoid lithium; if a mood stabilizer is needed, carbamazepine might be safer to control mania.

Direct Effect on Newborn (3rd trimester)

- During second and third trimesters, lithium and carbamazepine seem equally safe.

- Valproic acid known to cause hepatotoxicity when serum levels exceed 60 μg/ml; keep serum concentrations < 60 μg/ml.

Lactation

- Carbamazepine present in milk at about 60% of maternal plasma concentration.

- Valproic acid excreted in small amounts into breast milk.

- Clonazepam enters breast milk. Although it does not accumulate, its long half-life may produce apnea. Infants exposed *in utero* or during breast feeding should have clonazepam serum levels monitored and CNS depression observed.

Drug Dosage in Mother's Milk

Generic Names	Milk/ Plasma Ratio	Time of Peak Concentration in Milk (hours)	Infant Dose (mg/kg/day)	Maternal Dose (%)	Safety Rating*
Carbamazepine	0.36	?	0.38	2.8	C
Clonazepam	?	?	2 μg†	1.3–3.0‡	C
Valproic acid	0.01–0.07	?	0.27**	1.8	B

* B: Reasonably unsafe before 34 weeks, but safer after 34 weeks; C: Reasonably unsafe before week 44, but safer after 44 weeks; † Infant therapeutic dose 20–200 μg/kg/day; ‡ Maternal dose not specified, but assumed to be 20–200 μg/kg/day; ** Therapeutic dose for neonates 20–40 mg/kg/day.

DRUG-DRUG INTERACTIONS

Drug-Drug Interactions

Drugs (X) Interact with:	Carbamazepine (C)	Comments
Antipsychotics	X↓ C↓	Decreased neuroleptic and carbamazepine effects. See haloperidol.
Barbiturates	C↓	Phenobarbital can lower serum carbamazepine in 5 days, but without causing major clinical effects. Other barbiturates probably act similarly.
Birth control pills	X↓	Diminished oral contraceptives.
*Cimetidine	C↑	Increases carbamazepine by 30% to produce toxicity in 2 days. Chronically taking both drugs poses no particular risk. When cimetidine stopped, carbamazepine toxicity dissipates in about one week. Ranitidine can substitute for cimetidine.
Clonazepam	X↓	Diminishes clonazepam level.
*Corticosteroids	X↓	Carbamazepine may chronically reduce actions of most steroids. May need to increase steroid dose.
*Danazol	C↑	Danazol greatly raises carbamazepine levels, at times to toxicity. Other androgen derivatives (e.g., methyltestosterone) may act similarly. If used together, closely monitor carbamazepine level and adjust dose of one or both drugs.
*Diltiazem	C↑	On adding diltiazem toxicity may occur in 1–4 days. Halting diltiazem can ignite seizures because carbamazepine declines. Nifedipine, which does not affect carbamazepine clearance, is a safer calcium channel blocker.
Diuretics	X↓	Symptomatic hyponatremia. May need periodic electrolytes.
*Doxycycline	X↓	Carbamazepine may reduce doxycycline's level; it may occur with other tetracyclines.

ANTICONVULSANTS

Drugs (X) Interact with:	Carbamazepine (C)	Comments
†Erythromycin	C ↑	May double or triple carbamazepine levels in one day. After erythromycin stopped, it may subside in 2–3 days. Do not combine, but if must, use lower doses.
Ethosuximide	X ↓	Diminished ethosuximide.
*Haloperidol	X ↓	Carbamazepine curtails haloperidol by 50–60%, which may, or may not, induce symptoms in 24 hours (in rapid-cyclers) to 3 weeks. Serum levels of both drugs may be normal or low. Monitor serum levels of both drugs closely.
†Isoniazid (INH)	C ↑	Carbamazepine may increase to toxicity usually in 1–2 days of INH; frequently happens on INH doses > 200 mg/day. Symptoms stop 2 days after INH is halted. INH often reduces therapeutic dose of carbamazepine. When isoniazid is reduced or stopped, serum carbamazepine decreases.
*Lithium	L ↑	On normal lithium, carbamazepine may induce lithium toxicity. Neurotoxicity vanishes after stopping one agent for a few days. Other patients improve on the combination.
*Mebendazole	X ↓	On high mebendazole doses, carbamazepine may impair mebendazole's therapeutic effect. No special precautions needed. Valproic acid may be safer than carbamazepine.
*Methadone	X ↓	Carbamazepine may lower serum methadone and increase withdrawal symptoms. Patients may need more methadone or should be switched to valproic acid.
Phenytoin	X ↑↓ C ↓	Monitor serum levels.
*Primidone	X ↓ C ↑↓	Monitor levels of both drugs and phenobarbital.
*Propoxyphene	C ↑	Consistently raises carbamazepine, at times to toxicity.
Propranolol	X ↓	Theoretically, carbamazepine could speed metabolism of propranolol and other β blockers.
*Tetracyclines	X ↓	See doxycycline.
Theophylline	X ↓	Decreased theophylline.
*Thyroid hormone	X ↓	Accelerates thyroid hormone's elimination and may induce hypothyroidism. Add thyroid.
TCAs	T ↓ C ↓	Carbamazepine may lower imipramine actions, and probably other TCAs. Monitor serum levels. Increase TCA doses.
Troleandomycin	C ↑	Troleandomycin may increase carbamazepine level to toxicity. Measure plasma carbamazepine.
Valproic acid	X ↓	Diminished valproic acid.
*Verapamil	C ↑	On adding verapamil toxicity may occur in 1–4 days. Halting verapamil can ignite seizures because carbamazepine declines. Nifedipine may be safer.
*Warfarin	X ↓	Impaired hypoprothrombinemic response in several days to a week. Adjust anticoagulants when carbamazepine changed.

Drugs (X) Interact with:	Valproic Acid (V)	Comments
Benzodiazepines	X ↑	Valproic acid may elevate diazepam; with clonazepam, valproic acid may cause absence seizures; importance unclear.
Carbamazepine	V ↓	Decreased valproic acid.
*Phenobarbital	X ↑	Increases serum phenobarbital; may prompt toxicity. Cut phenobarbital dose by 30–75%. Monitor for decreased valproic acid.
*Phenytoin	X ↑↓ V ↓	Valproic acid initially lowers serum phenytoin by 30%, but in several weeks phenytoin may exceed pre-valproic acid levels with ataxia, nystagmus, mental impairment, involuntary muscular movements, and seizures. Do not increase phenytoin unless seizures occur. Phenytoin may decrease serum valproic acid, but clinical importance remains unclear.
*Primidone	X ↑	Valproic acid raises serum phenobarbital, which primidone substantially produces. Valproic acid inhibits phenobarbital metabolism, increases the risk of phenobarbital intoxication.
*Salicylates	X ↑ V ↑	Salicylate may increase unbound serum valproic acid concentrations to prompt valproic acid toxicity. Symptoms resolve when salicylate is stopped. Bleeding time is prolonged; may yield bleeding, bruising, and petechiae.

Codes: * Moderately important interaction; † Extremely important interaction; ↑ Increases; ↓ Decreases; ↑↓ Increases or decreases.

EFFECTS ON LABORATORY TESTS

Generic Names	Blood/Serum Tests	Results	Urine Tests	Results
Carbamazepine	BUN	↑	Albuminuria	↑
	Thyroid function	↓	Glycosuria	↑
	LFT	↑		
	RBC, WBC, platelets	↓↓↓		
	Sodium	↓		
Clonazepam	LFT	↑	None	
Valproic acid	LFT	↑	Ketone	False ↑
	WBC	↓		
	Thyroid function	↓		

Codes: ↑ Increases; ↓ Decreases; LFT tests are SGOT, SGPT, alkaline phosphatase, LDH, and bilirubin.

WITHDRAWAL

In nonepileptics carbamazepine and valproic acid do not produce

- Psychic dependence
- Tolerance
- Addiction

When suddenly withdrawing a psychiatric patient from carbamazepine or valproic acid, no symptoms emerge. Yet it is safest to withdraw them by 10% qod.

Clonazepam, a benzodiazepine, readily causes withdrawal.

- Hard to get patients off it.
- Withdrawal over months (see pages 232–36).

OVERDOSE: TOXICITY, SUICIDE, AND TREATMENT

Carbamazepine

Acute carbamazepine overdoses produce

- Difficulties in 1–3 days
- In lower doses, AV block is common; cardiac monitoring is useful.
- In higher overdoses, respiratory depression, stupor, and coma are more frequent.

Other problems include

- Nausea, vomiting, dry mouth, diarrhea, constipation, glossitis, stomach pain
- Agitation, restlessness, irritability
- Irregular breathing
- Vertigo
- Mydriasis, nystagmus, blurred vision, transient diplopia
- Anuria, oliguria, urinary retention
- Inability to perform rapidly alternating movements
- Hypotension, dizziness, hypertension, tachycardia
- Flushing, cyanosis
- Tremor, twitching, involuntary movements, opisthotonos, athetoid movements, ataxia
- Visual hallucinations
- Speech disturbances
- Hypoactive or hyperactive reflexes
- Seizures (especially in children)

The general management of carbamazepine overdoses is supportive. (see page 37)

- Dialysis is useless.
- Hemoperfusion of questionable help.

- Treat seizures with diazepam or barbiturate, but beware of aggravating respiratory depression.

Valproic Acid

Valproic acid causes little toxicity

- Most serious action is hepatotoxicity in children under 2 years old. (see page 163)

Other symptoms include

- Anorexia, nervosa, and vomiting.
- Somnolence, ataxia, and tremor. All respond to reduced dose.
- Rash, alopecia, stimulated appetite.
- Coma.

Management

- Supportive therapy. (see page 37)
- Because valproic acid is rapidly absorbed, gastric lavage of little value; divalproex sodium delayed-release tablets are absorbed more slowly, gastric lavage or emesis may help if started early enough.
- Hemodialysis and hemoperfusion have reduced valproic acid levels.
- Naloxone may reverse a coma, but it may trigger a seizure.

Toxicity and Suicide Data

Generic Names	Toxicity Doses Average (Largest) (g)*	Mortality Doses Average (Lowest) (g)	Toxic Levels Average (Largest) (µg/ml)	Lethal Levels (mg/l)
Carbamazepine	(> 30)	(> 60)	> 14	—
Clonazepam	0.10 0.060	—	> 80 (ng/ml)	—
Valproic acid	—	—	> 100 (2000)	1970

* Largest surviving dose in child was 10 grams (6-year-old boy); largest surviving dose in small child was 5 grams (3-year-old girl).

PRECAUTIONS

Carbamazepine levels vary since its hepatic metabolism changes between the third and eighth week on the same dose.

Thus, perform carbamazepine determinations

- Twice-weekly for first month
- Weekly for second month
- Every other week for third month
- Monthly thereafter

Avoid anticonvulsants in patients with

- Cardiovascular disease
- Bone marrow depression, leukopenia, thrombocytopenia
- Hepatic disease, especially if taking valproic acid or drinking excessive alcohol
- Hypersensitivity to drug
- Carbamazepine's manufacturer advises stopping MAOIs 14 days before starting carbamazepine, but the reason is theoretical, not practical.

Because of carbamazepine's moderate anticholinergic properties, watch for

- Intraocular pressure or
- Urinary retention.

NURSES' DATA

Insure patients on carbamazepine and valproic acid are aware of early toxicity, especially

- GI distress
- Liver disease
- Hematologic reactions, bleeding, weakness, fever, sore throat
- Rashes (may signal incipient blood dyscrasias)
- Renal impairment, urinary retention
- CNS depression, sedation
- Neurotoxicity (even on normal carbamazepine levels)

Because of valproic acid's hepatotoxicity, patients should inform doctors if they are using, or about to use

- Anticonvulsants
  - √ Phenobarbital
  - √ Phenytoin
  - √ Ethosuximide
- Alcohol, or
- Aspirin

PATIENT AND FAMILY NOTES

Note that with

- Depakene
  - √ If capsules chewed, they irritate the mouth and throat.
  - √ Swallow capsules whole.
  - √ Further reduce GI irritation by taking capsules and syrup with food or by slowly raising the dose.
- Divalproex (Depakote)
  - √ Sprinkle capsules may be swallowed whole.
  - √ They may also be opened carefully and sprinkled on a small teaspoon of soft food, such as applesauce or pudding. The drug-food mixture should be eaten immediately (avoid chewing) and *not* stored for future use.

When starting an anticonvulsant, patients should carefully drive cars, work around machines, and cross streets. When first on anticonvulsants, drive briefly in a safe place, since reflexes might be a tad off.

Patients may be mildly to considerably disorganized until the proper dose is found. Carbamazepine's metabolism may require 3–8 weeks to stabilize, prompting unexpected side effects on the same dose.

If on valproic acid, avoid aspirin unless approved by physician.

- Bleeding, bruises, and petechiae may arise.

Avoid during pregnancy, but at the first sign of being pregnant

- Do *not* stop drug,
- Consult with doctor.

Take anticonvulsants with meals.

- Food slightly delays absorption of valproic acid, but does not change its bioavailability.

Place anticonvulsants away from bedside or from any readily accessible area, where they might be taken by "accident." Keep safely away from hungry children.

Have a Medic Alert wallet-card or bracelet signifying anticonvulsant use. Also indicate that the patient is taking the agent for a psychiatric, not an epileptic, disorder.

Take anticonvulsants when doctor prescribes them.

- If forget dose, can consume in 2 hours.
- Otherwise wait for next regular dose and
- Do not double dose.

Do not suddenly stop anticonvulsants without talking to a physician.

COST INDEX

Generic Names	Brand Names	Equivalent Dosage (mg)	Dose Assessed (mg)	Cost Rating*
Carbamazepine	Tegretol	200	200	146
	generics	200	200	> 60
Clonazepam	Klonopin	0.5	0.5	98
Divalproex	Depakote	250	250	173
Valproic acid	Depakene	250	250	173
	generic			> 114

* The higher the number, the higher the cost.

7. Anti-Anxiety Agents

INTRODUCTION

Anti-anxiety agents (i.e., sedatives) and hypnotics share many characteristics and are known collectively as "hypnosedatives." Yet because anti-anxiety medications primarily treat daytime tension whereas hypnotics relieve insomnia, they are discussed separately.

This chapter presents

- Benzodiazepines
- Buspirone
- Clomipramine
- Clonidine
- Propranolol

Barbiturates are presented in the next chapter.

Medications examined in this chapter assist

- Agoraphobia (see page 190)
- Anticipatory anxiety (see pages 185–86)
- Generalized anxiety disorder (see page 187)
- Obsessive-compulsive disorder (see pages 191–92)
- Panic disorders (see page 188–90)
- Post-traumatic stress disorder (see page 192)
- School phobia (see page 191)
- Separation anxiety (see page 191)
- Social phobia (see pages 190–91)
- Tobacco abuse (see pages 192–93)

Anti-anxiety agents for disorders explored in other chapters include

- Aggression (Anticonvulsants, pages 158–60)
- Akathisia and dystonia (Antipsychotics, pages 18–20, 46)
- Alcohol and anti-anxiety withdrawal (Hypnotics, pages 232–37)

ANTI ANXIETY AGENTS

177

- Delirium (Antipsychotics, page 11)
- Dementia (Antipsychotics, pages 11–12)
- Depression (Antidepressants, pages 68–69)
- Mania (Lithium, page 132)
- Schizophrenia (Antipsychotics, page 11)

NAMES, CLASSES, MANUFACTURERS, DOSE FORMS, AND COLORS

Generic Names	Brand Names	Manu-facturers	Dose Forms (mg)*	Colors
		BENZODIAZEPINES		
Alprazolam	Xanax	Upjohn	t: 0.25/0.5/1/2	t: white (oval)/ peach/blue/ white (oblong)
Chlordiaze-poxide	Librium	Roche	c:5/10/25; p: 20 mg/ml	c: green-yellow/ green-black/ green-white
Clonazepam	Klonopin†	Roche	t: 0.5/1/2	t: orange/blue/ blue
Clorazepate	Tranxene	Abbott	t: 3.75/7.5/15;	t: blue/peach/ lavender;
	Tranxene-SD		t: 11.25/22.5	t: blue/tan
Diazepam	Valium	Roche	t: 2/5/10; p: 5 mg/ml	t: white/yellow/ blue
Lorazepam	Ativan	Wyeth-Ayerst	t: 0.5/1/2; p: 2/4 mg/ml	t: all white
Oxazepam	Serax	Wyeth-Ayerst	t: 15; c: 10/15/30	t: yellow; c: white/pink/ white-red/ white-maroon
Prazepam	Centrax	Parke-Davis	t: 10; c: 5/10/20	t: light blue; c: celery/aqua/ yellow
Azaspirodecanedione				
Buspirone	BuSpar	Mead Johnson	t: 5/10	t: all white
β Blocker				
Propranolol	Inderal	Wyeth-Ayerst	t: 10/20/40/ 60/80	t: orange/blue green/pink/ yellow
Tricyclic Antidepressant				
Clomipramine	Anafranil	CIBA	c: 25/50/75	c: ivory-melon-yellow/ivory-aqua-blue/ ivory-yellow
Miscellaneous				
Clonidine	Catapres	Boehringer Ingelheim	t: 0.1/0.2/0.3	t: tan/orange/ peach

Generic Names	Brand Names	Manu-facturers	Dose Forms (mg)*	Colors
Hydroxyzine	Atarax	Roerig	t: 10/25/50/100; s: 10 mg/5 ml	t: orange/green/yellow/red
	Vistaril	Pfizer	c: 25/50/100; su: 25 mg/5 ml	c: green/green-white/green-gray
Meprobamate	Equinil	Wyeth-Ayerst	t: 200/400	t: all white
	Miltown	Wallace	t: 200/400/600	t: all white

* c = capsules, p = parenteral; s = syrup, SD = single dose, su = suspension, t = tablets.
† Was called Clonopin.

PHARMACOLOGY

Benzodiazepines mediate the actions of GABA, the brain's major inhibitory neurotransmitter.

- GABA inhibits the firing of neurons by opening the chloride channels on the neuronal membrane.
- This causes a hyperpolarization that requires a greater depolarization to trigger an action potential.

Benzodiazepines of 3 chemical types

- 2-keto compounds
    √ Are prodrugs, which means they are inactive themselves, but have active metabolites (e.g., desmethyldiazepam).
    √ Are slowly oxidized in the liver and
    √ Have relatively long half-lives.
- 3-hydroxy compounds
    √ Are active compounds,
    √ Have short half-lives,
    √ Are metabolized rapidly via direct conjugation to a glucuronide radical, and
    √ Do not generate active metabolites.
- Triazolo compounds
    √ Are active,
    √ Have active metabolites,
    √ Have short half-lives, and
    √ Are oxidized.

Any agent that interferes with liver enzymes (e.g., cimetidine) can block the metabolism of 2-keto and triazolo compounds.

ANTIANXIETY AGENTS

Half-lives

- The longer the anti-anxiety agent's half-life, the more it affects daytime functioning (e.g., hangover).
- The shorter the half-life, the greater its withdrawal and anxiety between doses (rebound), and the greater its anterograde amnesia.
- For the elderly, shorter half-lives are safer than longer half-lives.

Lipophilic and hydrophilic properties

- More lipophilic drugs (e.g., diazepam)
  √ Enter the brain rapidly,
  √ Ignite effects promptly,
  √ Extinguish effects quickly, and
  √ Vanish into body fat.
- Less lipophilic drugs (e.g., lorazepam)
  √ Produce clinical effects more slowly, but
  √ Provide more sustained relief.
- Highly lipophilic drugs with longer half-lives (e.g., diazepam) give faster relief for shorter periods than would be expected by their half-life alone. On the other hand, the less lipophilic lorazepam has a shorter half-life, but sustains a longer action.

Potency

- High-potency benzodiazepines (e.g., alprazolam) with a relatively high receptor affinity have more withdrawal symptoms than would be expected by just half-life alone.

Duration of effects

- With acute doses, rates of absorption and distribution half-life are critical.
- With repeated doses, distribution is complete; the elimination half-life, which determines the drug's steady state levels, becomes critical.

Pharmacology of Oral Anti-Anxiety Agents

Generic Names	Speed of Onset (Peak Plasma Levels in Hours)	Speed of Distribution	Active Metabolites (Half-life, Hours)	Mean Elimination Half-life (Hours)*
2-Keto- Clorazepate	Rapid (1–2)	Rapid	Desmethyldiazepam (30–200), Oxazepam (3–21)	30–200
Chlordiazepoxide	Intermediate (0.5–4)	Slow	Desmethylchlor-diazepoxide (18), Demoxepam (14–95), Desmethyldiazepam (30–200), Oxazepam (3–21)	30–100
Diazepam	Rapid (0.5–2)	Rapid	Desmethyldiazepam (30–200), Oxazepam (3–21), 3-Hydroxydiazepam (5–20)	30–100
Prazepam	Slowest (2.5–6)	Intermediate	Desmethyldiazepam (30–200), Oxazepam (3–21)	30–100
3-Hydroxy- Clonazepam	Intermediate (1–2)	Intermediate	none	18–50

Pharmacology of Oral Anti-Anxiety Agents

Generic Names	Speed of Onset (Peak Plasma Levels in Hours)	Speed of Distribution	Active Metabolites (Half-life, Hours)	Mean Elimination Half-life (Hours)*
Lorazepam	Intermediate (1–6)	Intermediate	none	10–20
Oxazepam	Slow-Intermediate (1–4)	Intermediate	none	3–21
Triazolo- Alprazolam	Intermediate (1–2)	Intermediate	α-Hydroxy-alprazolam (6–10)	12–15
Other Buspirone	Rapid (0.6–15)	Rapid	1-Pyrimidinyl piperazine (6)	2–11
Clonidine	Rapid (3–5)	Slow-Intermediate	none	12–16
Hydroxyzine	Rapid (2–4)	Intermediate	none	< 4
Meprobamate	Rapid (1–3)	Intermediate	none	6–16
Propranolol	Rapid (2–4)	Intermediate	none significant	3–5

* Includes all active metabolites; longer in elderly; more important in chronic administration.

DOSES

General Anti-Anxiety Doses

Generic Names	Usual Dose for Anxiety (mg/day)	Dose Range for Anxiety (mg/day)	Therapeutic Plasma Level (µg/ml)	Geriatic Dose (mg/day)
Alprazolam	0.5–1.5	0.5–8	—	0.25–0.5
Buspirone	15–30	15–60	1–6†	15–30
Chlordiazepoxide	15–75	10–100	> 0.7	5–30
Clonazepam	1.5–10	0.25–20	5–70 ng/ml	0.5–5
Clonidine	0.2–0.6	0.1–2.0	500	0.2–0.4
Clorazepate	15–67½	7½–90	—	15–60
Diazepam	4–30	2–40	300–400 ng/ml	1–10
Hydroxyzine	200–400	100–600	—	10–50
Lorazepam	2–6	1–10	—	0.5–1.5
Meprobamate	400–1200	400–1600	5–20	200–600
Oxazepam	30–60	30–120	—	10–30
Prazepam	30–60	10–60	—	10–15
Propranolol	30–80	30–240	20 ng/ml	30–60

ANTI ANXIETY AGENTS

CLINICAL INDICATIONS AND USE

Anti-Anxiety Drug Indications

Generic Names	Anxiolytic	Panic Attacks	Obsessive-Compulsive Disorder	Hypnotic	Muscle Relaxant	Alcohol Withdrawal	Depression	EPS
Alprazolam	+	+	±	−	−	−	+	−
Buspirone	+	−	±	−	−	−	−	−
Chlordiazepoxide	+	−	−	+	−	+	−	−
Clomipramine	−	−	+	−	−	−	+	−
Clonazepam	±	+	±	−	−	−	−	±
Clonidine	±	+	−	±	−	−	+	−
Clorazepate	+	−	−	+	−	+	−	+
Diazepam	+	+	−	+	+	+	−	−
Hydroxyzine	+	−	−	+	+	−	−	+
Lorazepam	+	−	−	+	+	+	−	−
Meprobamate	+	−	−	+	+	−	−	−
Oxazepam	+	−	−	−	+	+	−	−
Prazepam	+	−	−	−	−	−	−	−
Propranolol	+	±	−	−	?	−	−	+

General Information

Benzodiazepines are potentially addictive, and therefore, should be

* Ideally aimed at anxiety from particular stressors.
* Time limited: 1–2 weeks.
* Chronically used for specific, identifiable, symptoms.

Benzodiazepine dependency may occur on

* 3–4 times the normal daily dose over several weeks or
* Smaller, therapeutic doses, over a month.

Avoid meprobamate and barbiturates because they

* Have a higher risk of addiction than benzodiazepines and
* Are more serious as overdoses.

Employ hydroxyzine for anxiety from physical conditions

* Pruritus due to allergic conditions, and for pre- and postoperative sedation.

Anticipatory Anxiety

General rule: treat patients with benzodiazepines if they have *exogenous* anticipatory anxiety, but not if they solely have *endogenous* anxiety from panic attacks.

Reduce short-term anticipatory anxiety with low doses of a short-acting benzodiazepine (e.g., alprazolam). If anxiety requires long-term medication, select a nonbenzodiazepine, which does not induce drug dependency (e.g., buspirone, propranolol).

Benzodiazepines

* For short-term treatment of anticipatory anxiety, best to prescribe benzodiazepines that are
  √ Short-acting
  √ Without active metabolites (e.g., oxazepam, lorazepam)
* In the elderly, generally employ 50% of the dose provided younger patients.

Propranolol

* Most useful against the "flight and fright" response—that is, the physical signs, of anxiety
  √ Palpitations
  √ Tachycardia
  √ GI upset

√ Tremors
√ Sweating
* Only mild improvement of psychological symptoms.
* Before using propranolol, examine patient for
  √ Cardiovascular problems
  √ Pulmonary difficulties
  √ Endocrine abnormalities
* Repeat these investigations while patient is on propranolol.
* Do not give propranolol to patients with h/o
  √ Bradyarrhythmias
  √ Asthma
  √ Congestive heart failure
* Start at 10 mg bid and increase to 80–160 mg/day.
  √ Most patients require small doses of propranolol (e.g., 10–20 mg tid-qid).
  √ Minimal doses minimally drop BP.
* Unlike benzodiazepines, propranolol does not dim consciousness, cause drowsiness, or produce drug dependency.

Clonidine

* May be useful, but has many side effects.
* For anticipatory anxiety, start at 0.1 mg bid.
  √ Increase by 0.1 mg every 1–2 days.
  √ Reach a final dose of 0.4–0.6 mg/day.

Neuroleptics

* Low neuroleptic doses (e.g., haloperidol 0.5 mg, chlorpromazine 25 mg, perphenazine 4 mg) tid quell anxiety.
  √ Neuroleptics do not generate drug dependency, but
  √ They may provoke EPS, especially akathisia which mimics anxiety.
* Thus, better to give benzodiazepines than neuroleptics.
* If neuroleptics used, prescribe more sedating neuroleptics, such as chlorpromazine or thioridazine, 25–50 mg qd-qid.

Antihistamines

* Sedating antihistamines reduce anxiety.
  √ Their anticholinergic effects may be dangerous to the elderly or the organically impaired.
* Nonaddicting
* Examples
  √ Hydroxyzine 10–50 mg qd-qid
  √ Diphenhydramine 10–25 mg bid-qid for daytime sedation

Generalized Anxiety Disorder (GAD)

Benzodiazepines

* Because short-acting, high-potency benzodiazepines (e.g., alprazolam) prompt more interdose rebound and dependency, long-acting, low-potency benzodiazepines (e.g., diazepam 15–30 mg/day) are preferred for GAD.

Buspirone

* Buspirone is a newer, nonbenzodiazepine, anti-anxiety agent that differs from benzodiazepines.

Buspirone	Areas	Benzodiazepines
No	Effect of single dose	Yes
2 Weeks	Full therapeutic effect	Days
No	Sedating	Yes
No	Impairs performance and motor coordination	Yes
No	Interacts with other hypnosedatives	Yes
No	Potentiates alcohol	Yes
No	Develops tolerance	Yes
No	Produces drug dependency	Yes
No	Suppresses hypnosedative withdrawal	Yes

Since buspirone does not cause drug dependency and since GAD is a long-term disorder, buspirone appears safer than benzodiazepines.

Unlike those taking benzodiazepines, patients ingesting buspirone rarely experience a "drug-calming" effect, and so they may think that buspirone is not working.

* Buspirone is *not* effective for prn anxiety.
  √ Initial effects occur in 1–2 weeks,
  √ Full effect often requires 4–6 weeks.
* Buspirone must be taken regularly.
* GAD patients improve most if free of benzodiazepines for one month.
* Buspirone does *not* prevent benzodiazepine withdrawal.
* Dose
  √ Start at 5 mg bid-tid for first week.
  √ Move dose up by 2½–5 mg every 2–4 days until achieving desired dose.
  √ Dose ranges from 15–30 mg/day, but may increase to 60 mg/day.

ANTI ANXIETY AGENTS

Panic Disorders

Three choices for treating panic disorders are

* TCAs
* MAOIs
* Benzodiazepines

Tricyclic Antidepressants

* TCAs are preferred for treating panic attacks.
  √ Unlike benzodiazepines, TCAs (and MAOIs) are not addicting.
  √ TCAs decrease panic attacks, but not the anxiety and phobias associated with panic attacks. Benzodiazepines help these latter symptoms.
* Patient does not need a depressed mood for TCAs (or MAOIs) to prevent panic attacks.
* Favored TCA is imipramine.
* Use same doses as in treating depression.
* Beneficial effect requires 1–6 weeks of TCA treatment.
* When patients with panic attacks are started on TCAs, they can initially experience "speediness," insomnia, or jitters. Therefore important to
  √ Start patient on a low dose of imipramine, around 10 mg.
  √ Increase dose by 10 mg qod.
  √ Perhaps add alprazolam ¼ mg when beginning imipramine and then gradually taper the alprazolam when the TCA works in 2–3 weeks.
  √ Counsel around this introductory period.
* Patient should initially remain on TCA (or MAOI) for at least 6 months.
  √ Taper drug only when patient is comfortable doing so.

Monoamine-oxidase Inhibitors

* MAOIs may be the drug of second choice (assuming patient follows diet).
* When depression is associated with panic attacks or severe anxiety, MAOIs may be more effective than TCAs.
* MAOIs require 4–6 weeks for improvement.
* All MAOIs thwart panic attacks, but
  √ Phenelzine is preferred, often up to 90 mg/day.
  √ May be the best drug for *severe* panic or phobic disorders.
* Phenelzine and tranylcypromine preferred over isocarboxazid, since the latter generates frequent hepatotoxicity.

Benzodiazepines

- Low-potency benzodiazepines induce too much sedation, and so high-potency benzodiazepines are recommended. These may be a
  √ Short-acting (e.g., alprazolam) or
  √ Long-acting (e.g., clonazepam) drug.
- Clonazepam may be superior to alprazolam because clonazepam
  √ Exhibits little interdose rebound,
  √ Acts more quickly than alprazolam,
  √ Produces less severe withdrawal than alprazolam, and
  √ Can be taken bid; alprazolam requires tid-qid dosage.
- For the above reasons, one study showed that 86% of panic patients preferred clonazepam over alprazolam.
- Alprazolam
  √ Start around $\frac{1}{4}$ mg tid; increase $\frac{1}{4}$ mg every 1–3 days.
  √ Usually effective at 3–5 mg/day.
  √ Therapeutic dose may require 10 mg/day.
  √ Range is from 1–10 mg/day.
  √ Can cause manic symptoms.
  √ Withdrawal of alprazolam may trigger panic attacks.
  √ Some patients describe the frequent alprazolam doses inducing a sense of "impending panic" after 1–2 hours of missing a dose.
    □ One option is to slowly discontinue alprazolam no faster than $\frac{1}{4}$–$\frac{1}{2}$ mg every 7 days for doses above 2 mg/day, and $\frac{1}{4}$–$\frac{1}{2}$ every 7–10 days for dosages below 2 mg/day.
    □ Another option is to switch from the short-acting alprazolam to the longer-acting clonazepam over a week.
- Clonazepam
  √ Start at $\frac{1}{4}$ mg bid for first 2 days; increase dose by $\frac{1}{4}$ mg qd or qod.
  √ Antipanic effect usually occurs around $1\frac{1}{2}$–$2\frac{1}{2}$ mg/day.
  √ Range is from $\frac{1}{2}$–$4\frac{1}{2}$ mg/day.
  √ Because clonazepam sedates, may dispense most of it at bedtime, with a smaller dose earlier in the day.
  √ Clonazepam can induce depression.
  √ Since clonazepam may cause liver damage, obtain periodic liver function tests.
- When stopping alprazolam or clonazepam, titrate *very* slowly— about 10% per week.
- Employ short-acting benzodiazepines without metabolites for anticipatory anxiety between panic attacks.
- Propranolol
  √ Although propranolol does not exert an antipanic effect, when low doses of propranolol (10–20 mg tid-qid) are added to a ben-

ANTI ANXIETY AGENTS

zodiazepine, there are benefits, especially in patients who cannot improve with TCAs or MAOIs.

Phobic Disorders

Three key drug-responsive types

- Agoraphobia
  - √ Persistent fears of open spaces, leaving home, or any place where it is difficult to escape or gain help.
  - √ Arises with, or without, panic attacks.
  - √ Often occurs in the elderly.
- Social phobia (e.g., "performance anxiety")
  - √ Persistent fears of being scrutinized by others.
  - √ Patients afraid of saying or doing something that will embarrass or humiliate them.
  - √ Afraid of public speaking, public eating, public performing, and public urinating in public bathrooms.
  - √ These patients often have physical signs of anxiety.
- School phobia and separation anxiety

Agoraphobia may be treated by

- Alprazolam 3–6 mg/day
- Imipramine 150–300 mg/day
- Other drugs curtailing agoraphobia include
  - √ Amitriptyline
  - √ Clomipramine
  - √ Trazodone
  - √ MAOIs
    - □ Patients may confuse MAOI's hypotensive and hypertensive effects with phobia.

Social phobia may be treated by

- Benzodiazepines, such as alprazolam or clonazepam, with or without adding propranolol
- β blockers include
  - √ Metoprolol 25–50 mg bid
  - √ Atenolol 50–100 mg qd, or primarily
  - √ Propranolol 10–40 mg tid-qid
    - □ A trial dose of 10–40 mg of propranolol should be given ½ hour before anxiety-instigating performance.
    - □ If this works, administer propranolol ½ hour before future stressful events.
    - □ If necessary, raise dose by increments of 10 mg.

- MAOI
  - √ Phenelzine seems more helpful than imipramine, amitriptyline, or atenolol.
    - □ A clear, identifiable, predictable, and specific social phobia did equally well on phenelzine and atenolol, but a more generalized social phobia showed phenelzine superior.
  - √ Phenelzine, 45–90 mg/day, works well in up to 6 weeks.
  - √ When patient taken off phenelzine, symptoms often reemerge.

School phobia and separation anxiety

- For school phobia
  - √ Start children ages 6–8 on 10 mg of imipramine at bedtime.
  - √ Start older children on 25 mg at bedtime.
  - √ Raise dose 10–50 mg/week, depending on child's age.
  - √ Maximum dose is 3.5 mg/kg/day of imipramine.
- For separation anxiety
  - √ May benefit from 25–50 mg/day of imipramine, but with school avoidance, may need 75 mg/day.
  - √ If patient does not respond to imipramine 125 mg/day, unlikely to improve on higher doses.
  - √ When children recover completely, it is in 6–8 weeks.
  - √ TCAs are rarely continued for longer than 3 months.

Obsessive-Compulsive Disorder (OCD)

Clomipramine is favored by more studies in treating this disorder.

- Obsessions improve more than compulsions.
- Doses 200–250 mg/day
  - √ > 250 mg/day prompts seizures.
  - √ Should wait 10 weeks for a full response.
- Clomipramine may reduce trichotillomania.
- Many patients cannot tolerate clomipramine's
  - √ Weight gain,
  - √ Excessive tremor,
  - √ Sweating, and
  - √ Serotonergic syndrome.

Fluoxetine

- The second-choice drug, often useful if patient cannot tolerate clomipramine.
- May require 20–120 mg/day, which is higher than antidepressant dose.

Overall clomipramine and fluoxetine work in up to 50% of cases.

Monoamine-oxidase inhibitors (phenelzine 45–90 mg/day, tranylcy-

ANTIANXIETY AGENTS

promine 10–50 mg/day) may help OCD with panic attacks or severe anxiety.

Anti-anxiety agents have not relieved OCD, but good results from

* Clonazepam (3–6 mg/day) and
* Buspirone (30 mg/day).

Augmenting agents for OCD include

* The anorectic fenfluramine (20–60 mg/day) and
* The antipsychotic pimozide (6 mg/day), especially for patients on TCAs or with schizotypal features.

Post-Traumatic Stress Disorder (PTSD)

There is no clear drug treatment for PTSD.

The positive symptoms of PTSD—re-experiencing the past and increased arousal—respond better than the negative symptoms—avoidance and withdrawal.

More positive findings stem from TCAs, especially

* Imipramine (150–350 mg/day)
* Fluoxetine (20–80 mg/day)
* Doxepin (300 mg/day).

Try the TCA for 6–8 weeks.
If it does not work, the next approach depends on the other symptoms.

Drug Treatment of PTSD

Symptoms	Drug	Dose
Persistent anger, vigilance, startle	Propranolol	120–160 mg/day
	Clonidine	0.2–0.4 mg/day
Persistent flashbacks	Carbamazepine	1200–1600 mg/day
Refractory and angry	Phenelzine	45–75 mg/day
	Lithium	900–1200 mg/day
Sleep disturbance	Trazodone	200–400 mg/day
	Alprazolam	0.5–6 mg/day
Significant distress on re-experience	Propranolol	120–160 mg/day

Tobacco Abuse

Hypnosis, nicotine gum, and gradual substitution with lower nicotine-containing cigarettes help only a few smokers.

Clonidine 0.2–0.4 mg may substantially decrease anxiety and craving—that is, the mental preoccupation with smoking. However, clonidine may generate sedation and hypotension, which restricts its use to normotensive patients.

Alprazolam 1.0 mg relieves anxiety, but risks benzodiazepine abuse.

Buspirone (started at 15–30 mg/day and increased to 40–50 mg/day) reduced, but did not stop, smoking in 7/8 subjects.

SIDE EFFECTS

Side Effects: Anti-Anxiety Agents

Side Effects	Benzodiazepines	Buspirone	Clonidine	Propranolol
CARDIOVASCULAR EFFECTS				
Hypotension	±	±	+	+
Dizziness, lightheadedness	+	+	+	+
Bradycardia	−	+	+	+
Tachycardia, palpitations	−	−	+	−
Arrhythmias	−	−	+	−
Congestive heart failure	−	+	+	+
Raynaud's phenomenon	−	−	+	+
Bronchospasm	−	−	−	+
Hyperventilation	−	+	−	−
GASTROINTESTINAL EFFECTS				
Dry mouth	±	±	+	−
Increased salivation	+	+	−	−
Decreased appetite	+	+	+	−
Nausea, upset stomach	+	+	+	+
Vomiting	−	−	+	+
Diarrhea	−	+	−	+
Incontinence	+	−	−	−
Constipation	+	−	+	+
Jaundice	+	−	−	−
Hepatitis	−	−	+	−
Weight gain	+	+	+	−
RENAL EFFECTS				
Urinary retention/frequency	+	+	+	−
Nocturia	−	+	+	−
ENDOCRINE AND SEXUAL EFFECTS				
Gynecomastia	−	−	+	−
Menstrual irregularities	−	+	−	−
Decreased sex drive	+	+	+	+
Impotence	+	+	+	+
HEMATOLOGIC EFFECTS				
Agranulocytosis	−	−	−	+
Purpura	−	+	−	+

Side Effects	Benzodiazepines	Buspirone	Clonidine	Propranolol
EYES, EARS, NOSE, AND THROAT				
Blurred vision	+	+	+	−
Burning/itching eyes	−	+	+	−
Dry eyes	−	−	+	+
Diplopia	+	−	−	−
Vertigo	+	−	−	−
Tinnitus	−	+	−	−
Painful neck glands	−	+	+	+
SKIN, ALLERGIES, AND TEMPERATURE				
Rash	+	+	+	+
Hives	−	−	+	−
Psoriasiform rash	−	−	−	+
Urticaria	−	−	+	−
Pruritus	−	+	+	−
Angioneurotic edema	−	−	+	−
Edema/facial edema	−	+	−	−
Hair loss	−	+	+	+
Pharyngitis	−	−	−	+
Sore throat	−	+	−	+
Laryngospasm	−	−	−	+
Erythematous rash	−	−	−	+
CENTRAL NERVOUS SYSTEM EFFECTS				
Spasms/cramps	+	+	−	−
Muscle/joint pain	−	+	+	−
Incoordination	+	−	−	−
Sedation, drowsiness	+	−	+	+
Fatigue (daytime)	+	−	+	+
Weakness	+	+	+	+
Agitation, anxiety	+	+	+	−
Tremor	+	+	−	−
Ataxia, nystagmus, dysarthria	+	−	−	−
Paresthesias	−	+	−	+
Numbness	−	+	−	−
Amnesia	+	−	−	+
Stuttering	+	−	−	−
Headache	+	+	+	−
Insomnia	+	−	+	+
Nightmares	+	+	+	+
Hallucinations	+	+	+	+
Rage reactions/anger	+	+	−	−
Excitement	+	+	−	−
Confusion, disorientation	+	+	+	+
Clouded sensorium	−	−	−	+
Depression	+	+	+	+
Mania	+	+	−	−

+ Occurs; − Does not occur; ± May or may not occur.

Key details about more important side effects include

Cardiovascular Effects

Hypotension, dizziness, lightheadedness

- Clonidine and propranolol can induce serious hypotension.
  - √ Hypotension milder with benzodiazepines and buspirone than with antipsychotics, TCAs, MAOIs, clonidine, or propranolol.
  - √ Hypotension becomes no worse after propranolol > 500 mg/day.
- Management
  - √ Measure BPs reclining and standing, before and during, the first few days of clonidine or propranolol.
  - √ Increase dose more slowly.
  - √ Have patient deal with hypotension by:
    - □ Sitting a full 60 seconds—or longer if at all lightheaded,
    - □ Standing slowly while holding onto stable object (e.g., bed), and
    - □ Waiting at least 30 seconds before walking.

Bradycardia

- Rarely a difficulty after reaching 300–500 mg/day.

Bronchospasm

- Do not give propranolol to asthmatics.
  - √ Stop propranolol if patients start wheezing.

Raynaud's phenomenon

- Cold fingers and toes.

Gastrointestinal Effects

Dry mouth, nasal congestion (see page 13)

- Also occurs with hydroxyzine.

Constipation (see page 14)

Renal Effects

Urinary hesitancy or *retention* (see page 14)

Eyes, Ears, Nose, and Throat

Blurred vision (see page 16)

- Mild and rare.
  - √ Bethanechol 5–10 mg po.

Dry eyes (see page 17)

ANTI ANXIETY AGENTS

Central Nervous System Effects

Stuttering

- Mainly with alprazolam.

Incoordination, ataxia

- Arises in 25% of patients on ≥ 10 mg/day of clonazepam.
- In regular doses, only with meprobamate.

Sedation

- Common for benzodiazepines, clonidine, and propranolol.
  √ For instance, clonazepam produces drowsiness 50% of the time.
  √ Buspirone does not normally sedate, although a single 20–40 mg dose can exhaust people.
- Management
  √ Reduce dose.

Confusion, disorientation, clouded sensorium

- Primarily in the elderly.
  √ Caused by small doses of benzodiazepines,
  √ Often reversible, and
  √ Misdiagnosed as dementia.
- On propranolol, not dose-related.

Amnesia

- Anterograde amnesia especially with IV diazepam and lorazepam.

Rage reactions, anger

- Violent episodes with, or without, a h/o violence.
- Often observed with alprazolam and diazepam.
  √ Less with oxazepam.
- Treat with haloperidol 5 mg/IM.

Excitement

- Often occurs in children and the elderly.

Depression

- Occurs most often with
  √ Propranolol (high doses)
  √ Clonazepam (most often among benzodiazepines)
  √ Diazepam
  √ Lorazepam

- Can escalate into
  - √ Neurovegetative signs of depression
  - √ Catatonia

Manic reactions

- Only alprazolam.

PERCENTAGES OF SIDE EFFECTS

Side Effects	Benzodiazepines	Buspirone	Clonidine	Propranolol
CARDIOVASCULAR EFFECTS				
Hypotension	4.7	< 1	11.5	9.9
Hypertension	0.0	< 1	—	0.0
Dizziness, lightheadedness	13.4 (6.8–30)	13.6 (10–30)	18 (10–30)	10.5 (1.5–30)
Fainting, syncope	3.1	< 1	—	5
Tachycardia	7.7	1.3	0.5	—
Palpitations	7.7	1	0.5	—
Bradycardia	< 1	< 1	0.5	20.7 (2.2–40)
Shortness of breath	< 1	< 1	—	5.6
Chest pain	—	1.5	3.3	4
Cold hands and feet	—	—	—	20
Cardiac arrhythmias	0.0	—	5.5	—
GASTROINTESTINAL EFFECTS				
Dry mouth and throat	12.6 (10.5–14.7)	5.3 (1–10)	22.8 (1–40)	—
Salivation	4.2	< 1	—	—
Anorexia, lower appetite	—	< 1	5.5	16.6 (1.5–23.5)
Increased appetite	—	< 1	—	—
Nausea, vomiting	7.4 (1–10)	10.8 (6–30)	5.4 (1–10)	14.8 (1.5–30)
Dyspepsia, upset stomach	—	2.5	—	16.7 (1.5–23.5)
Gas	—	< 1	—	4
Diarrhea	7 (1–10.1)	2.5	—	12.5
Constipation	7.1 (1–10.4)	1.3	7.8 (1–10)	3.8 (1–10)
Jaundice	< 1	—	—	—
Hepatitis	—	—	1	—
Weight gain	2.7	—	3.3	—
Weight loss	2.3	—	—	—
Edema	—	—	—	9 (2–16)

ANTI ANXIETY AGENTS

Side Effects	Benzodiazepines	Buspirone	Clonidine	Propranolol
RENAL EFFECTS				
Urinary hesitancy or retention	< 1	—	0.1	—
Painful urination	< 1	—	—	—
Urinary frequency	—	—	0.2	1
Nocturia	—	—	1	—
ENDOCRINE AND SEXUAL EFFECTS				
Breast swelling	—	—	2.8	—
Disturbed sexual function	11	1	4.3	8.7 (1–11.8)
HEMATOLOGIC EFFECTS				
Bleeding, bruising easily	—	< 1	—	< 1
EYES, EARS, NOSE, AND THROAT EFFECTS				
Blurred vision	10.6 (1–20.8)	2	—	1.5
Dry eyes	—	—	5.5	—
Tinnitus	—	5.5	—	—
Nasal stuffiness	7.3	—	—	—
SKIN, ALLERGIES, AND TEMPERATURE				
Allergies	3.8	—	—	0.4
Rashes	5.5	1	< 1	1.4
Itch	5.5	—	< 1	—
Abnormal skin pigment	—	—	0.2	—
Joint pain	—	—	—	5.5
Fever, hyperthermia	—	< 1	—	< 1
Sweating	—	1	—	—
CENTRAL NERVOUS SYSTEM EFFECTS				
Weakness, fatigue	17.7 (7.7–42)	7.6 (4–16)	6.3 (4–10)	17 (1.5–29.4)
Clumsiness	20	—	—	—
Muscle Cramps	—	1	0.6	2
Uncontrollable limb jerks	—	< 1	—	—
Seizures	—	< 1	—	—
Paresthesias	—	< 1	—	20
Numbness	—	1.4	—	20
Headache	9.1 (5.3–12.9)	10.6 (6–30)	3.3 (1–30)	8.4 (1–17.6)
Ataxia, incoordination	17.6 (5–79)	2.5	—	—
Slurred speech	—	< 1	—	—
Tremor	4	1	—	—
Memory loss	—	—	—	11.8
Drowsiness, sedation	35.1 (6.8–77)	12.4 (1–24)	30.8 (10–64)	15 (1.5–30)

Side Effects	Benzodiazepines	Buspirone	Clonidine	Propranolol
Confusion, disorientation	6.9 (1–10)	1.4	—	4.5
Insomnia	6.4 (3.9–8.9)	6.7 (3–12.2)	3 (0.5–10)	5.3 (0.0–9.6)
Weird dreams	—	5.5	—	4.3 (1–10)
Hallucinations	5.5	< 1	—	5.5
Anxiety, nervousness (i.e., mental)	4.1	5	3	—
Agitation, restlessness (i.e., motoric)	—	20	3	—
Irritable, hostile, angry	5.5	2	—	0.0
Excitement	—	2	—	—
Depression	8.3 (1–13.9)	1.4	0.8	8.9 (0.1–50)

PREGNANCY AND LACTATION

Teratogenicity (1st trimester)

- Chlordiazepoxide-taking mothers have 11.4% of newborns with anomalies, including mental retardation, spastic diplegia, deafness, microcephaly, congenital heart defects, duodenal atresia, and Meckel's diverticulum.

- Avoid diazepam during pregnancy. In first trimester, 6.3% of children born to mothers using diazepam developed cleft palates, whereas only 1.1% of controls did. Diazepam also associated with inguinal hernia, cardiac defects, and pyloric stenosis.

- Alprazolam linked to congenital defects, abortions, and miscarriages.

- Patients should stop benzodiazepines at least 1–2 months before attempting to conceive; they should remain off them until the first trimester ends.

- Meprobamate produces critical anomalies in 1.9–12.1% of newborns.

- Hydroxyzine, clonidine, and propranolol infrequently generate serious anomalies.

- Since anti-anxiety agents are rarely necessary, there are few reasons to prescribe them during pregnancy.

ANTI ANXIETY AGENTS

- For panic attacks, better to dispense imipramine than benzodiazepines; if cannot taper off alprazolam, try clonazepam with its longer half-life and uncommon congenital defects.

Direct Effect on Newborn (3rd trimester)

- High dose of benzodiazepines during third trimester may precipitate newborn withdrawal, with jitters, tremors, irritability, vomiting, diarrhea, lost weight, high-pitched crying, CNS depression, and lowered Apgar.

- Chlordiazepoxide induces neonatal withdrawal around weeks 3–4.

- Diazepam is generally safe at birth, but if mother ingests > 30–40 mg/day for extended periods, a floppy infant syndrome (with hypotonia, lethargy, and sucking difficulties) may ensue; if mother consumes > 15 mg/day of diazepam for over 12 weeks during the second or third trimester, withdrawal may erupt. Diazepam ingested in second trimester can create hemangiomas, cardiac defects, and vascular problems.

- Clonazepam can promulgate in newborns (at 6 hours) cyanosis, lethargy, and hypotonia, as well as (at 12 hours) apneic episodes lasting 16–43 seconds. Hypotonia and lethargy typically resolve in 5 days; apnea may persist for 10 days. Before stopping clonazepam in pregnancy, weigh the risks of seizures against those of withdrawal.

- Oxazepam may be safer than diazepam for preeclampsia.

- Lorazepam potentiates the effects of narcotic analgesics in labor; may induce floppy infant syndrome.

- Meprobamate can intensify the infant's drug withdrawal.

- Propranolol in low and high doses may foster intrauterine growth retardation, hypoglycemia, bradycardia and respiratory depression at birth, and hyperbilirubinemia in newborns. If mother on β blockers, closely monitor birth for 24–48 hours.

Lactation	• Benzodiazepines enter breast milk, may addict newborn, and induce withdrawal.
	• Benzodiazepines can impair alertness and temperature regulation.
	• With longer-acting benzodiazepines, effects persist 2–3 weeks in infants.
	• Diazepam accumulates in breast milk, causing sedation, lost weight, respiratory depression, and withdrawal in newborns. Women on diazepam should avoid breast-feeding.
	• Clonazepam flows into breast milk. Although it does not accumulate, its half-life is extended, which might encourage apnea. For any infant exposed to clonazepam, useful to monitor serum levels and to check for CNS depression.
	• Meprobamate in milk is 2–4 times that of maternal plasma.
	• Propranolol is excreted in breast milk; effects unclear.

Drug Dosage in Mother's Milk

Generic Names	Milk/ Plasma Ratio	Time of Peak Concentration in Milk (hours)	Infant Dose (μg/kg/day)	Maternal Dose (%)	Safety Rating*
Clonazepam	?	?	2†	1.3–3.0‡	C
Clonidine	?	?	0.41	7.8	E
Clorazepate	?	?	2.3	?	?
Diazepam	0.16	?	3.3–11.7	2–2.3	C
Hydralazine	?	?	20	0.8	A
Lorazepam	?	?	1.3	2.2	B
Oxazepam	?	1½	4½	0.9	A
Prazepam	0.11	22	13.4**	3.2***	B
Propranolol	0.32–0.76	2–5	1.4–11.2	0.2–0.9	A

* A: Safe throughout infancy; B: Reasonably unsafe before 34 weeks, but safer after 34 weeks; C: Reasonably unsafe before week 44, but safer after 44 weeks; E: Unsafe up to 34th week because infant plasma concentration approaches and may exceed the mother's, reasonably unsafe from weeks 34–68, and safest after 68th week.
† Infant therapeutic dose 20–200 μg/kg/day.
‡ Maternal dose not specified, but presumed to be 20–200 μg/kg/day.
** Metabolite N-desmethyldiazepam measured.
*** Assuming 100% conversion to metabolite.

ANTI ANXIETY AGENTS

DRUG-DRUG INTERACTIONS*

Drugs (X) Interact with:	Benzodiazepines (B)	Comments
*Alcohol	X↑ B↑	Potentiate each other. With alcohol, shorter-acting benzodiazepines produce less harm than longer-acting benzodiazepines. Alcohol escalates suicide risk from benzodiazepines.
Aluminum hydroxide	B↓	Antacids decrease GI absorption of benzodiazepines, but clinical effects unclear.
Aminophylline	B↓	Aminophylline rapidly antagonizes diazepam, lorazepam, and probably other benzodiazepine effects. Increase benzodiazepine dosage.
*Birth control pills	B↑↓	Oral contraceptives may increase 2-keto and triazolo compounds while reducing 3-hydroxy agents.
Caffeine	B↓	Caffeine (250–500 mg) antagonizes benzodiazepines, especially diazepam and lorazepam.
*Cimetidine	B↑	Cimetidine may increase most benzodiazepines—not lorazepam or oxazepam—and raise benzodiazepine's side effects. Ranitidine or famotidine appear less apt to interact with benzodiazepines than cimetidine.
Digitalis	B↑	Increased benzodiazepines, including diazepam and clonazepam.
*Disulfiram	B↑↓	Enhances most benzodiazepine levels (not 3-hydroxy compounds) and sedation. May need to lower benzodiazepines or switch to 3-hydroxy agents.
Levodopa (L-dopa)	X↓	Benzodiazepines may exacerbate parkinsonism in patients on L-dopa. Oxazepam has not caused this problem. Carbidopa-levodopa agents may help. Monitor, and if parkinsonism worsens, stop benzodiazepines.
Isoniazid (INH)	B↑	INH increases benzodiazepine effect; lower benzodiazepines.
Magnesium hydroxide	B↓	Antacids decrease GI absorption of benzodiazepines, but clinical effects unclear.
MAOIs	B↑	Greater intoxication with increased benzodiazepine levels.
Metoprolol	B↑	Metoprolol may slightly increase 3-keto compounds. Minimal clinical changes noted. Does not occur with atenolol.
Phenytoin	B↑	Increased benzodiazepines, including diazepam and clonazepam.
Probenecid	B↑↓	Probenecid may increase lorazepam and its side effects. May affect other benzodiazepines, but more likely it affects only 3-hydroxy compounds.
Propranolol	B↑	Propranolol may slightly increase 3-keto compounds. Minimal clinical changes noted. Does not occur with atenolol.
Rifampin	B↑↓	Reduces diazepam's effects, and probably other benzodiazepines (not 3-hydroxy agents). May need to increase rifampin.

Drugs (X) Interact with:	Benzodiazepines (B)	Comments
Theophylline	B ↓	Theophylline rapidly antagonizes diazepam, lorazepam, and probably other benzodiazepine effects. Increase benzodiazepine dosage.
Tobacco smoking	B ↓	Decreased benzodiazepine sedation. More benzodiazepines or don't smoke.
Valproic acid	B ↑	Valproic acid may increase diazepam levels; importance unclear.

Drugs (X) Interact with:	Alprazolam (A)	Comments
Digitalis	X ↑	Alprazolam may increase digoxin; unclear evidence.
TCAs	—	When patients on alprazolam switched to TCAs, seizures have occurred.

Drugs (X) Interact with:	Buspirone (B)	Comments
Cimetidine	B ↑	May see more minor side effects (e.g., light-headedness).
MAOI	X ↑	Case reports of elevated BP. May insert 10 days between buspirone and MAOI.

Drugs (X) Interact with:	Chlordiazepoxide (C)	Comments
Ketoconazole	C ↑	Ketoconazole increases chlordiazepoxide; side effects unclear.
TCAs	X ↑	Chlordiazepoxide may increase TCAs' sedation and atropine effects.

Drugs (X) Interact with:	Clonazepam (C)	Comments
Barbiturates	C ↑	Phenobarbital slightly decreases clonazepam level, but effect is unclear.
Carbamazepine	C ↓	In 5–15 days, carbamazepine may diminish clonazepam by 19–37%. Seizure effect unknown. Unclear if other benzodiazepines react to carbamazepine like clonzepam. 3-hydroxy compounds are less apt to react similarly. If combine drugs, check carbamazepine levels.
Phenytoin	C ↓	Phenytoin lowers plasma clonazepam, but effect is unclear.
Primidone	C ↓	Primidone may slightly decrease clonazepam level; effect is unknown.

Drugs (X) Interact with:	Clonidine (C)	Comments
Acebutolol	X ↑ C ↑	Potentiate each other.
Alcohol	X ↑ C ↑	Enhanced sedation and decreased BP.
Antipsychotics	X ↑ C ↑	Isolated severe hypotension or delirium, but scanty evidence. More common in patients with impaired cardiac function.

ANTI-ANXIETY AGENTS

Drugs (X) Interact with:	Clonidine (C)	Comments
Caffeine	C ↓	Diminished clonidine effect. ·
Cocaine	X ↑ C ↓	BP rise.
Diuretics	X ↑ C ↑	BP drop.
Enalapril	X ↑	May accelerate potassium loss.
Fenfluramine	C ↑	Possible increased clonidine effect.
Insulin	X ↓	Hyperglycemia. Alert patient.
Labetolol	X ↓ C ↓	Precipitous BP drop if both drugs are stopped together.
Levodopa	X ↓	Parkinsonian symptoms may emerge. Combine carefully.
Marijuana	X ↑ C ↑	Weakness on standing.
Naloxone	C ↓	May reduce clonidine's antihypertensive action. If so, change clonidine to another antihypertensive or stop the narcotic antagonist.
Nicotinic acid (Niacin)	X ↓	Clonidine may inhibit nicotinic flushing. No special precautions.
Nitrates	C ↑	BP drop.
Nitroprusside	C ↑	A few cases of severe hypotensive reactions. Be alert to them.
*Propranolol	X ↑	(See propranolol-clonidine below.)
*TCAs	C ↑	TCAs, especially imipramine and desipramine, may lead to hypotension. TCAs may augment the hypertensive response to abrupt clonidine withdrawal. Maprotiline may interfere less with clonidine then might TCAs, although little clinical evidence. Methyldopa may be a preferred antihypertensive with TCAs. Carefully monitor patients when clonidine is reduced. Gradually tapering clonidine might lower risk.

Drugs (X) Interact with:	Clorazepate (C)	Comments
Primidone	X ↑	Combined use may cause depression, irritability, and aggressive behavior.

Drugs (X) Interact with:	Diazepam (D)	Comments
Digitalis	X ↑	Diazepam may increase digoxin.
Gallamine	X ↑	Prolonged neuromuscular blockade.
Isoniazid (INH)	D ↑	INH may increase diazepam. Observe combination.
Succinylcholine	X ↑	Prolonged neuromuscular blockade.

Drugs (X) Interact with:	Hydroxyzine (H)	Comments
Alcohol	X ↑ H ↑	CNS depression.
Antipsychotics	X ↓	Hydroxyzine might block antipsychotic actions.
Narcotics	X ↑ H ↑	CNS depression.
TCAs	X ↑	CNS depression.

Drugs (X) Interact with:	Lorazepam (L)	Comments
Loxapine	X↑ L↑	Isolated respiratory depression, stupor, and hypotension. Switch one drug.

Drugs (X) Interact with:	Meprobamate (M)	Comments
*Alcohol	X↑ M↑	Concurrent use induces CNS depression. More than 2 drinks (90–120 ml of 100-proof whiskey) and 200–400 mg of meprobamate usually causes problems. Long-term alcohol ingestion raises tolerance to meprobamate.

Drugs (X) Interact with:	Propranolol (P)	Comments
Acebutolol	X↑ P↑	Increased antihypertensive effects of both drugs. Adjust doses.
Albuterol	X↓ P↓	Decreased albuterol and β-adrenergic blocking effects.
Alcohol	P↑↓	May see variable changes in BP. No special precautions.
Aluminum and magnesium hydroxides	P↓	Aluminum and magnesium hydroxides decrease β blockers, such as propranolol (60%), atenolol (35%), and metoprolol (25%). Clinical results unclear. Avoid combination; otherwise, ingest antacids and propranolol one hour apart.
*Anesthetics	X↑	β blockers and local anesthetics, particularly those containing epinephrine, can enhance sympathomimetic side effects. Acute discontinuation of β blockers prior to local anesthesia may increase anesthetic's side effects. Do not stop chronic β blockers before using local anesthetics. Avoid epinephrine-containing local anesthetics in patients on propranolol.
Anticholinergics	P↓	ACAs can block β blockers' bradycardia.
†Antidiabetics	X↑ P↓	β blockers may alter response to hypoglycemia by prolonging the recovery of normoglycemia, causing hypertension, and blocking tachycardia. May raise blood glucose and impair peripheral circulation. Cardioselective β blockers, such as metoprolol, acebutolol, and atenolol are preferable in diabetics, especially if prone to hypoglycemia.
Antihistamines	X↓	Decreased antihistaminic effect.
Antihypertensives	X↑	Increased antihypertensive effect.
Anti-inflammatory agents	X↓	Decreased anti-inflammatory effect.
*Antipsychotics	X↑ P↑	Some β blockers and neuroleptics (e.g., chlorpromazine, thioridazine, thiothixene) increase each other's effects, such as hypotension, toxicity, and seizures. Monitor serum levels or decrease dose.
Antipyrine	X↑	Propranolol and, possibly, metoprolol may increase antipyrine.
*Barbiturates	P↓	Barbiturates may lower propranolol.

ANTI ANXIETY AGENTS

Drugs (X) Interact with:	Propranolol (P)	Comments
Benzodiazepines	X ↑	(See Benzodiazepine-propranolol above.)
Carbamazepine	P ↑	Might induce β-blocker metabolism. Combine with caution.
*Cimetidine	P ↑	Cimetidine may double β blockers; pulse rate declines. Beginning or ending cimetidine may influence metoprolol and labetalol, but not atenolol or pindolol. Ranitidine (and possibly famotidine) may substitute for cimetidine.
*Clonidine	X ↑	β blockers can aggravate hypertension in patients withdrawn from clonidine within 24–72 hours. Symptoms may include tremor, insomnia, nausea, flushing, and headaches. Patients receiving propranolol with clonidine should have their propranolol withdrawn *before* the clonidine to reduce danger of rebound hypertension. Noncardioselective β blockers more likely to cause this reaction than cardioselective β blockers. Labetalol or another cardioselective β blocker may be preferable to propranolol.
Cocaine	X ↑	Irregular heartbeat.
Dicumarol	X ↑	Propranolol may produce small increases in dicumarol; effect on prothrombin times is unknown.
Digitalis	X ↑ P ↑	Propranolol can potentiate bradycardia from digitalis. Monitor heart rate.
*Diltiazem, *Verapamil	P ↑	Calcium channel blockers, such as diltiazem or verapamil, generally potentiate β blockers. Using nifedipine precludes increase of β-blocker effects on atrioventricular node conduction. β blockers not metabolized (e.g., atenolol) should also prevent this pharmacokinetic interaction.
†Epinephrine	X ↑	Noncardioselective β blockers (e.g., propranolol, timolol) substantially raise systolic and diastolic BPs and drop heart rate, sometimes resulting in arrhythmias and stroke. Cardioselective β blockers (e.g., metoprolol) are safer. Whereas α-agonist sympathomimetics (e.g., epinephrine) are dangerous, pure β-agonist sympathomimetics (e.g., isoproterenol) are safer. Avoid combining noncardioselective β blockers and α-agonist sympathomimetics; this includes injecting epinephrine in a local anesthetic.
Ergot alkaloids	X ↑	Propranolol may increase vasoconstriction. Using an ergotamine suppository, a patient on 30 mg/day of propranolol developed purple and painful feet. ADRs more common with noncardioselective β blockers. Employ cardioselective β blockers.
Furosemide	P ↑	Furosemide may increase propranolol levels.
Glucagon	X ↓	Propranolol may blunt the hyperglycemic action.
*Indomethacin	P ↓	Indomethacin, as do other nonsteroidal anti-inflammatory agents (NSAIAs), diminish propranolol's hypotensive effect. NSAIAs and other β blockers can be unpredictable. If BP

Drugs (X) Interact with:	Propranolol (P)	Comments
		increases, may need to increase propranolol or to decrease or stop indomethacin.
*Isoproterenol	P ↑↓	Noncardioselective β blockers (e.g., propranolol) are risky to join with isoproterenol to treat asthma. Safer to employ cardioselective β blockers (e.g., labetalol and metoprolol). No β blocker is absolutely safe in treating asthma.
*Lidocaine	X ↑	Lidocaine level may escalate with propranolol, metoprolol, or nadolol.
Marijuana	X ↓	Propranolol delays the increases in heart rate and BP from marijuana. Propranolol may prevent marijuana's impairment of learning tasks and eye reddening.
*Methyldopa	X ↓	Patients getting a β blocker and methyldopa may develop hypertension. Monitor. Hypertensive reactions may be helped by IV phentolamine.
MAOIs	X ↓ P ↓	Depression may escalate on β blockers. Highly anti-cholinergic MAOIs block β blockers' influence on myocardial tissue.
Nylidrin	X ↓	Propranolol may reduce nylidrin's greater gastric acid secretion and volume. No special precautions.
*Phenylephrine	X ↑	Phenylephrine added to propranolol may trigger hypertensive episode. A woman on chronic propranolol 160 mg/day developed a fatal intracerebral hemorrhage after dropping 10% phenylephrine in each eye. Phenylephrine 10% eye drops have produced acute hypertensive episodes without propranolol. Until this reaction is proved, observe patient.
Phenytoin	P ↑	Increased propranolol effect.
Prazosin	X ↑	β blockers may increase the "first-dose" hypotensive response to prazosin. Start prazosin cautiously in patients on β blockers.
Propoxyphene	P ↑	Propoxyphene increases extensively metabolized β blockers (e.g., propranolol, metoprolol), but not β blockers excreted by kidneys (e.g., atenolol, nadolol).
Quinidine	X ↑ P ↑	Propranolol may raise quindine level and foster lightheadedness, hypotension, slower heart rate and fainting. Other blockers probably act similarly.
*Rifampin	P ↓	Rifampin may decrease propranolol and metoprolol, which may need changing when rifampin altered.
Reserpine	X ↑	Increased reserpine effect with excessive sedation, hypotension, fainting, vertigo, and depression.
Terbutaline	X ↑↓	Propranolol may antagonize terbutaline-induced bronchodilatation, whereas cardioselective β-adrenergic blockers have little effect on terbutaline.
*Theophylline	X ↑	Propranolol raises theophylline levels; avoid in bronchospastic pulmonary disease. Cardioselective agents are safer.

ANTI ANXIETY AGENTS

Drugs (X) Interact with:	Propranolol (P)	Comments
Tobacco smoking	P ↓	Smoking decreases propranolol and may produce irregular heartbeats. If smoking halted, propranolol increases. Smoking patients need higher propranolol doses. Atenolol, and other β blockers not dependent on liver metabolism, are safer.
Tocainide	X ↓	May worsen congestive heart failure.
TCAs	X ↓ P ↓	Depression may escalate on β blockers. Highly anti-cholinergic TCAs block β blockers' influence on myocardial tissue. Maprotiline toxicity may arise after propranolol added.
Tubocurarine	X ↑	Propranolol may prolong neuromuscular blockade.
Warfarin	X ↑	Propranolol may produce small increases in warfarin; effect on prothrombin times is unknown.

* Moderately important interaction; † Extremely important interaction; ↑ Increases; ↓ Decreases; ↑↓ Increases and decreases.

EFFECTS ON LABORATORY TESTS

Generic Names	Blood/Serum Tests	Results	Urine Tests	Results
Benzodiazepines	WBC, RBC LFT	↓r↓r ↑	None	
Buspirone	LFT, WBC	↑ ↑↓	None	
Clonazepam	LFT	↑	None	
Clonidine	Glucose (transient), Plasma renin activity	↑ ↓	Aldosterone, Catecholamines	↑ ↑
Hydroxyzine	None		17-Hydroxycorticosteroids	↑ f
Meprobamate	WBC, Platelets	↓r↓r	17-Hydroxycorticosteroids	↑ f
Propranolol	LFT T_4, rT_3, T_3 BUN (with severe heart disease)	↑ ↑↑↓ ↑	None	

* ↑ Increases; ↓ Decreases; f = falsely; r = rarely; LFT = SGOT, SGPT, LDH, bilirubin, and alkaline phosphatase.

WITHDRAWAL

Anti-anxiety agents, barbiturates, and nonbarbiturate hypnotics share many withdrawal characteristics; these are discussed in the next chapter.

Clonidine

* If suddenly withdrawn, serious symptoms of
  √ Hypertension
  √ Nervousness
  √ Headache
  √ Stomach pain
  √ Tachycardia
  √ Sweating
  √ Other sympathetic overactivity
* Occurs in patients on 0.6 mg/day of clonidine.
  √ Life-threatening withdrawal from higher doses.
* Starts 18–20 hours after the last dose.
* Hypertension may persist 7–10 days.
* Management
  √ Do not
    □ Halt drug abruptly.
    □ Use β blockers; may exaggerate hypertension.
  √ Do
    □ Taper patient gradually (2–4 days).
    □ Readminister clonidine.
    □ If severe, IV vasodilators.
    □ Patients on clonidine and propranolol should halt propranolol before stopping clonidine to avoid hypertensive supersensitivity.
    □ Warn patients about abruptly stopping drug.

Propranolol

* Safe to withdraw in psychiatric patients without cardiac problems.

Buspirone

* No withdrawal from buspirone.
* Because buspirone has *no* cross-tolerance with benzodiazepines, withdrawal from benzodiazepines is not relieved by buspirone.

OVERDOSE: TOXICITY, SUICIDE, AND TREATMENT

Benzodiazepines

Benzodiazepine overdoses are relatively safe, but if benzodiazepines are consumed with alcohol, barbiturates, or other CNS depressants, they can be fatal. One study showed that only 2 of 1,239 deaths occurred from benzodiazepine overdoses alone.

More rapidly absorbed benzodiazepines (e.g., diazepam, clorazepate) may generate a "buzz," thereby encouraging abuse.

The effects of a chronic benzodiazepine overdose partly depends on how tolerant the patient has already become on benzodiazepines: the more tolerant, the fewer symptoms.

Chronic benzodiazepine overdoses demonstrate

- Drowsiness
- Ataxia
- Slurred speech
- Vertigo

Acute benzodiazepine overdoses manifest with chronic symptoms *and*

- Somnolence, confusion, lethargy, diminished reflexes
- Hypotension
- Hypotonia
- Coma
- Cardiac arrest (rare)
- Death (rarer)

The general management of benzodiazepine overdoses includes (see page 37)

- Many benzodiazepines (e.g., alprazolam, lorazepam, temazepam, triazolam) are not detected by urine tests.
- For hypotension
  - √ Norepinephrine 4–8 mg in 1000 ml 5% D/S or D/W by infusion, or
  - √ Metaraminol 10–20 mg SC/IM.
    - □ ½–5 mg by IV or
    - □ 25–100 mg in 500 ml 5% D/W by infusion.
    - □ Stay clear of caffeine or sodium benzoate because they are of questionable benefit.
- Hemodialysis does not alleviate benzodiazepine overdose.

Buspirone

Unlike most anti-anxiety compounds, buspirone is not a controlled substance, and its initial dysphoric effect may discourage overuse.
Acute buspirone overdoses can produce

- Nausea, vomiting, upset stomach
- Dizziness, drowsiness
- Miosis

Management (see page 37)

- Role of hemodialysis unknown.

Clonidine

Acute clonidine overdoses may present with

- Hypotension
- Bradycardia
- Lethargy, somnolence
- Irritability
- Weakness
- Absent or diminished reflexes
- Miosis
- Vomiting
- Hypoventilation

After large overdoses, also see

- Reversible cardiac conduction defects or arrhythmias
- Apnea
- Seizures
- Transient hypertension

Management

- As above, plus
- IV fluids, if indicated
- IV atropine 0.3–1.2 mg for bradycardia
- IV furosemide 20–40 mg over 1–2 minutes
  √ If this fails, consider IV tolazoline 10 mg at 30 minute intervals.
- Hemodialysis removes only 5% of clonidine; worthless.

Hydroxyzine

Overdoses propagate side effects, especially drowsiness and occasional hypotension.

Management (see page 37)

- Hemodialysis of little help.

Meprobamate

Even in low doses, meprobamate can be especially dangerous.

- A 7–10 day supply is often lethal,
- Particularly when mixed with alcohol or other CNS depressants.

Acute meprobamate overdose produces symptoms similar to barbiturate overdose.

ANTI ANXIETY AGENTS

- Drowsiness, lethargy, stupor
- Ataxia
- Coma
- Hypotension, shock, respiratory failure →
- Death

Meprobamate can be eliminated by peritoneal dialysis, hemodialysis, or with an osmotic diuretic, such as mannitol.

Propranolol

Acute propranolol overdoses present with, and are treated by

- Bradycardia
  - √ IV atropine 0.3–1.2 mg.
  - √ If no response to vagal blockade, cautiously administer isoproterenol 1 mg (5 mg) in 500 ml 5% D/S or D/W by infusion, generally at a rate of less than 10 µg/min.
- Cardiac failure
  - √ Provide digitalis and diuretics.
- Hypotension
  - √ Epinephrine—drug of choice in anaphylactic shock,
    - □ ½ ml 1:1000 in 10 ml saline IV.
    - □ If no response, give ½ ml q 5–15 minutes.
  - √ Levarterenol 4–8 mg in 1000 ml 5% D/S or D/W by infusion,
- Bronchospasm
  - √ Isoproterenol and
  - √ Aminophylline 500 mg IV slowly

Toxicity and Suicide Data

Generic Names	Toxicity Doses Average (Highest) (g)	Mortality Doses Average (Lowest) (g)	Toxic Levels % (ng/ml)	Fatal Levels % (ng/ml)
Alprazolam	—	—	—	—
Buspirone	—	—	—	—
Clonazepam	—	—	—	—
Clonidine	100		(370)	—
Chlordiazepoxide	6.230 (17.00)	0.6–1.0	—	(30)
Clorazepate	0.675	—	—	—
Diazepam	2	0.6–1.0	(900)	(> 50)
Lorazepam	—	—	—	—
Meprobamate	18.7 (40.0)	20–40 (0.375)	30–100 µg/ml	100–200 µ/ml (> 200 µg/ml)*
Oxazepam	—	—	—	(> 25)
Prazepam	—	—	—	—
Propranolol	2	—	—	—

* Almost always fatal.

PRECAUTIONS

Anti-anxiety agents are contraindicated in hypersensitive patients. Give anti-anxiety medications cautiously to

- Elderly and debilitated people
- Patients with liver disease (oxazepam and lorazepam are safer)
- People who drink alcohol excessively
- Patients who will not follow the time-limited restrictions on these medications

Buspirone

- May trigger restlessness.
- Does not prevent benzodiazepine or barbiturate withdrawal.

Clonidine should be used cautiously in

- Severe coronary insufficiency
- Recent myocardial infarction
- Chronic renal failure
- Generalized rash

Meprobamate contraindications include

- Allergic to meprobamate, or
  √ Carisoprodol or
  √ Carbromal.
- Meprobamate may trigger seizures in epileptics.

Propranolol

- Contraindicated in
  √ Cardiogenic shock
  √ Sinus bradycardia with greater first degree block
  √ Congestive heart failure
  √ Bronchial asthma
    □ Metoprolol and atenolol are less likely to produce broncho-spasm.
- Give cautiously in
  √ Congestive heart failure, persistent angina, Wolff-Parkinson-White syndrome, and impaired myocardial functioning—all can become worse with propranolol
    □ Gradually withdraw propranolol from angina patients over a few weeks.
  √ May interfere with glaucoma screen test
    □ Propranolol withdrawal can increase intraocular pressure.
  √ Hyperthyroidism
  √ Diabetes
  √ Chronic obstructive pulmonary disease

√ Hepatic failure
√ Renal failure
√ Depression
  □ May feel "washed out" or lethargic.
  □ Others develop neurovegetative signs of depression.

NURSES' DATA

Benzodiazepines' anti-anxiety actions arise in 15–40 minutes, and thus, whether the drug works can be determined after 1–2 doses.

Avoid other CNS depressants (e.g., antihistamines, neuroleptics, or alcohol) without consulting physician.

* Tell patients that they may be unaware of their diminished skills when mixing benzodiazepines and alcohol.
  √ Avoid alcohol 24–48 hours after lorazepam injection; this is probably good advice after any benzodiazepine injection.
* Drinking excessive caffeine counteracts anxiolytics.

Tolerance, physical addiction, and withdrawal can occur from antianxiety agents. These symptoms may be hard to distinguish from each other or from anxiety.

* Inform patients about withdrawal symptoms (see pages 209, 232–34).
* Inform patients about intoxication and overdose symptoms (see pages 210–11).
* Make sure patients realize that a sudden benzodiazepine withdrawal can be fatal, and more dangerous than narcotic withdrawal.
* It is dangerous to use anti-anxiety medication in high doses *or* in smaller doses for longer than 3–4 weeks continuously.
* There is no easy way to get off a benzodiazepine habit.
  √ Withdrawal can occur, yet must be done slowly under medical supervision.
* If there is an *acute* question between giving the patient too much or too little benzodiazepines, give too much; it's safer.

Techniques to administer benzodiazepines.

* IM injections
  √ Slowly into a single large muscle, especially deeply into the upper outer quadrant of the gluteus.
  √ Rotate sites and
  √ Insure the injection is for IM, not IV, use.
* IV injections
  √ Differ with different agents, but generally inject slowly, such as IV diazepam 2½ to 10 mg for anxiety.

□ May repeat in from 1–4 hours, but
□ IV diazepam should not exceed 30 mg in 8 hours.
* Protect parenteral drugs from light.

PATIENT AND FAMILY NOTES

Never stop these drugs suddenly—induces seizures.

* Suddenly stopping these agents is riskier than suddenly stopping narcotics. Narcotic withdrawal can produce sickness; benzodiazepine withdrawal can produce death.

Take anti-anxiety agent at prescribed time.

* If forget dose, can consume within 2 hours.
* Otherwise wait for the next regular dose.
* Do not double the dose.

When starting anti-anxiety agents, patients should be careful driving cars, working around machines, and crossing streets. When first on anti-anxiety agents, drive briefly in a safe place, since reflexes might be a tad off.

Benzodiazepines strongly potentiate alcohol: "One drink feels like 2–3 drinks." Buspirone, propranolol, and clonidine do not potentiate alcohol.

May take benzodiazepines, clonidine, and propranolol at any time; food does not interfere. Buspirone's absorption is delayed by food, but this does not alter its efficacy.

Maintain benzodiazepines away from bedside or any readily accessible place, where they might be taken by "accident." Keep safely away from children.

Patients on β blockers (e.g., propranolol) should inform doctor if they are traveling to high altitudes.

If doctor prescribes meprobamate or barbiturates, ask him if another agent would be superior, since benzodiazepines and other agents have largely superseded them.

ANTI ANXIETY AGENTS

COST INDEX*

Generic Names	Brand Names	Equivalent Dosage (mg)	Dose Assessed (mg)	Cost Rating*
Alprazolam	Xanax	0.5	0.5	160
Buspirone	BuSpar	5	5	167

Generic Names	Brand Names	Equivalent Dosage (mg)	Dose Assessed (mg)	Cost Rating*
Chlordiazepoxide	Librium	10	10	118
	generics	10	10	9
Clomipramine	Anafranil	25	75	18
Clonazepam	Klonopin	0.5	0.5	98
Clorazepate	Tranxene	7.5	7.5	201
	generics	7.5	7.5	> 147
	Tranxene-SD	7.5	11.25	285
Diazepam	Valium	5	5	146
	generics	5	5	> 5
Hydroxyzine	Atarax	25	25	214
	generics	25	25	> 27
Lorazepam	Ativan	1	1	193
	generics	1	1	> 42
Meprobamate	Equanil	200	200	45
	Miltown	200	200	164
	generics	200	200	> 5
Oxazepam	Serax	15	15	250
	generics	15	15	114
Prazepam	Centrax	10	10	176
Propranolol	Inderal	40	40	431
	generics	40	40	> 42

* The higher the number, the more costly the drug.

8. Hypnotics

INTRODUCTION

Hypnotics induce sleep. They are of three main types

- Benzodiazepines
- Barbiturates
- Barbiturate-like hypnotics

This chapter focuses on the benzodiazepine hypnotics; it also addresses

- Withdrawal from all hypnosedatives (see pages 233–37)
- Withdrawal from alcohol (see page 237)
- Disulfiram treatment of alcoholism (see pages 238–39)

Related topics detailed in other chapters are

- Cataplexy (Antidepressants, page 71)
- Narcolepsy (Stimulants, page 250)
- Night terrors (Antidepressants, pages 72–73)
- Sleep apnea (Antidepressants, page 72)
- Sleepwalking (Antidepressants, pages 71–72)

NAMES, CLASSES, MANUFACTURERS, DOSE FORMS, AND COLORS

Generic Names	Brand Names	Manufacturers	Dose Forms (mg)*	Colors
BENZODIAZEPINES				
Estazolam	ProSom	Abbott	t: 1/2	t: white-coral
Flurazepam	Dalmane	Roche	c: 15/30	c: orange-ivory/ red-ivory
Quazepam	Doral	Baker Cummins	t: 7.5/15	t: all light orange-white speckled
Temazepam	Restoril	Sandoz	c: 15/30	c: maroon-pink/ maroon-blue
Triazolam	Halcion	Upjohn	t: 0.125/0.25	t: white/blue
BARBITURATES				
Amobarbital	Amytal	Lilly	t: 15/30/50/ 100; c: 65/200; p: 250/500	t: green/ orange/yellow/ pink
Aprobarbital	Alurate	Roche	e: 40 mg/5 ml	e: red
Butabarbital	Butisol	Wallace	t: 15/30/50/ 100; e: 30 mg/5 ml	t: lavender/green/ orange/pink; e: green
Pentobarbital	Nembutal	Abbott	c: 50/100; su: 30; p: 50 mg/ml	c: orange/yellow
Phenobarbital	Luminal	Winthrop Many generic doses	t: 16/32/100	t: yellow/green/ brown
Secobarbital	Seconal	Lilly	c: 30/50/100; su: 30/60/120/ 200; p: 50 mg/ml	c: red/red/red
BARBITURATE-LIKE COMPOUNDS				
Chloral hydrate	Noctec	Squibb	c: 250/500; e: 500 mg/5 ml	c: red/red
Ethchlorvynol	Placidyl	Abbott	c: 200/500/ 750	c: red/red/ green
Methyprylon	Noludar	Roche	t: 200; c: 300	t: white; c: white

* c = capsules, e = elixir, p = parenteral, su = suppository, t = tablets.

PHARMACOLOGY

The preceding chapter presented the pharmacology of benzodiazepines. Benzodiazepine hypnotics exert similar effects on sleep.

- Decrease stage 1.
- Increase stage 2.
- Reduce stages 3 and 4.
  √ Temazepam prolongs stage 3 in depressed patients.
- REM sleep.
  √ Decrease REM sleep, except for temazepam and low doses of flurazepam.
  √ Prolong REM latency—the time to reach REM—except for flurazepam.
  √ Increase REM cycles, usually in the last part of sleep.
- Extend total sleep time.

Pharmacology of Oral Hypnotic Benzodiazepines

Generic Names	Speed of Onset (min)	Peak Plasma Levels (hours)	Duration of:		
			Half-Life (hours)	Action* (hours)	Active Metabolites
2-Keto-					
Flurazepam	30	½–1	67 (47–100)	LA > 40	N-Desalkylflurazepam
3-Hydroxy					
Temazepam	20–40	2–3	12 (9½–20)	SA 6–20	none
Triazolo-					
Estazolam	15–30	2	15 (10–24)	IA 6–8	4-Hydroxyestazolam, 1-Oxoestazolam
Triazolam	20	2	2–4 (1½–5½)	USA < 6	none
Other					
Quazepam	30	2	25–40 (2–73)	LA (2–100)	2-Oxoquazepam, N-Desalkylflurazepam
BARBITURATES					
Amobarbital	45–60	—	25 (16–40)	IA 6–8	—
Aprobarbital	45–60	3	24 (14–34)	IA (6–8)	—
Butabarbital	45–60	3–4	34–42 (34–140)	IA 6–8	—
Pentobarbital	15–60	30–60	22–50 (15–50)	SA 3–4	—
Phenobarbital	8–12	10–15	3–4 weeks	LA 80	—
Secobarbital	10–15	15–30	28–30 (15–40)	SA 3–4	—
BARBITURATE-LIKE COMPOUNDS					
Chloral Hydrate	30	—	4–14†	—	Trichloroethanol
Ethchlorvynol	15–60	—	10–25‡	5	—
Methyprylon	45	—	3–6	5–8	—

* LA = long-acting; IA = intermediate-acting; SA = short-acting; USA = ultra-short-acting hypnotics. The figures below represent the duration of action of the compound and its major active metabolites.
† Half-life for trichloroethanol—chloral hydrate's principal metabolite—is 7–10 hours.
‡ Half-lives for ethchlorvynol's free and conjugated forms of major metabolite are 10–20 hours.

DOSES

Generic Names	Usual Doses (mg)	Dose Ranges (mg)	When to Take Before Bedtime (hours)	Geriatric Dose (mg)
BENZODIAZEPINES				
Estazolam	1	1–2	0.5	0.5
Flurazepam	15–30	15–30	0.5	15
Quazepam	7.5–15	7.5–15	1.5	7.5
Temazepam	15–30	15–30	1–2	15
Triazolam	0.25	0.125–0.5	0.5	0.125
BARBITURATES				
Amobarbital	150–200	65–200	0.5	65
Aprobarbital	40–60	40–60	0.5	40
Butabarbital	50–100	50–100	0.5	50
Pentobarbital	100	50–200	0.5	50
Phenobarbital	100–200	15–600	1	16
Secobarbital	100–200	100–200	0.25	50
BARBITURATE-LIKE COMPOUNDS				
Chloral hydrate	500–1500	500–2000	0.5	500
Ethchlorvynol	500–750	500–1000	0.5	500
Methyprylon	200–400	200–800	0.5	200

CLINICAL INDICATIONS AND USE

Insomnia is defined as a difficulty sleeping *not* due to

- Drugs (e.g., prescription, over-the-counter, recreational, alcohol, caffeine)
- Sleep disorders (e.g., narcolepsy, sleep apnea)
- Medical ailments (e.g., pain)
- Mental disorders (e.g., depression, panic attacks, obsessive-compulsive disorder)
- Circadian rhythm difficulties (e.g., jet lag, shift changes)

Insomnia is insufficient sleep that renders the person consistently tired the next day.

- A person sleeping 3 hours a night who feels refreshed the next day is a brief sleeper but not a poor sleeper.
- A person who must sleep 9–10 hours a night to feel refreshed the next day is a healthy (albeit inefficient) sleeper.

Benzodiazepine hypnotics have largely replaced other hypnotics because benzodiazepines

- Are safer as overdoses,
- Cause less respiratory and CNS depression, and
- Induce less drug dependence.

Benzodiazepines are effective, but often for as little as 5–14 days.

- No hypnotic has been proven effective for over one month.

Hypnotics have 2 clear indications

- Brief (1–7 day) episode of insomnia
- Transitory insomnia incited by acute stress or by a marked diurnal rhythm change (e.g., jet lag)

Benzodiazepines most help patients with shorter total sleep time.

Hypnotics create 3 common problems

- If the hypnotic does not induce sleep, it fosters drowsiness, confusion, and agitation the next day.
- Longer-acting hypnotics can sedate and impede performance the following day.
- Hypnotics provoke tolerance, dependency, withdrawal insomnia, and rebound insomnia.

Withdrawal insomnia and rebound insomnia are separate.

- Withdrawal insomnia is a part of the *general* abstinence syndrome, which arises after the abrupt withdrawal of a *large* dose of any hypnotic taken over a *prolonged* period. (See precautions.)
- Rebound insomnia is a *specific* sleep disruption, which occurs after the sudden halting of a *normal* dose of any *briefly* taken and *quickly* eliminated hypnotic.
  - √ Hypnotics with rapid (e.g., triazolam) or intermediate (e.g., temazepam) elimination rates generate more rebound insomnia than do hypnotics with longer elimination rates (e.g., flurazepam, quazepam).
  - √ After abruptly stopping hypnotics, shorter-acting drugs produce a more aggravating rebound insomnia in 2 nights, whereas longer-acting hypnotics produce a calmer version in 5–7 nights.
  - √ Rebound insomnia is partly dose dependent.
  - √ From the greatest and fastest to the weakest and slowest rebound insomnia are
    - □ Temazepam
    - □ Triazolam
    - □ Flurazepam
    - □ Quazepam

✓ Greater rebound insomnia may increase hypnotic dosage, which
  □ Aggravates tolerance and
  □ Fosters drug dependency.
• When rebound insomnia occurs, clinicians should avoid resuming
  the same hypnotic, and
✓ Try to remove the patient from all hypnotics.
✓ If this is not possible,
  □ May prescribe a sedative antihistamine (e.g., diphenhydra-
    mine 50 mg) for a few nights.
  □ If this fails, try a sedating TCA (e.g., amitriptyline, doxepin)
    for a few nights, or
  □ Employ another benzodiazepine and gradually taper it.

Short-acting versus long-acting benzodiazepine hypnotics differ ac-
cording to these criteria

Characteristic	Short-Acting	Long-Acting
Accumulation with more use	No	Marked
Hangover	Mild	Moderate
Tolerance	Moderate	Mild
Anterograde amnesia	Moderate-Marked	Mild
Rebound insomnia risk	Moderate	No
Early morning awakening risk	Mild	No
Daytime anxiety risk	Mild	No
Anxiolytic the next day	No	Moderate
Full benefit on first night	Moderate	Moderate

Qualities of benzodiazepine hypnotics
• Estazolam
  ✓ Rapid absorption rate.
  ✓ Intermediate half-life.
  ✓ Duration of action between triazolam and temazepam.
• Flurazepam
  ✓ Rapid absorption rate
  ✓ Long half-life
  ✓ Sedates during the next day, which may, or may not, diminish
    with repeated doses.
• Quazepam
  ✓ Slow absorption rate
  ✓ Slower onset
  ✓ Long half-life
    □ A major metabolite, N-desalkylflurazepam (also called N-de-
      salkyl-2-oxoquazepam), has a half-life of 73 hours, range is
      47–100 hours.

□ Another key metabolite, 2-oxoquazepam, has a half-life of 2–3 hours.

□ Quazepam and 2-oxoquazepam together have a half-life of 39 hours.

√ Manufacturer claims it does not cause daytime sedation.

- Temazepam
  √ Slow absorption rate
  √ Intermediate half-life
  √ May take longer to induce sleep.
  √ Causes little or no daytime sedation.
- Triazolam
  √ Intermediate absorption rate
  √ Very short half-life
  √ No metabolites
  √ May provoke early morning awakening.
  √ No daytime sedation

Nonbenzodiazepines are solely indicated for patients who cannot tolerate benzodiazepines.

- Chloral hydrate is effective if used for 1–2 nights,
  √ Tolerance quickly develops thereafter.
- Barbiturates have an occasional use for daytime anti-anxiety effects.
  √ Most helpful to this end are
    □ Amobarbital
    □ Pentobarbital
    □ Secobarbital
- Antihistamines, which do not foster drug dependency, are weak hypnotics.
  √ Commonly employed are
    □ Diphenhydramine 50–100 mg (available over the counter in 25 mg capsules)
    □ Hydroxyzine 25–100 mg (see pages 185–86)
  √ Antihistamines are anticholinergic, which particularly troubles the elderly.
- Tryptophan, which is now off the market, was a fair hypnotic for mild to moderate insomnia.
  √ Not addictive
  √ Hypnotic dose is 1000–2000 mg (see pages 102, 268).

The choice of the "best" hypnotic for each patient depends on the patient's particular circumstances, in that some

- Hypnotics act more quickly (e.g., temazepam faster than quazepam),

- People wake up too early in the morning (e.g., triazolam more than flurazepam),
- Foster more drowsiness the next day (e.g., flurazepam more than triazolam),
- Shorter-acting hypnotics are more addictive than longer-acting hypnotics (e.g., triazolam more than flurazepam),
- Are more lethal or toxic than others (e.g., secobarbital more than triazolam),
- Exercise weird aberrations (e.g., triazolam's traveler's amnesia), and
- Promote rebound insomnia more than others (e.g., temazepam more than quazepam).

Historically, other medications have been prescribed for insomnia, but with modern choices none of these medications holds much value.

Dubious Hypnotics

		Hypnotic Ratings	
Generic Names	**Chemical Groups**	**Efficacy**	**Side Effects**
Amitriptyline	TCA	Strong	Serious
Chlorpromazine	Antipsychotic	Strong	Serious
Chlorprothixene	Antipsychotic	Strong	Serious
Chlordiazepoxide	Benzodiazepine	Considerable	Addictive
Clomipramine	TCA	Strong	Serious
Clonazepam	Benzodiazepine	Poor	Addictive
Diazepam	Benzodiazepine	Considerable	Addictive
Diphenhydramine*	Antihistamine	Minimal	Minimal
Doxepin	TCA	Strong	Serious
Ethinamate†	Barbiturate-like	Strong	Addictive
Fluoxetine	Antidepressant	Poor	Moderate
Glutethimide†	Barbiturate-like	Strong	Addictive
Hydroxyzine	Anti-anxiety agent	Poor	Moderate
Lorazepam	Benzodiazepine	Fair	Addictive
Meprobamate	Anti-anxiety agent	Fair	Addictive
Mesoridazine	Antipsychotic	Moderate	Serious
Methaqualone†	Barbiturate-like	Strong	Addictive
Paraldehyde	Hypnotic	Poor-Fair	Moderate
Thioridazine	Antipsychotic	Strong	Serious
Trazodone	TCA	Strong	Serious
Trimipramine	TCA	Strong	Serious
Tryptophan*‡	Amino acid	Good	Okay?

* Can be sold over the counter.
† No longer sold in United States, but doctor may distribute them from his free-drug supply.
‡ Removed from market in United States for medical reasons. Avoid until legal again.

SIDE EFFECTS

The side effects caused by benzodiazepine hypnotics are basically the same as those presented in the previous chapter for benzodiazepine anti-ànxiety agents.

Benzodiazepines' CNS effects follow a "U"-shaped time curve, with the most adverse consequences occurring in the first few days, and then reappearing a week or so later.

* This especially happens in the elderly as they accumulate the long-acting desalkylflurazepam.
* The degree of CNS side effects vary with drug, dose, and age. To illustrate, these percentages of CNS side effects emerge from oral flurazepam

Factor	CNS Side Effect (%)
15 mg/night	1.9
30 mg/night	12.3
Patients under 60	1.9
Patients over 80	7.1
Patients over 70, 15 mg doses	2.0
Patients over 70, 30 mg doses	39.0

Note these side effects

Respiratory ailments

* Insomniacs with chronic obstructive pulmonary disease, asthma, or other respiratory disorders should *not* receive sleeping pills. They might intensify sleep apnea in people who
  √ Snore
  √ Hypertensive
  √ Male
  √ Obese

Falls, fractures

* Often from *ataxia* and *confusion*

Hangover

* Common
* Aggravated by
  √ Alcohol consumption and
  √ Restricted fluid intake
* Management
  √ Reduce, halt, or switch hypnotic.

Amnesia

- Particularly common with triazolam.
- Because of its ultra-short half-life, triazolam is often taken for jet lag.
- Presents with
  - √ A single dose, often just ¼ mg.
  - √ May occur on, or off of, alcohol.
  - √ The person behaves normally; nobody notices any abnormality.
  - √ On awakening, the patient has no memory of events happening 6–11 hours after ingesting triazolam.
    - □ Memory loss is longer than sleep duration.
  - √ May swallow triazolam the following night without difficulty.
  - √ An apparently benign anterograde amnesia.

Warn patients about this hazard.

PERCENTAGES OF SIDE EFFECTS

Part I

Side Effects	Flurazepam	Quazepam	Temazepam	Triazolam
CARDIOVASCULAR EFFECTS				
Dizziness, lightheadedness	23.9	1.5	13.3	11.4 (4–19.5)
Fainting, syncope	—	—	< 1	—
Tachycardia	—	—	—	0.7
Palpitations	—	—	< 1	—
Shortness of breath	—	—	< 1	—
GASTROINTESTINAL EFFECTS				
Dry mouth and throat	3.4	1.5	—	0.6
Anorexia, lower appetite	—	—	1.5	—
Nausea, vomiting	0.7	—	5.5	2.8 (1.6–4.6)
Taste changes	3.4	—	—	0.6
Dyspepsia, upset stomach	0.7	1.1	—	1.5 (0.5–2.2)
Diarrhea	—	—	3.5	< 0.5
Constipation	0.7	—	5.5	1.4 (<0.5–2.2)
Jaundice	—	—	< 1	—
RENAL EFFECTS				
Urinary hesitancy or retention	—	—	5.5	—

Side Effects	Flurazepam	Quazepam	Temazepam	Triazolam
EYES, EARS, NOSE, AND THROAT EFFECTS				
Visual changes	4.6	—	5.5	3 (0.5–4.4)
Nystagmus	—	—	0.5	—
Tinnitus	4.6	—	—	2.9 ($<$0.5–4.4)
Mouth or throat sores	—	—	$<$ 1	—
SKIN, ALLERGIES, AND TEMPERATURE				
Allergies	—	—	—	$<$ 0.5
Rashes	0.6	—	5.5	0.2 (0–$<$0.5)
Itch	—	—	5.5	—
CENTRAL NERVOUS SYSTEM EFFECTS				
Weakness, fatigue	23.9	1.9	1–2	11.4 ($<$0.5–19.5)
Lethargy	23.9	—	5	11.8 ($<$0.5–19.5)
Clumsiness	—	—	20	13
Paresthesias	4.6	—	—	2.9 ($<$0.5–4.4)
Headache	4.6	4.5	—	5.9 (3.8–9.7)
Ataxia, incoordination	23.9	—	$<$ 1	12.8 (4.6–19.5)
Drowsiness, sedation	29.5 (23.9–36)	23 (12–34)	18.5 (10–30)	16.1 (14–19.5)
Confusion, disorientation	—	—	4 (1–10)	0.7
Decreased concentration	—	—	$<$ 1	—
Memory loss, amnesia	—	—	0.0	0.7 (0.5–0.9)
Insomnia	0.1	—	—	0.3
Nightmares	0.1	—	—	0.3
Hallucinations	—	—	3 ($<$0.5–10)	—
Anxiety, nervousness (i.e., mental)	—	—	—	5.2
Irritable	—	—	5.5	—
Depression	—	—	5.5	0.7
Euphoria	—	—	2.5	0.7
Paradoxical excitement	2.8	—	0.5	3.8

Part II

Side Effects	Barbiturates	Chloral Hydrate	Disulfiram
CARDIOVASCULAR EFFECTS			
Hypotension	< 1	—	—
Dizziness, lightheadedness	10.5 (<1–10)	5.5	—
Fainting, syncope	< 1	—	—
Apnea	< 1	—	—
Hypoventilation	< 1	—	—
Shortness of breath	< 1	—	—
GASTROINTESTINAL EFFECTS			
Nausea, vomiting	3.2	20	—
Bad taste	—	—	5.5
Dyspepsia, upset stomach	—	20	5.5
Diarrhea	5.5	—	—
Constipation	< 1	—	—
Jaundice	< 1	—	< 1
Liver disease	< 1	—	—
ENDOCRINE AND SEXUAL EFFECTS			
Disturbed sexual function	—	—	5.5
HEMATOLOGIC EFFECTS			
Anemia	< 1	—	—
Easy bruising	< 1	—	—
EYES, EARS, NOSE, AND THROAT EFFECTS			
Eye pain or swollen	5.5	—	5.5
Vision changes	—	—	5.5
Sore throat	5.5	—	—
SKIN ALLERGIES AND TEMPERATURE EFFECTS			
Allergies	< 1	—	—
Rashes	3.2	< 1	< 1
Itch	5.5	< 1	—
Fever, hyperthermia	3.2	—	—
CENTRAL NERVOUS SYSTEM EFFECTS			
Hyperkinesia	< 1	—	—
Clumsiness	—	5.5	—
Muscle cramps	5.5	—	—
Numbness of limbs	—	—	5.5
Headache	< 1	—	5.5
"Hangover"	20	5.5	—
Ataxia, incoordination	< 1	5.5	—
Slurred speech	5.5	—	—
Drowsiness, sedation	26.5 (10–>33)	5.5	20

Side Effects	Barbiturates	Chloral Hydrate	Disulfiram
CENTRAL NERVOUS SYSTEM EFFECTS			
Confusion, disorientation	3.2	< 1	—
Insomnia	< 1	—	—
Nighmares	< 1	—	—
Hallucinations	< 1	< 1	—
Anxiety, nervousness (i.e., mental)	< 1	—	—
Agitation, restlessness (i.e., motoric)	< 1	< 1	—
Depression	5.5	—	5.5

H Y P N O T I C S

PREGNANCY AND LACTATION

Teratogenicity (1st trimester)
- Patients should stop benzodiazepines at least 1–2 months before attempting to conceive; they should remain off of them until the first trimester ends.

- In a study of mothers taking amobarbital, 35% (95/273) of infants had congenital defects.

- Virtually no evidence that pentobarbital, secobarbital, or chloral hydrate are teratogenic.

- Ethchlorvynol may increase malformations.

- With little reason for hypnotics during pregnancy, and given hypnotics' potential risks, avoid them.

Direct Effect on Newborn (3rd trimester)
- Flurazepam linked to neonatal depression; mothers who receive 30 mg of flurazepam 10 days before delivery had sedated, inactive newborns during the first 4 days.

- Barbiturate-taking mothers are no more likely to produce congenitally defective children.

- No apparent harmful effects from secobarbital.

- Ethchlorvynol (500 mg/day) may induce infant withdrawal and/or mild hypotonia, poor suck, absent rooting, poor grasp, delayed-onset jitters, and CNS depression.

Lactation
- Benzodiazepines enter breast milk; may addict newborn and induce withdrawal.

- Benzodiazepines can impair alertness and temperature regulation.
- With longer-acting benzodiazepines, effects persist 2–3 weeks in infants.

Drug Dosage in Mother's Milk

Generic Names	Milk/ Plasma Ratio	Time of Peak Concentration in Milk (hours)	Infant Dose (µg/kg/day)	Maternal Dose (%)	Safety Rating*
Chloral hydrate	?	?	0.47 mg†	2	B
Glutethimide	?	8–12	41.0	½	A
Phenobarbital‡	?	?	1.56	23–156	D
Quazepam	4.13	3	14.4	5.8	C

* A: Safe throughout infancy; B: Reasonably unsafe before 34 weeks, but safer after 34 weeks; C: Unsafe before week 34, relatively safe from weeks 34–44, and safest after 44th week; D: Unsafe throughout infancy, largely because infant plasma concentrations may appear, and rarely exceed, those of mother.
† Infant therapeutic dose 15–50 µg/kg/day; maternal dose administered as 1.3 g suppository.
‡ Broad range in findings.

DRUG-DRUG INTERACTIONS

After reviewing the benzodiazepine interactions on pages 202–8, examine these interactions special for hypnotics.

Drugs (X) Interacts with:	Benzodiazepines (B)	Comments
Cimetidine	B↑	Cimetidine increases benzodiazepine hypnotics' (except temazepam) side effects. Ranitidine or famotidine are less likely to exert this effect.
*Disulfiram	B↑	Escalates benzodiazepine hypnotics (except temazepam), but degree is unknown.
*Erythromycin	B↑	Erythromycin increases triazolam, inducing psychomotor impairment, memory dysfunction, and drowsiness. May need to halt triazolam.
Isoniazid (INH)	B↑	INH may increase triazolam levels.
Levodopa (L-dopa)	X↓	Benzodiazepines may exacerbate parkinsonism in patients on L-dopa. Triazolam and temazepam have caused this interaction; flurazepam has not. Carbidopa-levodopa agents may act similarly. Monitor, and if parkinson's worsens, stop the benzodiazepine.
MAOIs	B↑	MAOIs may prolong triazolam's effects.
Rifampin	B↓	Reduces benzodiazepine hypnotics (except temazepam).
*Troleandomycin	B↑	Troleandomycin increases with triazolam, inducing psychomotor impairment, memory dysfunction, and drowsiness. May need to halt triazolam.

Drugs (X) Interacts with:	Chloral Hydrate (C)	Comments
*Alcohol	X↑ C↑	This "Mickey Finn" yields CNS depression. Patients can have fainting, sedation, flushing, tachycardia, headache, and hypotension. Avoid mixture, especially with cardiovascular problems.
*Dicumarol	X↑	Chloral hydrate may briefly accelerate hypo-prothrombinemic response to dicumarol. This effect quickly disappears. Adverse clinical responses are uncommon, but bleeding may occur. Benzodiazepines preferred. Don't give chloral hydrate to patients on anticoagulants.
Furosemide	X↑	Diaphoresis, hot flashes, and hypertension occur with IV furosemide. Give IV furosemide with caution to any patient on chloral hydrate in past 24 hours.
TCAs	X↓	Decreased antidepressant effect.
*Warfarin	X↑	Same as dicumarol.

Drugs (X) Interacts with:	Disulfiram (D)	Comments
†Alcohol	D↑	(See text, pages 238–39)
Amitriptyline	X↑	When amitriptyline was added to disulfiram, there appeared 2 cases of an organic brain syndrome with confusion, hallucinations, and memory loss in 1–4 weeks. Rapid improvement when one or both agents stopped. Avoid combination until more information.
Anticonvulsants	X↑	Excessive sedation.
Barbiturates	X↑	Excessive sedation.
*Benzodiazepines	X↑	Disulfiram enhances most benzodiazepine levels (not 3-hydroxy compounds); more sedation. Clinician can lower benzodiazepines or switch to 3-hydroxy compounds.
Cephalosporin	D↑	Disulfiram reaction.
Cocaine	D↓	Increased disulfiram effect.
†Dicumarol	X↑	See disulfiram-warfarin below.
*Isoniazid	D↑	Disulfiram and isoniazid produce ataxia, irritability, disorientation, dizziness, and nausea. Frequency unclear, but combine cautiously. Reduce or stop disulfiram.
*Metronidazole	D↑	The combination may cause CNS toxicity, psychosis, and confusion. Avoid combination.
MAOIs	D↑	Severe CNS reactions.
Paraldehyde	X↑	Disulfiram may inhibit paraldehyde's metabolism, leading to toxicity.
†Phenytoin	X↑	Disulfiram consistently increases phenytoin, causing phenytoin toxicity (e.g., ataxia, mental impairment, nystagmus). Often occurs about 4 hours after disulfiram's initial dose. After stopping disulfiram, symptoms may persist for 3 weeks. Avoid combination, but if must use together, observe patient carefully. Obtain serum phenytoin determinations. Monitor for reduced phenytoin response when disulfiram stopped.

HYPNOTICS

Drugs (X) Interacts with:	Disulfiram (D)	Comments
*Theophylline	X ↑	Disulfiram increases theophylline, which may prompt toxicity. Lower theophylline dose may be needed. If disulfiram is changed, monitor patient's theophylline effect.
†Warfarin	X ↑	Disulfiram increases response to warfarin, which induces bleeding. If disulfiram is started or discontinued in patients taking oral anticoagulants, monitor patient carefully. Similar interaction with dicumarol likely, but unproven.

Drugs (X) Interacts with:	Ethchlorvynol (E)	Comments
Amitriptyline	X ↑ E ↑	Transient delirium noted in patient taking one gram of ethchlorvynol and amitriptyline.
*Anticoagulants	X ↓	Ethchlorvynol may inhibit response to dicumarol and possibly warfarin. May need to adjust oral anticoagulants, or preferably, to replace ethchlorvynol with a benzodiazepine.

Codes: * Moderately important interactions. † Extremely important interaction; ↑ Increases; ↓ Decreases.

EFFECTS ON LABORATORY TESTS

Generic Names	Blood/Serum Tests	Results	Urine Tests	Results
Benzodiazepines	WBC, RBC LFT	↓ r ↓ r ↑	None	
Chloral Hydrate	WBC	↓	Ketonuria Glucose Catecholamines 17-hydroxycortico-steroids	↑ ↑ f ↑ ↓
Disulfiram	Cholesterol	↑	VMA	↓

Codes: ↑ Increases; ↓ Decreases; ↑↓ Increases or decreases; f = falsely; r = rarely; LFT = SGOT, SGPT, LDH, bilirubin, and alkaline phosphates.

WITHDRAWAL

Benzodiazepines, barbiturates, barbiturate-like hypnotics, and alcohol all produce

- Dependency
- Tolerance
- Addiction
- Withdrawal

This withdrawal can be fatal. For these reasons, *never* abruptly withdraw hypnosedatives.

These agents are all cross-reactive, although alprazolam and triazolam are not fully cross-reactive with diazepam.

In general, addiction occurs when the patient takes 3–4 times the normal daily therapeutic dose for at least 4–6 weeks.

Compared to patients who suddenly withdraw, patients who gradually withdraw have fewer symptoms and no seizures.

Hypnosedative withdrawal can arise up to 10 days from after the last dose. More typical presentations are

- 2–5 days from the last dose of diazepam or clorazepate
- 1–3 days from alprazolam
- 12–16 hours from barbiturates

Hypnosedatives with shorter half-lives (e.g., amobarbital, lorazepam, alprazolam) present more severe withdrawal symptoms and earlier peaks (2–3 days). Hypnosedatives with longer half-lives (e.g., chlordiazepoxide, diazepam, clorazepate, clonazepam) have less severe withdrawal symptoms and later peaks (5–10 days).

- Benzodiazepine half-lives are longer in older people because they metabolize them more slowly.

*Signs and Symptoms of Hypnosedative Withdrawal**

Stage	Signs and Symptoms	Timing	Patients (%)
I "SHAKES"	Tremor, bad dreams, insomnia, morning sweats, apprehension, blepharospasm, agitation, ataxia, dilated pupils, increased BP and respiration, nausea, vomiting, flushed, hypotension; atypically have transient hallucinations and illusions; rum fits—14%.†	4–8 hours after last dose; peaks at 24 hours; may last 2 weeks; may occur on any substance.	80
II HALLUCINATIONS	Auditory hallucinations both vague (e.g, buzzes, hums) and specific (e.g., accusatory voices); clear consciousness; fear, apprehension, panic, tinnitus; other atypical hallucinations and some clouded consciousness may arise; rum fits—3%.	Onset may happen on agent or up to 12–48 hours (and infrequently up to 7 days) after last dose; typically persists one week, but can exist over 2 months.	5

Stage	Signs and Symptoms	Timing	Patients (%)
III SEIZURES ("Rum fits")	Single or multiple grand mal convulsions; occasionally status epilepticus; muscle jerks.	Appears 6–48 hours after last dose; peaks at 12–24 hours; seizures usually erupt 16 hours into withdrawal.	10
IV DELIRIUM TREMENS (DTs)	Typical delirium: clouded and fluctuating consciousness, confusion, disorientation, loss of recent memory, illusions and hallucinations (of all types, often scary), agitation, emotional lability, persecutory delusions, severe ataxia, coarse tremor; REM rebound (up to 3–4 months); rum fits—41%; 1–15% of DT patients die.	Appears 48–96 hours after last dose; persists 4–7 days without complications; convulsions appear 16 hours into withdrawal, and psychotic symptoms, 36 hours into withdrawal.	15

* This withdrawal pattern applies most to alcohol, barbiturates, and barbiturate-like hypnotics (e.g., ethchlorvynol); happens less often and less severely with benzodiazepines. Stages may evolve gradually or leap ahead. May pass through any stage without going through a previous stage.

† "Rum fits" are convulsions that erupt during any stage. Stage III presents the most intense and frequent rum fits. About 20% of patients with DTs have already had a seizure.

Pentobarbital-Phenobarbital Tolerance Test

To withdraw people from hypnosedatives, the pentobarbital-phenobarbital test can determine the degree of dependence on hypnosedatives.

Step #1: The patient should not be intoxicated before receiving any pentobarbital.

- If the patient is already taking a hypnosedative, adding pentobarbital will increase the patient's tolerance.
- If patient has been consuming shorter-acting hypnosedatives, the hypnosedative test can be delayed 6–8 hours.
- If a patient has been using longer-acting hypnosedatives, the hypnosedative test can be delayed 1–2 days.

Step #2: Give the patient 200 mg of liquid pentobarbital, often the following morning.

Step #3: Examine the patient 50–60 minutes later. Signs of tolerance to a total daily dose of *pentobarbital-equivalents* are shown below.

Possible Findings One Hour After Pentobarbital Challenge

Patient's Condition One Hour After Text Dose	Degree of Tolerance	Estimated 24-Hour Pentobarbital Requirement After Test Dose (mg)
No signs of intoxication	Extreme	Over 850
Fine nystagmus only	Marked	700–850
Slurred speech, mild ataxia, fine nystagmus	Definite	450–700
Coarse nystagmus, positive Romberg, gross ataxia, drowsy	Moderate	300–450
Asleep, but can awake	None or minimal	< 300

Step #4: The patient's pentobarbital-equivalents can be altered by

- The patient has not ingested the full test dose of pentobarbital or has secretly taken other hypnosedatives.
- Tolerance escalates with greater anxiety or agitation.
- A 300 mg test dose is better for patients taking a pentobarbital-equivalent of over 1200 mg/day.
- For elderly patients, the test dose might be 100 mg.
- If the patient shows no intoxication to 200 mg of pentobarbital, the patient's tolerance is over 850 mg/day. If so,
  - √ Give patient pentobarbital 100 mg q2h until he manifests intoxication or total dose reaches 500 mg of pentobarbital in 6 hours (e.g., 200 + 100 + 100 + 100 = 500 mg).
  - √ The total dose given in the first 6 hours (e.g., 300–500 mg) is the patient's 6-hour requirement.

Step #5: Figure out the detoxification strategy.

- Establish the patient's phenobarbital-equivalent.
  - √ If the patient had nystagmus, mild ataxia, and some slurred speech, the patient might go on 150 mg qid (600 mg/day) of pentobarbital.
- However, it is better to calculate the initial 24-hour phenobarbital-equivalent.
  - √ Because phenobarbital has a longer half-life and greater anti-seizure activity than pentobarbital, this 24-hour pentobarbital-equivalent (600 mg/day) is converted to phenobarbital requirements by substituting 30 mg of phenobarbital for 100 mg of pentobarbital. In this example, the phenobarbital-equivalent is 180 mg.

Step #6: Divide the daily phenobarbital dose into thirds (60 mg) and provide each dose every 8 hours for the first 48 hours.

- After 2 days, phenobarbital dose is diminished by 30 mg/day or by 10%/day (whichever is less) from the original dose. In this case, 10% is less and equals 6 mg.
- If patient is oversedated, reduce the dose slightly.
- If the patient displays withdrawal signs, inch the dose up slightly.
- If unsure whether patient has received too much or too little phenobarbital, dispense too much rather than too little, since seizing is a greater risk than sleeping.

Other Withdrawal Methods

Benzodiazepines

Can be withdrawn by using the same agents and decreasing the dose 10% a day.

An alternative is to

- Eliminate the benzodiazepine by 50% during first week, and then
- Reduce the other half by doses of 1/8th to 1/16th of the remaining dose every 4–7 days.

Because withdrawing patients often have symptoms of depression, panic, and insomnia, clinicians might accompany withdrawal by adding either

- Imipramine (150–300 mg/day),
- Doxepin (25–50 mg/day) if patient has insomnia,
- Phenelzine (45–90 mg/day),
- Buspirone (25–45 mg/day), or
- Carbamazepine (200–600 mg/day).

Five weeks later, benzodiazepine-free states occurred in 79–92% of patients withdrawing with these added drugs, whereas 58% of the placebo-treated withdrawing patients were free of drugs.

- Carbamazepine gave the best (92%) results.
- Clonidine afforded no benefit.

It is best to withdraw patients on shorter-acting alprazolam and triazolam with benzodiazepines having a longer half-life.

- For instance, transfer patient from alprazolam to diazepam in 2–3 times the equivalent dose, such as ½ mg of alprazolam to 10 mg (not 5) of diazepam. Gradually make this change over a one-week period.
- Watch for withdrawal symptoms up to 5 weeks.

Buspirone

Does not create tolerance, dependence, or withdrawal. It does *not* stop or prevent withdrawal from benzodiazepines.

Hydroxyzine

May not produce physical dependence.

Meprobamate

Withdrawal no faster than 10% every 2–3 days.

Immediate withdrawal of 3200 mg/day can induce convulsions, agitation, delirium, or death.

Alcohol

Although alcohol withdrawal resembles hypnosedative withdrawal, a somewhat different procedure might address certain matters specific to alcohol.

Chlordiazepoxide provides an effective method because it is

- Relatively long-acting,
- Offers less euphoria than diazepam, and
- Affords fewer side effects than other agents.

Management of alcohol withdrawal involves

- Treat Wernicke's syndrome
  - √ Thiamine, 100 mg po or IM on admission and
  - √ Thiamine 50 mg/day po for one month.
- Manage alcohol withdrawal *per se*
  - √ Initiate chlordiazepoxide 200 mg/day for first 2 days.
  - √ Reduce total daily dose of chlordiazepoxide by 25% each day until reaching zero.
  - √ Give extra doses of chlordiazepoxide to prevent withdrawal symptoms.
- If there is adequate social support and a well-motivated patient, outpatient withdrawal can be implemented.
  - √ Start with chlordiazepoxide 25 mg taken q4h (or less often) for day #1.
  - √ Taper by 25% qd until no chlordiazepoxide remains.
  - √ In very tremulous outpatient, use 100 mg/day of chlordiazepoxide.
- Patients with hepatic problems are best withdrawn with oxazepam or lorazepam, which are not metabolized in the liver.

Alcohol Prevention

If the goal is to *prevent* the resumption of alcohol consumption, disulfiram might help.

If the disulfiram-taking patient drinks alcohol, he or she may experience in 5–10 minutes (usually in this order)

• Flushing
• Sweating
• Throbbing headache and neck pain
• Palpitations
• Dyspnea
• Hyperventilation
• Tachycardia
• Hypotension
• Nausea
• Vomiting

More serious reactions generate chest pain, difficulty breathing, more severe hypotension, confusion, and (especially in patients on >500 mg/day) an occasional death.
Reactions occur for ½-2 hours, often followed by drowsiness and sleep.

• The reaction's dangers increase with higher amounts of disulfiram (>500 mg/day) or ethanol.
• Reactions can occur up to 14 days after the last drink.

Disulfiram should be avoided in

• Masochistic or suicidal patients
• Organic patients who forget they have ingested disulfiram
• Patients with severe cardiac disease, moderate-to-severe liver disease, renal failure, peripheral neuropathies, or pregnancy
• Patients using drugs metabolized by the liver, including TCAs, MAOIs, neuroleptics, vasodilators, α- or β-adrenergic blockers, paraldehyde, or metronidazole
• Patients extremely sensitive to thiuram derivatives in pesticides or rubber vulcanization
• Patients who refuse to tell any relatives about their use of disulfiram
• Patients who will not (or cannot) avoid aftershave lotions, sauces, vinegars, cough syrup

Give disulfiram as follows

• Wait at least 12 hours after last drink.
• Start on 250 mg qd for 1–2 weeks, and then
   √ 250 mg to patients over 170 pounds or
   √ 125 mg to patients under 170 pounds.

Side effects include

- Drowsiness, fatigue
- Body odor or halitosis (dose-related)
- Also foul taste in mouth, headache, tremor, impotence, dizziness, and a rare hepatotoxicity, neuropathy, or psychosis.

Management

- If there is a severe disulfiram reaction, give diphenhydramine 50 mg IM/IV.
- Treat hypotension, shock, and arrhythmias symptomatically.
- Oxygen is useful for respiratory distress.

Treat alcohol-induced aggression and hallucinosis with high-potency antipsychotics, such as haloperidol 5 mg.

- Avoid low-potency neuroleptics (e.g., thioridazine) during alcohol withdrawal since they are more likely to prompt seizures and severe hypotension.

OVERDOSE: TOXICITY, SUICIDE, AND TREATMENT

Benzodiazepines

Benzodiazepine overdoses are discussed in the previous chapter.

Barbiturates and Barbiturate-like Hypnotics

Barbiturates and barbiturate-like hypnotics present high suicide risks.

- About 10 times the daily dose of a barbiturate can be severely toxic.
- Death occurs in $\frac{1}{2}$–12% of barbiturate overdoses. These fatalities may happen "on purpose" or from an "autonomous" state, in which the patient falls asleep, awakes in a fog, cannot remember how many pills he already has taken, and overconsumes.

Barbiturates, with a shorter half-life and high lipid solubility, are more lethal.

Chloral Hydrate

Chloral hydrate's lethal dose is 5–10 times its hypnotic dose of 1–2 grams. Acute chloral hydrate overdoses display:

Common	Less Common	Infrequent
Stomach distress	Miosis	Esophageal stricture
Hypotension	Vomiting	Gastric necrosis and perforation
Hypothermia	Areflexia	GI hemorrhage
Respiratory depression	Muscle flaccidity	Transient hepatic damage and
Cardiac arrhythmias		jaundice
Coma		

Management of chloral hydrate overdose

- General management as listed in the previous chapter for benzo-diazepines.
- Hemodialysis may eliminate the metabolite trichloroethanol.
  √ Peritoneal dialysis may assist.

Ethchlorvynol

Acute ethchlorvynol overdoses generate

- Hypotension
- Bradycardia
- Hypothermia
- Mydriasis
- Areflexia

This may lead to

- Pulmonary edema
- Severe infections
- Peripheral neuropathy
- Severe pancytopenia, hemolysis
- Severe cardiorespiratory depression, apnea
- Deep coma (lasting several weeks)

Management of ethchlorvynol overdoses involve (see page 37)

- Emphasis on pulmonary care and monitoring blood pressure gases.
- Value of hemodialysis is debated.
- Alkalinization of urine does not increase excretion.

Methyprylon

Acute methyprylon overdoses cause

- Somnolence
- Confusion
- Constricted pupils

* Hyperpyrexia or hypothermia
* Hypotension
* Coma

Management of methyprylon overdoses includes (see page 37) and

* Hypotension (see pages 74–75)
* Treat excitation and seizures with short-acting barbiturates (e.g., thiopental).

Hemodialysis may be useful in severe intoxication, especially if patient is unresponsive to supportive measures and cannot maintain adequate urinary output. Improvement is slower with peritoneal dialysis or forced diuresis.

Toxicity and Suicide Data

Generic Names	Toxic Doses Average (g)	Fatal Doses Average (Lowest) (g)	Toxic Levels* (µg/ml)	Fatal Levels* (µg/ml)
Benzodiazepines				
Flurazepam	—	—	—	—
Quazepam	—	—	—	—
Temazepam	—	—	—	—
Triazolam	2	—	—	—
Barbiturates				
Amobarbital	0.4	2–3	30–40	> 50
Butabarbital	—	—	40–60	> 50
Pentobarbital	—	2–3	10–15	> 30
Phenobarbital	—	6–10	50–80 (30–134)	> 80
Secobarbital	—	2–3	10–15	> 30
Miscellaneous				
Chloral hydrate	30	10 (4)	—	—
Ethchlorvynol	50	6	—	—
Methyprylon	> 20	6	—	—

* *Toxic levels* are comatose, difficult to arouse, significant respiratory depression; *fatal levels* are usually lethal.

PRECAUTIONS

All hypnotics contraindicated in

* Hypersensitivity to hypnotics or anti-anxiety agents
* Pregnancy
* Sleep apnea
* Porphyria (mainly barbiturates and chloral hydrate)

Barbiturates should be avoided in patients with

* Liver impairment
* Alcoholism
* Renal conditions

NURSES' DATA

Observe if patients have

- Trouble finding the bed after taking hypnotic
- Walking or falling
- Confusion
- Immediate sleepiness or overstimulation
- Skin rash
- Abdominal pain or
- Muscle weakness

Note symptoms of withdrawal, intoxication, or overdose (see pages 232-37, 239-41). Withdrawal symptoms may be difficult to distinguish from anxiety and vice versa.

Insure that patients do not take hypnotics for pain relief.

Also make sure patients understand the short-term value of hypnotics. Ingesting hypnotics outdoors produces needless risks.

PATIENT AND FAMILY NOTES

If taking a hypnotic, avoid

- Alcohol
  - √ With a hypnotic, one drink feels and acts like 2–3 drinks.
  - √ Worse with barbiturates and barbiturate-like hypnotics.
- Aspirin or other nonsteroidal anti-inflammatory agents for relieving hangovers, unless a physician has already approved of it
- Contraceptives or steroids unless doctor concurs
- Pregnancy
  - √ If become pregnant, do not stop hypnotics until deciding on a withdrawal schedule with clinician.
- Long-term use
- Suddenly stopping hypnotics after long-term use!
  - √ Abrupt hypnotic withdrawal is often more dangerous than abrupt opiate withdrawal—seizures, and worse.

If a doctor prescribes barbiturate or barbiturate-like hypnotic, ask if a benzodiazepine, which is safer, would be better short-term hypnotic.

If the elderly or debilitated are too confused to manage their hypnotics properly, family members may need to dispense them.

Store hypnotics away from the bedside or from any readily accessible location to avert accidental intake. Keep away from youngsters.

Within 6 hours of taking a hypnotic, do not work around machines, drive a car, or cross the street.

* The next morning, check if reflexes are a "tad off," such as by stepping down on the car break in the driveway.
* There is a 5–10 times higher driving-accident rate in patients ingesting benzodiazepines than nondrug takers.
* People on hypnotics are more likely to ignore fire alarms, pain, a full bladder, a crying baby, or telephones.

Triazolam induces traveler's amnesia.

The doctor should suggest a specific time before bedtime to take a hypnotic (e.g., ½ hour, 1½ hour).

If patient forgets a dose, he can safely consume it within 6 hours of awakening.

* Otherwise wait for next evening.
* Do not double dose.

May ingest with food.

COST INDEX

Generic Names	Brand Names	Equivalent Dosage (mg)	Dose Assessed (mg)	Cost Rating*
Chloral Hydrate	Noctec	500	500	22
	generic	500	500	>8
Estazolam	ProSom	1	1	122
Ethchlorvynol	Placidyl	500	500	139
Flurazepam	Dalmane	30	30	98
	generics	30	30	743
Methyprylon	Noludar	200	200	118
Quazepam	Doral	15	15	213
Temazepam	Restoril	30	30	111
	generics	30	30	40
Triazolam	Halcion	0.5	0.250	112

* The higher the number, the higher the cost.

9. Stimulants

INTRODUCTION

Although abused illegally, stimulants are used clinically to treat

- Attention-deficit hyperactivity disorder (ADHD) (see pages 247–49)
- Treatment-resistant depression (see page 249)
- Narcolepsy (see page 250)
- AIDS (see page 250)

NAMES, MANUFACTURERS, DOSE FORMS, AND COLORS

Generic Names	Brand Names	Manufacturers	Dose Forms (mg)*	Colors
Dextroamphetamine	Dexedrine	SmithKline Beecham	t: 5; SR-sp: 5/10/15; e: 5 mg/5 ml	t: orange;† SR-sp: all brown-clear; e: orange
Methylphenidate	Ritalin	CIBA	t: 5/10/20;	t: yellow/pale green/pale yellow;†
	Ritalin-SR generics	CIBA	SR-t: 20	SR-t: white
Pemoline	Cylert	Abbott	t: 18.75/37.5/ 75 c: 37.5	t: white/orange/ tan c: orange

* c = chewable tablet; e = elixir; sp = spansule; SR = sustained release; t = tablets; † scored.

PHARMACOLOGY

Stimulants act by

- Directly releasing catecholamines into synaptic clefts, and thus onto postsynaptic receptor sites.
- Efficiently blocking the reuptake of catecholamines, thereby prolonging their actions.
- Act on MAO enzymes to slow down metabolism.
- Serve as false neurotransmitters.

Dextroamphetamine

- Rapidly absorbed from GI tract.
- Causes
  - √ Increased BP and pulse rate
  - √ Decreased appetite, reduced weight
  - √ Delayed sleep
- Diminishes more weight gain than methylphenidate or pemoline.

Methylphenidate

- Rapidly absorbed from GI tract.
- Effects persist 2–4 hours from a single normal tablet and 3–5 hours after extended-release tablets.
  - √ Sustained-release tablets are absorbed more slowly and may yield a lower plasma level than regular tablets.
- Has less anorectic effect than dextroamphetamine.

Pemoline

- Is rapidly absorbed by GI tract.
- May be smoother and better tolerated.
- Is 80% bound to plasma protein.
- Reaches a steady state in 2–3 days.
- Has less stimulant effect than dextroamphetamine and methylphenidate.
- Reduces appetite and delays sleep in 30% of children.

Pharmacology of Stimulants in Children

Generic Names	Peak Serum Levels (hours)	Serum Half-Lives (hours)	Onset of Action (hours)	Duration of Action (hours)
Dextroamphetamine	3–4	11–12	1	4–6
Methylphenidate	1–3	2–4	1	3–6
Pemoline	2–4 (5–12)	2–12 (acute) 14–34 (chronic)	3–4	12–24

DOSES

Attention-Deficit Hyperactivity Stimulant Doses in Children

Generic Names	Usual Starting Dose (mg)	Single Dose Range (mg/kg/day)	Daily Dose Range (mg/kg/day)	Daily Dose Range (mg/day)
Dextroamphetamine	2½ qd or bid	0.15–½	0.6–1.7	5–40
Methylphenidate	5 qd or bid	0.3–0.7	0.3–1.25	10–60
Pemoline	18.75 daily	½–2½	½–3.0	37½–112½

Other Stimulant Doses

Generic Names	Adult Depression (mg/day)	Adult Narcolepsy (mg/day)	Geriatric Patients (mg/day)
Dextroamphetamine	5–40	20–30	10–15
Methylphenidate	40–60	10–30	10–30
Pemoline	37½–150	37½–75	—

S
T
I
M
U
L
A
N
T
S

CLINICAL INDICATIONS AND USE

Stimulants can

- Clearly effective
  - √ Attention deficit-hyperactivity disorder (in children)
  - √ Narcoleptic symptoms of daytime sleepiness and sleep attacks
- Probably effective
  - √ Treatment-resistant depressions
  - √ Apathy and withdrawal in medically ill and the elderly
- Possibly effective
  - √ Residual attention deficit disorder (in adults)
  - √ Affective and organic symptoms of AIDS

Attention-Deficit Hyperactivity Disorder (ADHD)

Roughly 75% of these children respond to stimulants.

Short-acting stimulants are the first choice.

- Dextroamphetamine or
- Methylphenidate

If one of these drugs fails, there is a 25% chance the other drug will succeed.

When a stimulant works, it

- Occurs early (often in 2 days),
- Persists, and
- Shows little or no tolerance over months to years.

Stimulants superior to placebo in 70–80% of patients.

- 30% exhibit marked improvement,
- 40% display some benefit, and
- 10–30% are refractory.

Stimulants generate

- Decreased motor activity
- Diminished impulsiveness
- Increased vigilance and attention
- Less emotional liability
- More "normal" behavior

Stimulants make some youngsters more active and others more withdrawn and despondent.

Dosing

- Dextroamphetamine uses bid-tid and methylphenidate tid-qid dosages.
- Pemoline can be dispensed once every morning.
- Can increase stimulant doses q 2–4 days.
- Scored tablets useful.
- Kids enjoy chewable pemoline.

Therapeutic responses do not jive directly with serum or saliva levels.

Safe to suddenly stop stimulants.

Safer to use sustained-release forms before TCAs.

TCAs may help if

- Single night dosing desirable for compliance,
- Mood disorder co-exists,
- Strong family h/o mood disorder,
- Prominent sleep symptoms, or
- Drug-abusing children or parents.

Drawbacks of TCAs are

- Hard to maintain beneficial effects, since TCAs may lose their efficacy over time.
- Serious cardiovascular hazards (especially in prepubertal children),
- Overdose—high risk or reality.

Antidepressants include.

- Imipramine—1st choice
- Desipramine, nortriptyline, bupropion—2nd choice
- Clomipramine not indicated for ADHD children because it sedates excessively and triggers seizures.
  - √ Clomipramine excellent for kids with obsessive-compulsive disorders.

Start imipramine at 10 mg hs and then gradually increase to 75 mg hs.

Improvement with TCAs happens in a few days or weeks.

Other drugs suggested for ADHD have important limitations.

- Benzodiazepines and barbiturates can trigger excitement; avoid.
- Diphenhydramine and chloral hydrate promote less agitation and may temporarily induce sleep.
- Neuroleptics (e.g., chlorpromazine 10–50 mg qid) nonspecifically calm and cause tardive dyskinesia.
- Lithium only assists bipolar patients with impulsiveness, low attention span, and hyperactivity.
  - √ Also helps conduct disorders.

Adults with residual attention deficit disorder (with inattention, impulsiveness, concentration difficulty, anxiety, irritability, and excitability) *plus* a childhood history of ADHD may improve with stimulants.

- Often have poor work or academic performance, temper outbursts, antisocial behavior, or alcohol abuse.
- Instead of a residual attention deficit disorder, the patient may have a mood, borderline, or antisocial disorder, and therefore, not respond to stimulants.

Treatment-Resistant Depression

Stimulants infrequently stop depression, yet they dramatically aid a small, *select* group, who

- Have failed on at least 2 other antidepressants (TCAs/MAOIs).
- Have a serious, often life-threatening, ailment (e.g., AIDS, cancer), who cannot tolerate antidepressants.
- Will be booted soon from a job or school, and who require a stimulant's boost until TCAs work.
- Need an adjunct to TCAs.

Childhood depressions may not respond to TCAs.

Never add a stimulant to MAOIs: Hypertensive crisis!

Narcolepsy

Treatments include

- Methylphenidate and dextroamphetamine for sleep attacks and daytime sleepiness.
  - √ Unlike with ADHD, tolerance to stimulant occurs with higher doses.
- Phenelzine for sleep attacks.
- TCAs (e.g., imipramine) for cataplexy.

AIDS

Methylphenidate or dextroamphetamine alone reduced affective and organic symptoms in patients with AIDS.

- No adverse effects.
- No tolerance developed.

SIDE EFFECTS

Stimulant side effects typically arise

- In 2–3 weeks after initiating drug and
- From dose reduction, causing rebound with symptoms.

Elderly develop more side effects.

From the greater to the lesser, stimulants exert

Subjective Side Effects	Objective Side Effects
Irritability, hyperalertness	Blood pressure changes (up or down)
Insomnia	Dysrhythmias
Nausea	Tremor
Appetite change	
Palpitations	
Blurred vision	
Dry mouth	
Constipation	
Dizziness	

Cardiovascular Effects

Blood pressure changes

- Highly variable
  - √ Black children more often hypertensive.

- Unclear if taking stimulants with meals alters BP,
- Reduce or stop drug.

Palpitations

Tachycardia

Gastrointestinal Effects

Dry mouth

- Mainly in adolescents

Anorexia

- Reduced appetite occurs in 30% of children given moderately high stimulant doses.

Weight loss

- Usually begins early in treatment,
- May last for up to 6 weeks and
  √ With pemoline, *weight gain* may follow in 3–6 months.

Hepatotoxicity

- Pemoline induces hepatotoxicity in 1–3% of children.
- SGOT and SGPT gradually increase over first 6 months of treatment.
  √ Enzymes return to normal after stopping pemoline.

Endocrine and Sex Effects

Suppressed growth

- Some stimulants suppress weight gain in some children; whether stimulants suppress height gain is debated.
  √ Suppressed growth happens more with dextroamphetamine > methylphenidate > pemoline.
- When methylphenidate (average dose 41 mg/day) was stopped for 2 summers in some ADHD children, the methylphenidate-treated group's average height was $1\frac{1}{2}$ cm shorter than the unmedicated group.
  √ Yet when methylphenidate is halted, compensatory growth occurs, which eliminates all growth difference between drug and nondrug-treated patients.
- Growth rebound appears during drug-free holidays.

Impotence

Changes in libido

Central Nervous System Effects

Insomnia

- Affects 30% of children on moderately high stimulant doses.
- Often arises early, at times before optimal dose reached.
  √ May be transient with pemoline.
- Management
  √ Give more of the stimulant earlier in the day.
  √ Reduce dose.

Overstimulation

Confusion, "Dopey feeling"

- Especially arises with > 1 mg/kg/day of methylphenidate.

Restlessness

- Reduce dose and/or
- Give earlier in day.

Headache

Dizziness

Choreoathetoid movements

- Common with pemoline

Dysphoria

- With all stimulants, but especially with methylphenidate patients who display
  √ Mild dysphoria
  √ Subtle social withdrawal
  √ Dulled affect, emotional blurting
  √ Cognitive "overfocusing"
  √ Perseveration
- Mild to moderate depression in children

Euphoria

Exacerbation of tics, exacerbation of Tourette's

- Avoid stimulants with these patients.

Psychosis

- Dextroamphetamine doses > 80 mg/day triggers psychosis with
  √ Agitation
  √ Tremor
  √ Toxicity
  √ Hallucinations
  √ Paranoid thinking

PERCENTAGES OF SIDE EFFECTS*

Side Effects	Dextroamphetamine	Methylphenidate	Pemoline
CARDIOVASCULAR EFFECTS			
Dizziness, lightheadedness	11.5 (1–23)	7.7 (0–13)	5.5
Lower blood pressure	—	< 1	< 1
Higher blood pressure	> 10	15.8 (1–26)	—
Tachycardia	5.5	15 (1–20)	5.5
Palpitations	5.5	4.4 (1–10)	5.5
Cardiac arrhythmias	< 1	5.5	—
Chest pain	< 1	4.4 (1–10)	—
GASTROINTESTINAL EFFECTS			
Dry mouth and throat	> 10	8.7 (0–17.4	—
Anorexia, lower appetite	23.1 (1–56)	26.9 (0–72)	14.5 (1–34)
Nausea	5.5	5.1 (1–10)	5.5
Vomiting	5.5	—	—
Bad taste	5.5	—	—
Dyspepsia, upset stomach	5.5	9.7 (1–28)	5.5
Diarrhea	5.5	—	—
Constipation	5.5	6.5	—
Hepatotoxicity	—	—	2
Weight loss	29.5 (1–63)	13.5 (3–27)	5.5
Weight gain	—	4.3	—
RENAL EFFECTS			
Enuresis	—	9 (3–20)	—
ENDOCRINE AND SEXUAL EFFECTS			
Impotence	5.5	—	—
Disturbed sexual function	5.5	—	—
Growth suppression	SEE TEXT	SEE TEXT	SEE TEXT
HEMATOLOGIC EFFECTS			
Easy bruising	—	5.5	—
EYES, EARS, NOSE, AND THROAT EFFECTS			
Blurred vision	5.5	< 1	—
Nystagmus	—	—	5.5

Side Effects	Dextroamphetamine	Methylphenidate	Pemoline
SKIN, ALLERGIES, AND TEMPERATURE			
Unusual sweating	5.5	—	—
Rashes	< 1	5.5	5.5
Hives	< 1	5.5	—
Exfoliative dermatitis	—	5.5	—
Fever, unexplained	—	5.5	—
Joint pain	—	5.5	—
CENTRAL NERVOUS SYSTEM EFFECTS			
Dyskinesias	<1	3	5.5
Tourette's syndrome	< 1	< 1	< 1
Tics	< 1	—	—
Headache	18.3 (1–31)	9.3 (0–15)	13.8 (1–22)
Drowsiness, less alert	5.5	5.7 (0–17)	5.5
Psychosis (normal dose)	< 1	< 1	< 1
Difficulty arousing	—	15 (11–19)	—
Insomnia	19 (5–43)	16.9 (0–52)	28.7 (<10–42)
Tremor	5.5	6.5	—
Confused, "dopey"	10.3 (8–12)	3.9 (2–10)	—
Mood changes	< 1	> 10	5.5
Depression	39	8.7 (0–16)	—
Agitation, restlessness (i.e., motoric)	> 10	6.7 (3.3–>10)	—
Irritable, stimulation	25 (17–29)	17.3 (11–19.6)	13.3 (1–21)

* These figures are primarily derived from children and adolescents being treated for ADHD.

PREGNANCY AND LACTATION

Teratogenicity (1st trimester)

- Dextroamphetamine may cause congenital malformations, such as cardiac abnormalities and biliary atresia.

- Methylphenidate not linked with congenital defects.

Direct Effect on Newborn (3rd trimester)

- One case of IV dextroamphetamine use reported in woman to produce withdrawal; experts strongly discourage dextroamphetamine during pregnancy.

Lactation	• One of 3 studies revealed infants of amphetamine-using mothers were more irritable and poor sleepers; no figures given.
	• Methylphenidate: no data.

Drug Dosage in Mother's Milk

Generic Name	Milk/ Plasma Ratio	Time of Peak Concentration in Milk (hours)	Infant Dose (μg/kg/day)	Maternal Dose (%)	Safety Rating*
Amphetamine	2.8–7½	?	20.7	6.2	C

* C: Unsafe before week 34, relatively safe from weeks 34–44, and safest after 44th week.

DRUG-DRUG INTERACTIONS

Virtually no drug-drug interactions have occurred with pemoline, but its combination with CNS depressants should be observed carefully.

Drugs (X) Interacts with:	Dextroamphetamines (D)	Comments
*Acetazolamide	D↑	Acetazolamide increases amphetamines. Monitor patients on acetazolamide or on other carbonic anhydrase inhibitors for excessive amphetamines.
Amantadine	X↑	Increased amantadine effect with stimulation and agitation.
Antihistamines	X↑	Amphetamine reduce antihistamine's sedation.
Antihypertensives	X↓	Amphetamines may antagonize antihypertensives.
Antipsychotics	X↓ D↓	Amphetamines restrain antipsychotic actions, while neuroleptics block amphetamines' anorectic effect. Chlorpromazine effectively treats amphetamine overdose, but amphetamines should never treat a chlorpromazine overdose.
Ethosuximide	X↓	Amphetamines delay absorption of anticonvulsant ethosuximide.
Fluoxetine	X↑ D↑	Increased agitation.
†Furazolidone	D↑	Amphetamines induce hypertensive crisis in patients given furazolidone, especially after 5 days. Avoid.
*Guanethidine	X↓ D↑	Amphetamines inhibit guanethidine's antihypertensive action. Does hypertensive patient need amphetamines? Use another agent.
Lithium	D↓	Lithium slows weight reduction and stimulatory effects of amphetamines. No special precautions.
Meperidine	X↑	Amphetamine potentiates analgesic action.

Drugs (X) Interacts with:	Dextroamphetamines (D)	Comments
†MAOIs	X ↑	Hypertensive crisis. Tranylcypromine is the most dangerous MAOI.
Norepinephrine	X ↑	Amphetamine abuse may increase pressor response to norepinephrine. Combine with caution.
Phenytoin	X ↓	Amphetamines delay phenytoin absorption.
*Sodium bicarbonate	D ↑	Hefty sodium bicarbonate can increase amphetamine's effect.
*TCAs	X ↑	Amphetamines may increase TCA effect; it can also produce arrhythmias, agitation, and psychosis.

Drugs (X) Interacts with:	Methylphenidate (M)	Comments
*Guanethidine	X ↓ D ↑	Methylphenidate inhibits guanethidine's antihypertensive action. Try another antihypertensive.
*MAOIs	X ↑	Methylphenidate poses less risk than amphetamines for hypertensive crisis, but methylphenidate should still be avoided with MAOIs.
Phenytoin	X ↑	Isolated cases of phenytoin intoxication. No special precautions.
TCAs	X ↑	Methylphenidate may facilitate TCA antidepressant and toxic effects.

Codes: * Moderately important interactions; † Extremely important interaction; ↑ Increases; ↓ Decreases.

EFFECTS ON LABORATORY TESTS

Generic Names	Blood/Serum Tests	Results	Urine Tests	Results
Dextroamphetamine	Corticosteroids	↑	Steroids determinations	Interferes
	Growth hormone	?		
	Prolactin	?		
Methylphenidate	RBC, WBC	↓ r ↓ r	None	
	Growth hormone	?		
	Prolactin	?		
Pemoline	LFT	↑	None	

Codes: ↑ Increases; ↓ Decreases; ? Inconsistent; r = rarely; LFT are SGOT, SGPT, LDH, alkaline phosphatase, and bilirubin.

WITHDRAWAL

Stimulants do not seem to induce

- Physical dependence
- Tolerance
- Addiction
- Physical withdrawal

Stimulants may cause

- Psychic dependence
- Drug misuse

From the most to the least abused are

- Dextroamphetamine
  √ Dextroamphetamine > 50 mg/day can often generate a serious, but not life-threatening, withdrawal.
- Methylphenidate
  √ Abused orally when mixed with other drugs.
  √ Addicts grind up tablets, inject, and develop emboli.
- Pemoline
  √ Is rarely an addiction problem.

Dextroamphetamine and methylphenidate withdrawal symptoms include

- Increased appetite, weight gain
  √ Appetite may be huge for several days.
- Increased sleep
  √ Sleep may be extensive at first.
- Decreased energy, fatigue
  √ Rapid withdrawal, especially from high doses, can lead to profound inertia, depressed mood ("crashing"), and suicide.
- Paranoid symptoms may persist during withdrawal, but this is uncommon.

Management

- Observe patient.
- Prevent suicide.
- Frequently reassure patient.
- TCAs, if patient is depressed.
  √ Since amphetamine withdrawal depletes noradrenergic activity, TCAs (e.g., desipramine) that increase noradrenergic over serotonin function are preferred.

OVERDOSE: TOXICITY, SUICIDE, AND TREATMENT

Death rarely occurs from overdoses of prescribed stimulants, since there is a large difference between the therapeutic and toxic doses of the drug. Nevertheless, a 10-day supply taken at once can be very toxic, even lethal, especially with children.

Virtually all amphetamine overdoses are from illegal, not clinically, used drugs.

Amphetamine overdoses produce

- Agitation (21%)
- Suicidal ideation (12%)
- Chest pain (9%)
- Hallucinations (auditory > visual) (7%)
- Confusion (6%)
- Dysphoria, weakness, lethargy (5%)
- Delusions (5%)

Other symptoms (< 5%) include

- Seizures, aggression, headache, palpitations, abdominal pain, rashes, dyspnea, leg pain, and paresthesias.

The general management of stimulant overdoses involve (see page 37)

For specific symptoms of stimulant overdoses, other treatments are

- For seizures
  √ Short-acting barbiturates (e.g., amobarbital) or
  √ IV diazepam.
- For agitation
  √ Haloperidol and diazepam equally effective.
- For psychosis
  √ Isolate patients from environmental stimuli, which aggravate psychosis.
  √ Haloperidol 2½–5 mg IM prn q2h, or
  √ Chlorpromazine 25–50 mg IM prn q2h.
- For high blood pressure
  √ Hasten excretion by acidifying urine with ammonium chloride.
  √ If hypertension is severe, may inject phentolamine 5 mg IV.
  √ May employ hypothermic measures if intracranial pressure rises.
  √ Combat cerebral edema and congestion.

Chronic amphetamine abuse may be treated best with desipramine.

Toxicity and Suicide Data

Generic Names	Toxicity Doses Average (Highest) (mg)	Mortality Doses Average (Lowest) (mg)	Fatal Supplies (days)	Toxic Levels (ng/ml)
Dextroamphetamine	20 (1½ mg/kg)	400	—	—
Methylphenidate	—	—	—	—
Pemoline	—	—	—	—

PRECAUTIONS

Contraindications

- Anxiety and agitation
- h/o drug abuse (unless a solid clinical reason)
- Advanced arteriosclerosis, cardiovascular disease, hypertension
- Hyperthyroidism
- Allergy to stimulants
- Glaucoma
- Tics, or Tourette's syndrome (in patients or family members)
- MAOIs
- Psychotic patients

After several months, if patients on pemoline has decreased appetite, fatigue, and stomach fullness, hepatotoxicity should be suspected and liver function tests ordered.

Decrements in predicted growth with premoline are reported after long-term use; observe.

NURSES' DATA

Stress that stimulants have different medical and recreational uses.

- The medical stimulant alleviates specific symptoms, whereas the recreational stimulant triggers a "buzz."
- Patients given medical stimulants often do not develop a "high" or experience tolerance.

If a question exists about whether an adult or child is illegally trying (or hyping) the drug, raise the issue in a reasonable perspective.

Closely monitor the patient's

- Cardiovascular symptoms and vital signs,
- Blood glucose in diabetics,

- Signs of dextroamphetamine or methylphenidate withdrawal, intoxication, or overdose, and
- Slowing of growth; consider drug-free holidays.

PATIENT AND FAMILY NOTES

A 10-day supply of stimulants can be lethal for children.

- Patients who take stimulants also become depressed.
  - √ Patients who suddenly stop taking stimulants also become depressed.
  - √ Ergo, if necessary, monitor the youngster's use of the drug, just as one would with any other drug.

Keep stimulants away from bedside or from any readily accessible place to deter accidental intake. For safety, protect pills from other children in a proper place.

Family and patients should not make a "big deal" about taking stimulants: "It's a medication, like any medication."

Proper stimulant use avoids

- Excessive sodium bicarbonate because it alkalinizes the urine, which reduces amphetamine excretion and prolongs its effect.
- Starvation and unprescribed dietary changes since they acidify the urine, which induces ketosis, accelerates amphetamine elimination, and lowers its effect.

Stimulants have no effective role overcoming lethargy or losing weight.

If anxiety erupts, excessive caffeine may be the culprit.

If patient neglects a dose,

- Can consume the medication for up to 2 hours.
- Otherwise, wait for next dose.
- Never double the dose.

If patient forgets a long-acting (sustained-release) pill,

- Take it the next morning.

Dosage times

- Dextroamphetamine
  - √ Give tablet or elixir at early morning—possibly on awakening— or 30–60 minutes before breakfast.

√ Offer other doses at 4–6 hour intervals.
  □ Do not take within 6 hours of bedtime, especially sustained-acting products.
  □ Doses gobbled after breakfast or lunch do not alter sleep.
√ If stimulant's side effects (e.g., insomnia, anorexia) arise, try the once-a-day dextroamphetamine spansule.

- Methylphenidate
  √ First dose with breakfast, which might reduce stomach aches.
  √ Do not swallow methylphenidate within 6 hours of sleep.
  √ If insomnia or anorexia develop, consider the (8-hour) methylphenidate-SR tablet taken in morning.
  √ Avoid the methylphenidate-SR tablet at first; try it later.
- Pemoline
  √ Give as a single morning tablet, and increase the morning strength.

COST INDEX

Generic Names	Brand Names	Equivalent Dosage (mg)	Dose Assessed (mg)	Cost Rating*
Dextroamphetamine	Dexedrine	5	5	60
	generics	5	5	>9
Methylphenidate	Ritalin	5	5	11
	generics	5	5	>3
	Ritalin (sustained release)	5	20	9
Pemoline	Cylert	37.5	37.5	24

* The higher the number, the higher the cost.

S
T
I
M
U
L
A
N
T
S

Appendices

DRUG IDENTIFICATION

Generic*	Brand Name	Chief Action
acebutolol	Sectral	β blocker (CS)
acetaminophen*	Tylenol	Analgesic
acetazolamide	Diamox	Carbonic anhydrase inhibitor
acetophenazine	Tindal	Neuroleptic
albuterol	Proventil	Sympathomimetic (DA) β
alprazolam	Xanax	Anti-anxiety
aluminum hydroxide*	Gelusil	Antacid
amantadine	Symmetrel	Antiparkinsonian
amiloride	Midamor	Potassium-sparing diuretic
aminophylline	Mudrane	Bronchodilator
amitriptyline	Elavil	TCA
amobarbital	Amytal	Hypnotic
amoxapine	Asendin	HCA
ampicillin	Ampicillan	Penicillin
atenolol	Tenormin	β blocker (CS)
atropine	Atropine sulfate	Anticholinergic
beclomethasone	Vanceril	Corticosteroid
benztropine	Cogentin	Antiparkinsonian
bethanechol	Urecholine	Cholinergic
biperiden	Akineton	Antiparkinsonian
bromocriptine	Parlodel	Prolactin inhibitor
bupropion	Wellbutrin	HCA
buspirone	BuSpar	Anti-anxiety
butabarbital	Butisol	Anti-anxiety
calcium carbonate*	Tums	Antacid
captopril	Capoten	Antihypertensive
carbamazepine	Tegretol	Anticonvulsant
carbidopa-levodopa	Sinemet	Antiparkinsonian
carisoprodol	Soma	Muscle relaxant
casanthranol*	Peri-Colace	Laxative
chloral hydrate	Noctec	Hypnotic

Generic*	Brand Name	Chief Action
chloramphenicol	Chloromycetin	Antibiotic
chlordiazepoxide	Librium	Anti-anxiety
chlorothiazide	Diuril	Thiazide diuretic
chlorpheniramine*	Chlortrimeton	Antihistamine
chlorpromazine	Thorazine	Neuroleptic
chlorprothixene	Taractan	Neuroleptic
choline mg trisalicyate	Trilisate	NSAIA
cimetidine	Tagamet	H_2-Receptor antagonist
clomipramine	Anafranil	TCA
clonidine	Catapres	Antihypertensive
clorazepate	Tranxene	Anti-anxiety
clozapine	Clorazil	Neuroleptic
cyclobenzaprine	Flexeril	Muscle relaxant
cyclophosphamide	Cytoxan	Antineoplastic agent
cyclosporine	Sandimmune	Immunosuppressant
cyproheptadine	Periactin	Antihistamine
danazol	Danocrine	Androgen derivative
desipramine	Norpramin	TCA
dextroamphetamine	Dexedrine	Stimulant
dextromethorphan*	Contac	Cough suppressor
diazepam	Valium	Anti-anxiety
dichloralphenazone	Midrin	Analgesic-Sedative
dicumarol	Dicumarol	Anticoagulant (oral)
digoxin	Lanoxin	Cardiac glycoside
diltiazem	Cardizem	Calcium channel blocker
diphenhydramine*	Benadryl	Antihistamine
disopyramide	Norpace	Antiarrhythmic
disulfiram	Antabuse	Alcohol blockade
divalproex	Depakote	Anticonvulsant
dobutamine	Dobutrex	Sympathomimetic (DA) $\alpha\beta$
docusate*	Colate	Stool softener
dopamine	Intropin	Sympathomimetic (MA) $\alpha\beta$
doxapram	Dopram	Respiratory stimulant
doxepin	Sinequan	TCA
doxorubicin	Adriamycin	Antineoplastic antibiotic
doxycycline	Vibramycin	Tetracycline
dronabinol	Marinol	Antiemetic
enalapril	Vasotec	Antihypertensive
enflurane	Ethrane	Anesthetic (general)
ephedrine*	Primatene	Sympathomimetic (IA) $\alpha\beta$
epinephrine*	Lidocaine	Sympathomimetic (DA) $\alpha\beta$
ergotamine tartrate	Cafergot	Ergot alkaloid
estazolam	ProSom	Hypnotic
ethacrynic acid	Edecrin	Loop diuretic
ethchlorvynol	Placidyl	Hypnotic
ethosuximide	Zarontin	Anticonvulsant
famotidine	Pepcid	H_2-Receptor antagonist
fenfluramine	Pondimin	Sympathomimetic (IA) $\alpha\beta$

APPENDICES

Generic*	Brand Name	Chief Action
fludrocortisone	Florinef	Corticosteroid
fluoxetine	Prozac	HCA
fluphenazine	Prolixin	Neuroleptic
flurazepam	Dalmane	Hypnotic
furazolidone	Furoxone	Antibiotic
furosemide	Lasix	Loop diuretic
glucagon	Glucagon	Antihypoglycemic
glutethimide	Doriden	Hypnotic
griseofulvin	Fulvicin	Antibiotic
guanabenz	Wytensin	Antihypertensive
guanadrel	Hylorel	Antihypertensive
guanethidine	Ismelin	Antihypertensive
haloperidol	Haldol	Neuroleptic
halothane	Fluothane	Anesthetic
hydralazine	Apresoline	Antihypertensive
hydrochlorthiazide	Aldoril	Thiazide diuretic
hydroxyzine	Atarax	Anti-anxiety
ibuprofen*	Advil	Analgesic
imipramine	Tofranil	TCA
indomethacin	Indocin	NSAIA
insulin*	Humulin	Antihyperglycemic
ipecac*	Ipecac Syrup	Induces vomiting
isocarboxazid	Marplan	MAOI
isoflurane	Forane	Anesthetic (general)
isoniazid	Rifamate	Antibiotic
isoproterenol	Isuprel	Sympathomimetic (DA) β
ketamine	Ketalar	Anesthetic (general)
ketoconazole	Nizoral	Antifungal agent
labetalol	Normodyne	β blocker (NCS)
lecithin*	Pro-Hepatone	Multivitamin
levodopa	Larodopa	Antiparkinsonian
lidocaine*	Xylocaine	Anesthetic (local)
liothyronine	Cytomel	Thyroid
lithium	Eskalith	Mood regulator
lorazepam	Ativan	Anti-anxiety
loxapine	Loxitane	Neuroleptic
magnesium hydroxide*	Maalox	Antacid
maprotiline	Ludiomil	HCA
mazindol	Mazanor	Anorectic agent
mebendazole	Vermox	Anthelmintic agent
meperidine	Demerol	Narcotic
meprobamate	Miltown	Anti-anxiety
mesoridazine	Serentil	Neuroleptic
metaproterenol	Alupent	Sympathomimetic (DA) β
metaraminol	Aramine	Sympathomimetic (MA) αβ
methadone	Dolophine	Narcotic

Generic*	Brand Name	Chief Action
methenamine	Mandelamine	Antibiotic
mephabarbital	Mebaral	Anti-anxiety
methoxyflurane	Penthrane	Anesthestic (general)
methyldopa	Aldomet	Antihypertensive
methylphenidate	Ritalin	Stimulant
methyltestosterone	Estratest	Androgen derivative
methyprylon	Noludar	Hypnotic
metoclopramide	Reglan	Anti-emetic
metoprolol	Lopressor	β blocker (CS)
metronidazole	Flagyl	Antibiotic
molindone	Moban	Neuroleptic
morphine	Roxanol	Narcotic
nadolol	Corgard	β blocker (NCS)
naloxone	Narcan	Narcotic antagonist
naltrexone	Trexan	Narcotic antagonist
naproxen	Anaprox	NSAIA
neostigmine	Prostigmine	Anticholinesterase
nifedipine	Procardia	Calcium channel blocker
nitrofurantoin	Macrodantin	Antibiotic
nitroprusside	Nipride	Antihypertensive
nizatidine	Axid	H_2-Receptor antagonist
norepinephrine	Levophed	Sympathomimetic (DA) αβ
nortriptyline	Pamelor	TCA
orphenadrine	Norflex	Analgesic
oxazepam	Serax	Anti-anxiety
pancuronium	Pavulon	Neuromuscular blocker
paraldehyde	Paral	Hypnotic
pargyline	Eutonyl	MAOI
pemoline	Cylert	Stimulant
pentazocine	Talwin	Narcotic agonist-antagonist
pentobarbital	Nembutal	Hypnosedative
perphenazine	Trilafon	Neuroleptic
phenelzine	Nardil	MAOI
phenmetrazine	Preludin	Anorectic agent
phenobarbital	Luminal	Anticonvulsant
phentolamine	Regitine	Antihypertensive
phenylbutazone	Butazolidin	NSAIA
phenylephrine*	Neo-Synephrine	Sympathomimetic (MA) αβ
phenylpropanolamine*	Acutrim	Sympathomimetic (IA) αβ
phenytoin	Dilantin	Anticonvulsant
physostigmine	Antilirium	Anticholinesterase
pimozide	Orap	Neuroleptic
pindolol	Visken	β blocker (NCS)
piroxicam	Feldene	NSAIA
prazepam	Centrax	Anti-anxiety
prazosin	Minipress	Antihypertensive
primidone	Mysoline	Anticonvulsant
probenecid	Benemid	Uricosuric agent

APPENDICES

Generic*	Brand Name	Chief Action
procainamide	Pronestyl	Anesthetic (local)
prochlorperazine	Compazine	Anti-emetic
procyclidine	Kemadrin	Antiparkinsonian
promethazine	Phenergan	Antihistamine
propoxyphene	Darvon	Analgesic
propranolol	Inderal	β blocker (NCS)
protriptyline	Vivactil	TCA
pseudoephedrine*	Sudifed	Sympathomimetic (IA) αβ
psyllium*	Metamucil	Laxative
quazepam	Doral	Hypnotic
quinidine	Quinidine	Antiarrhythmic
ranitidine	Zantac	H_2-Receptor antagonist
reserpine	Serpasil	Antihypertensive
rifampin	Rifadin	Antibiotic
secobarbital	Seconal	Hypnotic
selegiline	Eldepryl	MAOI
spectinomycin	Trobicin	Antibiotic
spironolactone	Aldactone	Potassium-sparing diuretic
succinylcholine	Anectine	Neuromuscular blocker
sulfinpyrazone	Anturane	Uricosuric agent
temazepam	Restoril	Hypnotic
terbutaline	Brethine	Sympathomimetic (DA) β
terfenadine	Seldane	Antihistamine
tetracycline	Achromycin	Antibiotic
theophylline*	Bronkaid	Bronchodilator
thiopental	Pentothal	Anesthetic (general)
thioridazine	Mellaril	Neuroleptic
thiothixene	Navane	Neuroleptic
timolol	Blocadren	β blocker (NCS)
tocainide	Tonocard	Antiarrhythmic
tolazoline	Priscoline	Antihypertensive
tranylcypromine	Parnate	MAOI
trazodone	Desyrel	HCA
triazolam	Halcion	Hypnotic
trifluoperazine	Stelazine	Neuroleptic
trihexyphenidyl	Artane	Antiparkinsonian
trimethaphan	Arfonad	Antihypertensive
trimethobenzamide	Tigan	Antiemetic
trimipramine	Surmontil	TCA
troleandomycin	Tao	Antibiotic
tryptophan*[1]	Saave	Amino acid
tubocurarine	Tubocurarine	Neuromuscular blocker
tyramine		Sympathomimetic (IA) αβ
urea*	Debrox	Earwax drops
valproic acid	Depakene	Anticonvulsant
verapamil	Isoptin	Calcium channel blocker

Generic*	Brand Name	Chief Action
warfarin	Coumadin	Anticoagulant (oral)
yohimbine*	Yocon	Mydriatic

Codes:
* Can be sold in nonprescription drug.
¹The American government withdrew tryptophan on 9/19/90 after it caused a potentially fatal eosinophilia myalgia syndrome. The problem exists with the nontryptophan ingredients, since tryptophan is a naturally occurring amino acid.
NSAIA = nonsteroidal anti-inflammatory agent.
β blockers: (CS) = Cardioselective; (NCS) = Noncardioselective
Sympathomimetics: (DA) = Direct acting; (IA) = Indirect acting; (MA) Mixed acting; α = alpha agonist; β = beta agonist

SYMPTOM CHECK LIST

When patients gripe about side effects, do their complaints stem from the medication or from another problem, such as a psychiatric or a medical disorder?

The symptom check list helps answer this question. Patients fill it out *before* they start on a medication so the clinician can detect symptoms unrelated to the medication. Subsequently, patients complete it every week or month to uncover symptoms that occurred only *after* the medication was begun. ("Side effects" often decline on medication.)

For patients and doctors alike, the list saves office time for exploring more personal matters, while insuring that clinicians still know about any key side effects.

A
P
P
E
N
D
I
C
E
S

SYMPTOM CHECK LIST

Patient's name _____ Date _____

			Does It Make You Uncomfortable?	
Do You Have Any of the Following Symptoms?	**Yes**	**No**	**Yes**	**No**
Dizziness/lightheadedness	☐	☐	◇	◇
Faint	☐	☐	◇	◇
Rapid or pounding heart	☐	☐	◇	◇
Dry mouth, throat, or nose	☐	☐	◇	◇
Always hungry	☐	☐	◇	◇
Diminished appetite	☐	☐	◇	◇
Nausea or vomiting	☐	☐	◇	◇
Upset stomach	☐	☐	◇	◇
Diarrhea	☐	☐	◇	◇
Constipation	☐	☐	◇	◇
Jaundice	☐	☐	◇	◇
Weight gain	☐	☐	◇	◇
Edema	☐	☐	◇	◇
Frequent or difficult urination	☐	☐	◇	◇
Increased thirst	☐	☐	◇	◇
Different menstruation	☐	☐	◇	◇
Swollen breasts	☐	☐	◇	◇
Fluid discharge from breast	☐	☐	◇	◇
Decreased sexual interest	☐	☐	◇	◇
Lack of energy	☐	☐	◇	◇
Bruising easier	☐	☐	◇	◇
Sores in mouth	☐	☐	◇	◇
Blurred vision	☐	☐	◇	◇
Ringing in the ears	☐	☐	◇	◇
Skin rash	☐	☐	◇	◇
Increased sweating	☐	☐	◇	◇
Insomnia	☐	☐	◇	◇
Excessive sleeping	☐	☐	◇	◇
Weird dreams/nightmares	☐	☐	◇	◇
Stiff tongue	☐	☐	◇	◇
Body stiff or rigid	☐	☐	◇	◇
Difficulty in swallowing	☐	☐	◇	◇
Tremors, shakes, jitters	☐	☐	◇	◇
Unsteady gait	☐	☐	◇	◇
Slurred speech	☐	☐	◇	◇
Headache	☐	☐	◇	◇
Drowsiness	☐	☐	◇	◇
Poor memory	☐	☐	◇	◇
Nervousness	☐	☐	◇	◇

CURRENT MEDICATIONS: DRUG NAME AND DOSE

_____   _____

_____   _____

_____   _____

_____

References

Albeck, J. H. (1987). Withdrawal and detoxification from benzodiazepine dependence: A potential role for clonazepam. *Journal of Clinical Psychiatry, 49,* 43–48 (suppl).

Allen, M. D. (1980). Overdosage with antipsychotic agents. *American Journal of Psychiatry, 137,* 234–236.

American Psychiatric Association. (1987). *Diagnostic and statistical manual of mental disorders* (3rd ed. rev.). Washington, DC: Author.

American Psychiatric Association. (1989). *Treatment of psychiatric disorders: A task force report of the American Psychiatric Association.* Washington, DC: Author.

Andreasen, N. C., & Akiskal, H. S. (1983). The specificity of Bleulerian and Schneiderian symptoms: A critical reevaluation. *Psychiatric Clinics of North America, 6,* 41–54.

Ankier, S. I., & Goa, K. L. (1988). Quazepam: A preliminary review of its pharmacodynamic and pharmacokinetic properties and therapeutic efficacy in insomnia. *Drugs, 35,* 42–62.

Anton, R. F., & Burch, E. A. Jr. (1990). Amoxapine versus amitriptyline combined with perphenazine in the treatment of psychotic depression. *American Journal of Psychiatry, 147,* 1203–1208.

Arana, G. W., & Hyman, S. E. (1991). *Handbook of psychiatric drug therapy* (2nd ed.). Boston: Little, Brown.

Baastrup, P. C., et al. (1976). Adverse reactions in treatment with lithium carbonate and haloperidol. *Journal of the American Medical Association, 236,* 2645–2646.

Baldessarini, R. J. (Ed.). (1985). *Chemotherapy in psychiatry: Principles and practice* (rev.). Cambridge, MA: Harvard University Press.

Baldessarini, R. J. (1989). Current status of antidepressants: Clinical pharmacology and therapy. *Journal of Clinical Psychiatry, 50,* 117–126.

Ballenger, J. C. (1988). The clinical use of carbamazepine in affective disorders. *Journal of Clinical Psychiatry, 49,* 13–19 (suppl).

Bartels, M., et al. (1987). Treatment of akathisia with lorazepam: An open clinical trial. *Pharmacopsychiatry, 20,* 51–53.

Bauer, M. S., & Whybrow, P. C. (1986). The effect of changing thyroid function of cyclic affective illness in a human subject. *American Journal of Psychiatry, 143,* 633–636.

Belpaire, F. M., Vanderheeren, F. A. J., & Bogaert, M. G. (1975). Binding of thioridazine and some of its metabolites to human serum and human albumin. *Drug Research, 25,* 1969–1971.

Bernstein, J. G. (1988). *Handbook of drug therapy in psychiatry* (2nd ed.). Littleton, MA: PSG Publishing Co.

Bernstein, J. G. (1988). Psychotropic drug induced weight gain: Mechanisms and management. *Clinical Neuropharmacology, 11,* 194–206 (suppl).

Bezchlibnyk-Butler, K. Z., & Jeffries, J. J. (Eds.). (1990). *Clinical handbook of psychotropic drugs* (2nd ed.). Lewiston, NY: Hogrefe & Huber Publishers.

Blackwell, B., et al. (1967). Hypertensive interaction between monoamine oxidase inhibitor, and food stuffs. *British Journal of Psychiatry, 113,* 349–365.

Blackwell, B., & Mabbitt, L. A. (1965). Tyramine in cheese related to hypertensive crises after monoamine oxidase inhibition. *Lancet,* 1(7392), 938–940.

Bone, S., et al. (1980). Incidence of side effects in patients on long-term lithium therapy. *American Journal of Psychiatry, 137,* 103–104.

Briggs, G. G., Freeman, R. K., & Yaffe, S. J. (1986). *Drugs in pregnancy and lactation* (2nd ed.). Baltimore: Williams & Wilkins.

Briggs, N. C., Jefferson, J. W., & Koenecke, F. H. (1990). Tranylcypromine addiction: A case report and review. *Journal of Clinical Psychiatry, 51,* 426–429.

Brophy, J. J. (1967). Suicide attempts with psychotherapeutic drugs. *Archives of General Psychiatry, 17,* 652–657.

Brown, W. T. (1976). Side effects of lithium therapy and their treatment. *Canadian Psychiatric Association Journal, 21,* 13–21.

Browne, T. R. (1976). Clonazepam: A review of a new anticonvulsant drug. *Archives of Neurology, 33,* 326–332.

Cain, R. M., & Cain, N. N. (1975). A compendium of psychiatric drugs. *Drug Therapy,* January/February, 1–16.

Cassano, G. B., Perugi, G., & McNair, D. M. (1988). Panic disorder: Review of the empirical and rational basis of pharmacological treatment. *Pharmacopsychiatry, 21,* 157–165.

Castaneda, R., & Cushman, P. (1989). Alcohol withdrawal: A review of clinical management. *Journal of Clinical Psychiatry, 50,* 278–284.

Charney, D. S., et al. (1986). Drug treatment of panic disorder: The comparative efficacy of imipramine, alprazolam, and trazodone. *Journal of Clinical Psychiatry, 47,* 580–586.

Chouinard, G., et al. (1982). Alprazolam in the treatment of generalized anxiety and panic disorders: A double-blind placebo-controlled study. *Psychopharmacology, 77,* 229–233.

Clinical Pharmacokinetics. (1990). *Drug data handbook* (2nd ed.). G. J. Mammen (Ed.) Auckland, New Zealand: AIDS Press.

Cohen, L. S., Heller, V. L., & Rosenbaum, J. F. (1989). Treatment guidelines for psychotropic drug use in pregnancy. *Psychosomatics, 30,* 25–33.

Conant, J., et al. (1989). Central nervous system side effects of β-adrenergic blocking agents with high and low lipid solubility. *Journal of Cardiovascular Pharmacology, 13,* 656–661.

Coplan, J. E., & Gorman, J. M. (1990). Treatment of anxiety disorder in patients with mood disorders. *Journal of Clinical Psychiatry, 51,* 9–13 (suppl).

Davidson, J. (1989). Seizures and bupropion: A review. *Journal of Clinical Psychiatry, 50,* 256–261.

Davis, J. M. (1973). Overdose of psychotropic drugs. *Psychiatric Annuals, 3*(4), 6–11.

Davis, J. M., Janicak, P. G., & Bruninga, K. (1987). The efficacy of MAO inhibitors in depression: A meta-analysis. *Psychiatric Annals, 17,* 825–831.

Delisle, J. (1990). A case of amitriptyline abuse (letter). *American Journal of Psychiatry, 147,* 1377–1378.

Deng, M. Z., Chen, G. Q., & Phillips, M. R. (1990). Neuroleptic malignant syndrome in 12 of 9,792 Chinese inpatients exposed to neuroleptics: A prospective study. *American Journal of Psychiatry, 147,* 1149–1155.

Derlet, R. W., et al. (1989). Amphetamine toxicity: Experience with 127 cases. *Journal of Emergency Medicine, 7,* 157–161.

Detre, T. P., & Jarecki, H. G. (1971). *Modern psychiatric treatment.* Philadelphia: J. B. Lippincott.

Dilsaver, S. C. (1989). Antidepressant withdrawal syndromes: Phenomenology and pathophysiology. *Acta Psychiatrica Scandinavica, 79,* 113–117.

Dunner, D. L., & Fieve, R. R. (1974). Clinical factors in lithium carbonate prophylaxis failure. *Archives of General Psychiatry, 30,* 229–233.

Ereshefsky, L., Watanabe, M. D., & Tran-Johnson, T. K. (1989). Clozapine: An atypical antipsychotic agent. *Clinical Pharmacy, 8,* 691–709.

Facts and Comparisons. (1990). *Drug facts and comparisons.* St. Louis: Author.

Facts and Comparisons. (1991). *Drug facts and comparisons.* St. Louis: Author.

Family Physician's Compendium of Drug Therapy: 1989. (1988). New York: McGraw-Hill.

Fernandez, F., et al. (1987). Methylphenidate for depressive disorders in cancer patients. *Psychosomatics, 28,* 455–461.

Fisch, R. Z. (1987). Trihexyphenidyl abuse: Therapeutic implications for negative symptoms of schizophrenia? *Acta Psychiatrica Scandinavica, 75,* 91–94.

Fishbain, D. A. (1989). Priapism and neuroleptics: A case report. *Acta Psychiatrica Scandinavica, 79,* 207.

Freedberg, K. A., et al. (1979). Antischizophrenic drugs: Differential plasma protein binding and therapeutic activity. *Life Sciences, 24,* 2467–2474.

Freudenheim, M. (1990, December 6). Maker of schizophrenia drug bows to pressure of cut cost. *New York Times,* pp. A1, D3.

Frishman, W., et al. (1979). Clinical pharmacology of the new beta-adrenergic blocking drugs: Part 4. Adverse effects. Choosing a β-adrenoreceptor blocker. *American Heart Journal, 98,* 256–262.

Gawin, F., Compton, M., & Byck, R. (1989). Buspirone reduces smoking. *Archives of General Psychiatry, 46,* 989–990.

Gelenberg, A. J. (1989). New perspectives on the use of tricyclic antidepressants. *Journal of Clinical Psychiatry, 50,* 3.

Gelenberg, A. J., Bassuk, E. L., & Schoonover, S. C. (Eds.). (1991). *The practitioner's guide to psychoactive drugs* (3rd ed.). New York: Plenum Medical.

Gillin, J. C., & Byerley, W. F. (1990). The diagnosis and management of insomnia. *New England Journal of Medicine, 322,* 239–248.

Gilman, A. G., et al. (1985). *The pharmacological basis of therapeutics* (7th ed.). New York: Macmillan.

Glassman, A. H., & Bigger, J. T. (1981). Cardiovascular effects of therapeutic doses of tricyclic antidepressants: A review. *Archives of General Psychiatry, 38*, 424–427.

Glassman, A. H., & Roose, S. P. (1987). Cardiovascular effects of tricyclic antidepressants. *Psychiatric Annals, 17*, 340–342.

Gold, M. S., Lydiard, R. B., & Carman, J. S. (Eds.). (1984). *Advances in psychopharmacology: Predicting and improving treatment response.* Boca Raton, FL: CRC Press.

Goodwin, F. K., et al. (1982). Potentiation of antidepressant effects by 1-triiodothyronine in tricyclic nonresponders. *American Journal of Psychiatry, 139*, 34–38.

Greenblatt, D. J., et al. (1984). Adverse reactions to triazolam, flurazepam, and placebo in controlled clinical trials. *Journal of Clinical Psychiatry, 45*, 192–195.

Greenblatt, D. J., & Koch-Weser, J. (1973). Adverse reactions to propranolol in hospitalized medical patients: A report from the Boston Collaborative Drug Surveillance Program. *American Heart Journal, 86*, 478–484.

Greenhill, L. L., et al. (1987). Methylphenidate salivary levels in children. *Psychopharmacology Bulletin, 23*, 115–119.

Greist, J. H., Jefferson, J. W., & Spitzer, R. L. (Eds.). (1982). *Treatment of mental disorders.* New York: Oxford University Press.

Griffith, H. W. (1988). *Complete guide to prescription and non-prescription drugs* (5th ed.). Los Angeles: Body Press.

Gunderson, J. G. (1986). Pharmacotherapy for patients with borderline personality disorder. *Archives of General Psychiatry, 43*, 698–700.

Guzé, B. H., & Baxter, L. R. Jr. (1985). Neuroleptic malignant syndrome. *New England Journal of Medicine, 313*, 163–166.

Haller, E., & Binder, R. L. (1990). Clozapine and seizures. *American Journal of Psychiatry, 147*, 1069–1071.

Hansten, P. D., & Horn, J. R. (1989). *Drug interactions: Clinical significance of drug-drug interactions* (6th ed.). Philadelphia: Lea & Febiger.

Haring, C., et al. (1990). Influence of patient-related variables on clozapine plasma levels. *American Journal of Psychiatry, 147*, 1471–1475.

Harrison, W. H., et al. (1989). MAOIs and hypertensive crisis: The role of OTC drugs. *Journal of Clinical Psychiatry, 50*, 64–65.

Hauger, R., et al. (1990). Lithium toxicity: When is hemodialysis necessary? *Acta Psychiatrica Scandinavica, 81*, 515–517.

Hemstrom, C. A., Evans, R. L., & Lobeck, F. G. (1988). Haloperidol decanoate: A depot antipsychotic. *Drug Intelligence and Clinical Pharmacy, 22*, 290–295.

Herman, J. B., Brotman, A. W., & Rosenbaum, J. F. (1987). Rebound anxiety in panic disorder patients treated with shorter-acting benzodiazepines. *Journal of Clinical Psychiatry, 48*, 22–26 (suppl).

Himmolhoch, J. M., et al. (1977). Adjustment of lithium dose during lithium-chlorothiazide therapy. *Clinical Pharmacology and Therapeutics, 22*, 225–227.

Holmes, V. F., Fernandez, F., & Levy, J. K. (1989). Psychostimulant response in AIDS-related complex patients. *Journal of Clinical Psychiatry, 50*, 5–8.

Horowitz, D., et al. (1964). Monoamine oxidase inhibitors, tyramine, and cheese. *Journal of the American Medical Association, 188*, 1108–1110.

Hudson, J. I., & Pope, H. G. Jr. (1990). Affective spectrum disorder: Does antidepressant response identify a family of disorders with a common pathophysiology? *American Journal of Psychiatry, 147,* 552–564.

Jefferson, J. W. (1989). Cardiovascular effects and toxicity of anxiolytics and antidepressants. *Journal of Clinical Psychiatry, 50,* 368–378.

Jefferson, J. W. et al. (1987). *Lithium encyclopedia for clinical practice* (2nd ed.). Washington, DC: American Psychiatric Press.

Judd, F. K., et al. (1987). The dexamethasone suppression test in panic disorder. *Acta Psychiatrica Scandinavica, 20,* 99–101.

Kahn, D. A., Silver, J. M., & Opler, L. A. (1989). The safety of switching rapidly from tricyclic antidepressants to monoamine oxidase inhibitors. *Journal of Clinical Psychopharmacology, 9,* 198–202.

Kales, A., et al. (1986). Quazepam and temazepam: Effects of short- and intermediate-term use and withdrawal. *Clinical Pharmacology and Therapeutics, 39,* 345–352.

Kales, A., et al. (1986). Comparison of short and long half-life benzodiazepine hypnotics: Triazolam and quazepam. *Clinical Pharmacology and Therapeutics, 40,* 376–386.

Kales, A., et al. (1983). Rebound insomnia and rebound anxiety: A review. *Pharmacology, 26,* 121–137.

Kane, J., et al. (1978). Extrapyramidal side effects with lithium treatment. *American Journal of Psychiatry, 135,* 851–853.

Kane, J. M. (1989). The current status of neuroleptic therapy. *Journal of Clinical Psychiatry, 50,* 322–328.

Kaplan, H. I., & Sadock, B. J. (Eds.). (1983). *Comprehensive textbook of psychiatry/IV.* Baltimore: Williams & Wilkins.

Keck, P. E., et al. (1989). Frequency and presentation of neuroleptic malignant syndrome in a state psychiatric hospital. *Journal of Clinical Psychiatry, 50,* 352–355.

Kinon, G., et al. (1979). Mesoridazine in treatment-refractory schizophrenics. *Current Therapeutic Research, 25,* 534–539.

Klein, D. F., & Davis, J. M. (1969). *Diagnosis and drug treatment of psychiatric disorders.* Baltimore: Williams & Wilkins.

Klein, D. F., et al. (1980). *Diagnosis and drug treatment of psychiatric disorders* (2nd ed.). Baltimore: Williams & Wilkins.

Klein, R. G., et al. (1988). Methylphenidate and growth in hyperactive children: A controlled withdrawal study. *Archives of General Psychiatry, 45,* 1127–1130.

Klein, R. G., & Mannuzza, S. (1988). Hyperactive boys almost grown up: III. Methylphenidate effects on ultimate height. *Archives of General Psychiatry, 45,* 1131–1134.

Kotin, J., et al. (1976). Thioridazine and sexual dysfunction. *American Journal of Psychiatry, 133,* 82–85.

Kranzler, H. R., & Cardoni, A. (1988). Sodium chloride treatment of antidepressant-induced orthostatic hypotension. *Journal of Clinical Psychiatry, 49,* 366–368.

Kushner, M. J., et al. (1988). You don't have to be a neuroscientist to forget everything with triazolam—but it helps. *Journal of the American Medical Association, 259,* 350–352.

Lazarus, A. (1985). Neuroleptic malignant syndrome: Detection and management. *Psychiatric Annals, 15,* 706–711.

Lederle Laboratories. (1985). *Loxitane*. Pearl River, NY: Author.

Lederle Laboratories. (1987). *Asendin*. Pearl River, NY: Author.

Levenson, J. L., & Fisher, J. G. (1988). Long-term outcome after neuroleptic malignant syndrome. *Journal of Clinical Psychiatry, 49,* 154–156.

Levinson, D. F., & Simpson, G. M. (1986). Neuroleptic-induced extrapyramidal symptoms with fever. *Archives of General Psychiatry, 43,* 839–847.

Levy, R. H., & Kerr, B. M. (1988). Clinical pharmacokinetics of carbamazepine. *Journal of Clinical Psychiatry, 49,* 58–61 (suppl).

Lieberman, J. A., Kane, J. M., & Johns, C. A. (1989). Clozapine: Guidelines for clinical management. *Journal of Clinical Psychiatry, 50,* 329–338.

Liebowitz, M. R., et al. (1984). Phenelzine vs. imipramine in atypical depression: A preliminary report. *Archives of General Psychiatry, 41,* 669–677.

Lion, J. R. (1979). Benzodiazepines in the treatment of aggressive patients. *Journal of Clinical Psychiatry, 2,* 25–26.

Lipinsky, J. F., et al. (1989). Fluoxetine-induced akathisia: Clinical and theoretical implications. *Journal of Clinical Psychiatry, 50,* 339–342.

Ludwig, A. M. (1980). *Principles of clinical psychiatry.* New York: Free Press.

Maany, I., et al. (1989). Increase in despiramine serum levels associated with methadone treatment. *American Journal of Psychiatry, 146,* 1611–1613.

Maxmen, J. S. (1986). *Essential psychopathology.* New York: Norton.

McCann, U. D., & Agras, W. S. (1990). Successful treatment of nonpurging bulimia nervosa with desipramine: A double-blind, placebo-controlled study. *American Journal of Psychiatry, 147,* 1509–1513.

McClusky, H. Y., et al. (1991). Efficacy in behavioral versus triazolam treatment in persistent sleep-onset insomnia. *American Journal of Psychiatry, 148,* 121–126.

McElroy, S. L., et al. (1989). Valproate in psychiatric disorders: Literature review and clinical guidelines. *Journal of Clinical Psychiatry, 50,* 23–29 (suppl).

McEvoy, G. K. (Ed.). (1990). *AHFS Drug Information 90.* Bethesda, MD: American Society of Hospital Pharmacists.

M. M. (1990). Sandoz compromises on Clozaril. *Psychiatric News, 25*(24), 1, 8–9.

Morris, H. H. III, & Estes, M. L. (1987). Traveler's amnesia: Transient global amnesia secondary to triazolam. *Journal of the American Medical Association, 258,* 945–946.

Murphy, D. L. (1977). The behavioral toxicity of monoamine oxidase-inhibiting antidepressants. In S. Garattini et al. (Eds.), *Advances in pharmacology and chemotherapy* (vol. 14), 71–103. New York: Academic Press.

Neppe, V. N., Tucker, G. J., & Wilensky, A. J. (1988). Introduction: Fundamentals of carbamazepine use in neuropsychiatry. *Journal of Clinical Psychiatry, 49,* 4–6 (suppl).

Nikaido, A. M., & Elinwood, E. H. (1987). Comparison of the effects of quazepam and triazolam on cognitive-neuromotor performance. *Psychopharmacology, 92,* 459–464.

Noyes, R., et al. (1984). Diazepam and propranolol in panic disorder and agoraphobia. *Archives of General Psychiatry, 41,* 287–292.

Ontiveros, A., & Fontaine, R. (1990). Social phobia and clonazepam. *Canadian Journal of Psychiatry, 35,* 439–441.

Peer to Peer. (1990). Refractory depression: Treatment strategies for the problem patient. *2,* 3–10.

Pellock, J. M. (1987). Carbamazepine side effects in children and adults. *Epilepsia, 28,* S64–S70 (suppl).

Perényi, A., et al. (1987). Dexamethasone suppression test and depressive symptoms in schizophrenia and endogenous depressed patients. *Acta Psychiatrica Scandinavica, 20,* 48–50.

Perse, T. (1988). Obsessive-compulsive disorder: A treatment review. *Journal of Clinical Psychiatry, 49,* 48–55.

Petersdorf, R. G., et al. (1983). *Principles of internal medicine* (10th ed.). New York: McGraw-Hill.

Pies, R. (1990). Anticholinergic agents and psychiatric practice. *The Psychiatric Times, 7*(12), 44–46.

Pinder, R. M., et al. (1976). Clonazepam: A review of its pharmacological properties and therapeutic efficacy in epilepsy. *Drugs, 12,* 321–361.

Pope, H. G. Jr., et al. (1986). Frequency and presentation of neuroleptic malignant syndrome in a large psychiatric hospital. *American Journal of Psychiatry, 143,* 1227–1233.

Post, R. M. (1988). Time course of clinical effects of carbamazepine: Implications for mechanisms of action. *Journal of Clinical Psychiatry, 49,* 35–46 (suppl).

Post, R. M., Trimble, M. R., & Pippenger, C. E. (1989). *Clinical use of anticonvulsants in psychiatric disorders.* New York: Demos.

Prien, R. F., & Kupfer, D. J. (1986). Continuation drug therapy for major depressive episodes: How long should it be maintained? *American Journal of Psychiatry, 143,* 18–23.

Razani, J., et al. (1983). The safety and efficacy of combined amitriptyline and tranylcypromine antidepressant treatment. *Archives of General Psychiatry, 40,* 657–661.

Reiter, S. (1990). Social phobia: Diagnosis and pharmacotherapy. *Massachusetts General Hospital Progress Notes, 1*(2), 1–4.

Remington, G. J., et al. (1990). Prevalence of neuroleptic-induced dystonia in mania and schizophrenia. *American Journal of Psychiatry, 147,* 1231–1233.

Richelson, E., & Nelson, A. (1984). Antagonism by antidepressants of neurotransmitter receptors of normal human brain *in vitro. Journal of Pharmacology and Experimental Therapeutics, 230,* 94–102.

Rickels, K., et al. (1972). Methylphenidate in mildly depressed outpatients. *Clinical Pharmacology and Therapeutics, 13,* 595–601.

Rickels, K., et al. (1988). Long-term treatment of anxiety and risk of withdrawal. *Archives of General Psychiatry, 45,* 444–450.

Rickels, K., et al. (1990). Benzodiazepine dependence: Management of discontinuation. *Psychopharmacology Bulletin, 26,* 63–68.

Roose, S. P., et al. (1987). Cardiovascular effects of imipramine and bupropion in depressed patients with congestive heart failure. *Journal of Clinical Psychiatry, 7,* 247–251.

Roose, S. P., et al. (1987). Tricyclic antidepressants in depressed patients with cardiac conduction disease. *Archives of General Psychiatry, 44,* 273–275.

Roose, S. P., Glassman, A. H., & Dalack, G. W. (1989). Depression, heart disease, and tricylic antidepressants. *Journal of Clinical Psychiatry, 50,* 12–16 (suppl).

Rosenfeld, B. G. (Ed.). (1972). *Manual of medical therapeutics* (20th ed.). St. Louis, MO: Little, Brown, & Company.

Satel, S. L., & Nelson, J. C. (1989). Stimulants in the treatment of depression: A critical overview. *Journal of Clinical Psychiatry, 50,* 241–249.

Scharf, M. B., Fletcher, A. C. P. K., & Graham, J. P. (1988). Comparative amnestic effects of benzodiazepine hypnotic agents. *Journal of Clinical Psychiatry, 49,* 134–137.

Schatzberg, A. F., & Cole, J. O. (1987). *Manual of clinical psychopharmacology.* Washington, DC: American Psychiatric Press.

Schneider, L. S., Syapin, P. J., & Pawluczyk, S. (1987). Seizures following triazolam withdrawal despite benzodiazepine treatment. *Journal of Clinical Psychiatry, 48,* 418–419.

Schou, M. (1990). Lithium treatment during pregnancy, delivery, and lactation: An update. *Journal of Clinical Psychiatry, 51,* 410–413.

Shader, R. I. (1964). Sexual dysfunction associated with thioridazine hydrochloride. *Journal of American Medical Association, 188,* 1007–1009.

Shalev, A., Hermesh, H., & Munitz, H. (1989). Mortality from neuroleptic malignant syndrome. *Journal of Clinical Psychiatry, 50,* 18–25.

Shaw, E. (1986). Lithium noncompliance. *Psychiatric Annals, 16,* 583–587.

Sheehy, L. M., & Maxmen, J. S. (1978). Phenelzine-induced psychosis. *American Journal of Psychiatry, 135,* 1422–1423.

Shinn, A. F., & Hogan, M. J. (Eds.). (1988). *Evaluations of drug interactions.* New York: Macmillan.

Shlafer, M., & Marieb, E. N. (Eds.). (1989). *The nurse, pharmacology, and drug therapy.* Redwood City, CA: Addison-Wesley Publishing.

Shopsin, B., & Gershon, S. (1975). Cogwheel rigidity related to lithium maintenance. *American Journal of Psychiatry, 132,* 536–538.

Shulman, K. I. (1989). Dietary restriction, tyramine, and the use of monoamine oxidase inhibitors. *Journal Clinical Psychopharmacology, 9,* 397–401.

Silver, J. M., Sandberg, D. P., & Hales, R. E. (1990). New approaches in the pharmacotherapy of posttraumatic stress disorder. *Journal of Clinical Psychiatry, 51,* 33–38 (suppl).

Silverstone, T., Smith, G., & Goodall, E. (1988). Prevalence of obesity in patients receiving depot antipsychotics. *British Journal of Psychiatry, 153,* 214–217.

Snyder, S. H. (1981). Dopamine receptors, neuroleptics, and schizophrenia. *American Journal of Psychiatry, 138,* 460–464.

Steardo, L., et al. (1987). Is the dexamethasone suppression test predictive of response to specific antidepressant treatment in major depression? *Acta Psychiatrica Scandinavica, 76,* 129–133.

Sullivan, E. A., & Shulman, K. I. (1984). Diet and monoamine oxidase inhibition: A reexamination. *Canadian Journal of Psychiatry, 29,* 707–711.

Sussman, N. (1987). Treatment of anxiety with buspirone. *Psychiatric Annals, 17,* 114–120.

Swett, C. Jr. (1975). Drug-induced dystonia. *American Journal of Psychiatry, 132,* 532–534.

Talbott, J. A., Hales, R. E., & Yudofsky, S. C. (Eds.). (1988). *Textbook of psychiatry.* Washington, DC: American Psychiatric Press.

Task Force on the Use of Laboratory Tests in Psychiatry. (1985). Tricyclic antidepressants-blood level measurements and clinical outcome: An APA Task Force Report. *American Journal of Psychiatry, 142,* 155–162.

Tesar, G. E., et al. (1987). Clonazepam versus alprazolam in the treatment of panic disorder: Interim analysis of data from a prospective, double-blind, placebo-controlled trial. *Journal of Clinical Psychiatry, 48,* 16–19 (suppl).

Thienhaus, O. J., & Vogel, N. (1988). Despiramine and testicular swelling in two patients. *Journal of Clinical Psychiatry, 49,* 33–34.

Thompson, J. W., Ware, M. R., & Blashfield, R. K. (1990). Psychotropic medication and priapism: A comprehensive review. *Journal of Clinical Psychiatry, 51,* 430–433.

Trimble, M. R. (1990). Worldwide use of clomipramine. *Journal of Clinical Psychiatry, 51,* 51–54 (suppl).

Tupin, J. P., et al. (1973). Long-term use of lithium in aggressive prisoners. *Comprehensive Psychiatry, 14,* 311–317.

Vestergaard, P. (1983). Clinically important side effects of long-term lithium treatment: A review. *Acta Psychiatrica Scandinavica, 305,* 11–33 (suppl).

Walsh, B. T. (1989). Use of antidepressants in bulimia. *Clinical Pediatrics, 28,* 127–128.

Watts, V. S., & Neill, J. R. (1988). Buspirone in obsessive-compulsive disorder (letter). *American Journal of Psychiatry, 145,* 1606.

Wender, P. H., & Klein, D. F. (1981). *Mind, mood and medicine: A guide to the new biopsychiatry.* New York: Meridian.

Woods, S. W., et al. (1986). Psychostimulant treatment of depressive disorders secondary to medical illness. *Journal of Clinical Psychiatry, 47,* 12–15.

Yadalam, K. G., & Simpson, G. M. (1988). Changing from oral to depot fluphenazine. *Journal of Clinical Psychiatry, 49,* 346–348.

Yassa, R., et al. (1988). Lithium-induced thyroid disorders: A prevalence study. *Journal of Clinical Psychiatry, 49,* 14–16.

Yesavage, J. A., Tanke, E. D., & Sheikh, J. I. (1987). Tardive dyskinesia and steady-state serum levels of thiothixene. *Archives of General Psychiatry, 44,* 913–915.

Yudofsky, S. C., Silver, J. M., & Hales, R. E. (1990). Pharmacologic management of aggression in the elderly. *Journal of Clinical Psychiatry, 51,* 22–28 (suppl).

Index of Drugs
by Brand Names

Brand Name	Generic Name	Chief Action	Page Numbers
Akineton	biperiden	Antiparkinsonian	43–55
Amytal	amobarbital	Hypnotic	217–243, 249
Anafranil	clomipramine	TCA	57–97, 105, 176, 190–191, 224, 249
Antabuse	disulfiram	Alcohol blockade	217–243
Antilirium	physostigmine	Cholinergic	25
Artane	trihexyphenidyl	Antiparkinsonian	43–55
Asendin	amoxapine	HCA	57–97
Atarax	hydroxyzine	Anti-anxiety	177–215, 224, 249
Ativan	lorazepam	Anti-anxiety	22, 44–45, 55, 158, 177–215, 224, 237, 249
Aventyl	nortriptyline	TCA	57–97
Benadryl*	diphenhydramine	Antiparkinsonian/ Antihistamine	43–55, 186, 223–224, 249
BuSpar	buspirone	Anti-anxiety	107, 159, 177–215, 236–237
Butisol	butabarbital	Anti-anxiety	217–243, 249
Catapres	clonidine	Anti-smoking	22, 177–215
Centrax	prazepam	Anti-anxiety	177–215, 249
Cibalith-S	lithium	Bipolar disorder	24, 68–69, 71, 102–103, 127–152, 155–156, 159–160, 168, 249
Clozaril	clozapine	Neuroleptic	1–41
Cogentin	benztropine	Antiparkinsonian	43–55
Compazine	prochlorperazine	Anti-emetic	1–41
Corgad	nadolol	Anti-aggression	160
Cylert	pemoline	Stimulant	71, 245–261
Cytomel	liothyronine	Thyroid	68–69, 140
Dalmane	flurazepam	Hypnotic	217–243, 249
Dantrium	dantrolene	Anti-NMS	22, 43–55
Demerol	meperidine	Narcotic	107
Depakene	valproic acid	Anticonvulsant	11, 24, 107, 133, 153–176
Depakote	divalproex	Anticonvulsant	11, 153–176
Desyrel	trazodone	HCA	57–97, 105
Dexedrine	dextroamphetamine	Stimulant	68, 107, 245–261
Dilantin	phenytoin	Anticonvulsant	153–176
Doral	quazepam	Hypnotic	217–243, 249
Doriden	glutethimide	Hypnotic	107, 217–243
Elavil	amitriptyline	TCA	57–97, 106
Eldepryl	selegiline	MAOI	69, 99–126, 133–134, 188, 191
Equanil	meprobamate	Anti-anxiety	177–215, 224, 236
Eskalith	lithium	Bipolar disorder	24, 66, 68–69, 71, 102–103, 127–152, 156–157, 159–160, 168, 249

Brand Name	Generic Name	Chief Action	Page Numbers
Eutonyl	pargyline	MAOI	69, 71, 99–126, 133–134, 188, 191
Inderal	propranolol	Anti-social phobia	44–45, 159–160, 177–216
Janimine	imipramine	TCA	57–97, 106, 190, 192, 236, 249–250
Halcion	triazolam	Hypnotic	217–243, 249
Haldol	haloperidol	Neuroleptic	1–41, 132, 158, 186, 258
Kemadrin	procyclidine	Antiparkinsonian	43–55
Klonopin	clonazepam	Anticonvulsant/ Anti-anxiety	11, 132, 134, 153–215, 224, 236
Larodopa	levodopa	Antiparkinsonian	22, 24, 107
Librium	chlordiazepoxide	Anti-anxiety	177–215, 237, 249
Lithane	lithium	Bipolar disorder	24, 68–69, 71, 102–103, 127–152, 155–156, 159–160, 168, 249
(lithium: See Cibalith-S, Eskalith, Lithane, Lithobid)			
Lithobid	lithium	Bipolar disorder	24, 68–69, 102–103, 127–152, 155–156, 159–160, 168, 249
Lopressor	metoprolol	Anti-social phobia	190
Loxitane	loxapine	Neuroleptic	1–41
Ludiomil	maprotiline	HCA	57–97
Luminal	phenobarbital	Anticonvulsant	153–176, 217–243
Marplan	isocarboxazid	MAOI	69, 71, 99–126, 133–134, 188, 191
Mebaral	methabarbital	Anti-anxiety	217–243, 249
Mellaril	thioridazine	Neuroleptic	1–41, 77, 136, 186, 224
Miltown	meprobamate	Anti-anxiety	177–215, 224, 237
Moban	molindone	Neuroleptic	1–41
Mysoline	primidone	Anticonvulsant	153–176
Nardil	phenelzine	MAOI	68–72, 99–126, 133–134, 188, 191, 236, 250
Navane	thiothixene	Neuroleptic	1–41
Nembutal	pentobarbital	Hypnosedative	217–243
Nipride	nitroprusside	Anti-MAOI-induced headache	106
Noctec	chloral hydrate	Hypnotic	217–243
Noludar	methyprylon	Hypnotic	217–243
Norpramin	desipramine	TCA	57–97, 249, 258
Orap	pimozide	Neuroleptic	1–41, 192
Pamelor	nortriptyline	TCA	57–97, 249
(paraldehyde: no brand name)		Hypnotic	217–243
Parlodel	bromocriptine	Antiparkinsonian	15, 43–55
Parnate	tranylcypromine	MAOI	66, 69, 71–72, 99–126, 133–134, 188, 191–192
Periactin	cyproheptadine	Appetite stimulant	70–71, 77, 82
Permitil	fluphenazine	Neuroleptic	1–41
Pertofrane	desipramine	TCA	57–97, 249, 258
Placidyl	ethchlorvynol	Hypnotic	217–243

Brand Name	Generic Name	Chief Action	Page Numbers
Procardia	nifedipine	Anti-MAOI-induced headache	106
Prolixin	fluphenazine	Neuroleptic	1–41
(physostigmine: See Antilirium)			
ProSom	estazolam	Hypnotic	217–243, 249
Prostigmine	neostigmine	Cholinergic	77
Prozac	fluoxetine	HCA	57–97, 105, 191–192, 224
Regitine	phentolamine	Anti-MAOI-induced headache	106, 258
(reserpine: See Serpasil)			
Restoril	temazepam	Hypnotic	217–243, 249
Ritalin	methylphenidate	Stimulant	68, 245–261
Saave*	tryptophan	Hypnotic (now off the market)	82, 102, 124, 223–224
Seconal	secobarbital	Hypnotic	217–243, 249
Serax	oxazepam	Anti-anxiety	177–215, 237, 249
Serentil	mesoridazine	Neuroleptic	1–41
Serpasil	reserpine	Antihypertensive	1–41, 107
Sinemet	carbidopa-levodopa	Neuroleptic	22
Sinequan	doxepin	TCA	57–97, 105, 190, 192, 224, 236
SK-Pramine	imipramine	TCA	57–97, 106, 190–192, 236, 249–250
Stelazine	trifluoperazine	Neuroleptic	1–41, 66
Surmontil	trimipramine	TCA	22, 57–97, 224
Symmetrel	amantadine	Antiparkinsonian	24, 43–55
Taractan	chlorprothixene	Neuroleptic	1–41, 224
Tegretol	carbamazepine	Anticonvulsant	11, 24, 69, 132–134, 136, 145, 153–176, 236
Tenormin	atenolol	Anti-social phobia	190
Thorazine	chlorpromazine	Neuroleptic	1–41, 70, 77, 105–106, 132, 156, 186, 224, 258
Tindal	acetophenazine	Neuroleptic	1–41, 224
Tofranil	imipramine	TCA	57–97, 106, 188, 190, 192, 236, 250, 259–260
Tranxene	clorazepate	Anti-anxiety	177–215, 249
Trexan	naltrexone	Narcotic antagonist	70–71
Trilafon	perphenazine	Neuroleptic	1–41, 69, 186
(tryptophan: See Saave*)			
Urecholine	bethanechol	Cholinergic	13–14, 16, 77
Valium	diazepam	Anti-anxiety	44–45, 177–215, 224, 249, 258
Vistaril	hydroxyzine	Anti-anxiety	177–215, 223–224, 237
Vivactil	proptriptyline	TCA	57–97
Wellbutrin	bupropion	HCA	57–97, 249
Xanax	alprazolam	Anti-anxiety	68–69, 177–215, 236, 249
Zarontin	ethosuximide	Anticonvulsant	153–176

* Sold as nonprescription drugs